London Dialogues

Hans Ulrich Obrist
Rem Koolhaas

Serpentine Gallery 24-Hour Interview Marathon

London
Dialogues

SKIRA

Editor
Luca Molinari

Design
Marcello Francone

Editorial coordination
Emma Cavazzini

Copy editor
Emanuela di Lallo

First published in Italy in 2012
by Skira Editore S.p.A.
Palazzo Casati Stampa
via Torino 61
20123 Milano
Italy
www.skira.net

Printed and bound in Italy.
First edition

ISBN: 978-88-572-0059-0

Distributed in USA, Canada,
Central & South America by
Rizzoli International Publications,
Inc., 300 Park Avenue South,
New York, NY 10010, USA.
Distributed elsewhere
in the world by Thames
and Hudson Ltd., 181A High
Holborn, London WC1V 7QX,
United Kingdom.

List of Contents

FOREWORD

The Serpentine Gallery 24-Hour Interview Marathon: London Dialogues was a highlight of *Time Out Park Nights at the Serpentine Gallery*, the programme of events that accompanied and took place within the Serpentine Gallery Pavilion 2006, designed by Rem Koolhaas and Cecil Balmond, with Arup.

This annual architectural commission is an ongoing programme of temporary structures by internationally acclaimed architects and individuals. The project, initiated in 2000, is unique worldwide. The commission is not decided by competition but is a curatorial choice, and only international architects who have not completed a building in the UK at the time of our invitation are eligible, as a means of introducing the British public to their designs. The project is an extension of the way in which we commission work for the Gallery, so that architecture can sit alongside Exhibitions, Education and Public Programmes as an integrated part of the programme, with the participating architects encouraged to alter perceptions of the Gallery and its surroundings.

This foreword provides an opportunity to focus on the evolution of the Pavilion commission by examining its history, as well as to thank the people who were involved in both the extraordinary structure of 2006, and the remarkable *24-Hour Interview Marathon* that took place within it.

It is our intention with the Pavilion to give people an idea of the extraordinary richness of contemporary architecture and allow them to compare works that they have personally experienced. In this way they become engaged and involved in the debate surrounding this field, which can often be perceived as aloof or forbidding, surrounded by a formal language that is obscure and exclusive.

The first Pavilion in 2000 was designed by Zaha Hadid and was the genesis of the architectural commission, becoming the prototype for future structures. Hadid's Pavilion employed the architectural language of the canopy: the roof folded and dipped in a series of angular moves, supported by a structure of props and struts. She stated that, 'The nature of the folding planes engages with the site by extending itself to the ground at points whilst at the same time undulating to create a variety of internal spaces. These undulations are further exploited by the positioning of lighting between the two roof fabrics, which incurs gradual changes over time by shifting contrast through the roof planes. The internal ground plan is occupied by a field of specially designed tables, which create a movement through the space where their colour graduates from white to black, reinforcing a sense of movement dissipating through the tent.'

The following year, Daniel Libeskind with Arup was invited to design the Pavilion. Entitled *Eighteen Turns*, his structure was an exploration of folding techniques, perhaps the most eloquent exposition of his spiralling, collapsing structural and spatial design. Origami-like panels curled around to meet themselves at their own beginning. 'Each of the four interlocking sections of the structure is made from three panels attached to the floor base to form a complete unit', Libeskind explained. 'The first panel rises from ground level, forming a natural arch and "folds" into the next section, which "folds" into the next, until the final arch and last panel return to the ground level. The structure, with walls, floor and roof, creates a continuous spiral that moves across the ground creating labyrinths and viewing panels from within the structure.'

Toyo Ito's and Cecil Balmond's Pavilion, with Arup, which followed Libeskind's in 2002, was, like its predecessor, a collaboration in design terms but in this case it was also an exploration of the column-less box. The whole concept of the permeable, temporary structure seemed to appeal to Ito's fondness for lightness and ethereality. 'There is something very attractive', he wrote, 'about the idea of it existing only temporarily for three months. Whereas just the thought that the buildings I design might stand for a hundred years or more wears heavily on me, the notion of a temporary project is liberating in many ways. One need not be so strict about function nor worry about how it will age. And it seems to me, it just might offer the clearest expression of the concepts I habitually imagine.' Ito concluded that the Pavilion was 'a curious art object that is clearly architecture, yet at the same time non-architecture. The reason being that, while offering the bare minimum of functions as a space for people's activities, it on the other hand has no columns, no windows, no doors – that is, it has none of the usual architectural elements.'

In 2003, Oscar Niemeyer wanted to express the main characteristics of his architecture through a simple and small-scale work. In order to achieve the Pavilion's distinctive lightness, he suspended its weight one and a half metres above the ground. His other objective was to attain unity in the interiors through good use of colours and coverings. He included a number of elements that he saw as characteristic of his oeuvre: the ramp, the signature roof profile, a semi-submerged auditorium, a view of the grass from the auditorium, and a grand staircase. Among his principal problems was that, perhaps more than any architect alive, he is known for his concrete constructions. Here he had to design an essentially lightweight, demountable pavilion. The final outcome, a steel-framed structure clad in aluminium, achieved the desired result.

If Niemeyer's Pavilion attempted miniscule monumentality, the subsequent design, by the radical Dutch practice MVRDV, went to the opposite extreme – the scale of a mountain. After Niemeyer, we deliberately approached a younger practice to create a balance in the annual programme. More experimental and with an entirely different working practice, MVRDV seemed an interesting counterpoint. Just as Niemeyer's roof profile had emerged at the very beginning, so MVRDV's idea for the mountain was there from the outset. The idea was simply to cover the Serpentine in a faux mountain structure. Of all the proposals, it is this one that forced the most complete re-interpretation of the built and spatial form of the Gallery, and it is the only one that has proved too ambitious for the moment. (The nature of commissioning visual art is risky and the risk is implicit in the process.) Yet it remains no less a project than any of those completed. Time, thought and effort went into it, and at its heart is an integrity concerning the process and a seriousness of intent. This remains a project in development and a remarkable scheme.

The 2005 Pavilion was designed by Álvaro Siza and Eduardo Souto de Moura, with Cecil Balmond, involving his team at Arup and their long-term Portuguese colleagues at AFA. They are both internationally respected for their subtlety and inventiveness that delicately approaches the small scale and the everyday rather than monumentality. The Pavilion was constructed from an undulating, organic timber grid above the lawn. Coming to a halt 1m 30cm above the ground, it gave the effect of a floating structure but also one with the visual and physical permeability of a marquee roof. The building was anchored to the ground by a carpet of grey bricks, which provided a hard floor surface, while the visual metaphor was maintained by the retention of turf around the carpet's edges, leaving it clearly defined within the covered space, but never touching the Pavilion's almost non-existent edge. Sitting in a bowl like a lurking reptile, the structure was about negative space and absence. This scheme was the first to have focused on the grounds around the Pavilion, which were gently re-landscaped for the occasion.

To be truly appreciated, architecture needs to be experienced firsthand; the space needs to be felt, the colours seen, and the textures engaged with. Being in a building, absorbing the space, seeing the light, is the only way to get a true understanding of it. The 2006 Pavilion designed by Rem Koolhaas and Cecil Balmond with Arup developed this concept even further to create an architecture that, as Koolhaas explains, 'facilitates the inclusion of individuals in communal dialogue and shared experience'. The central design was a spectacular ovoid-shaped inflatable canopy that floated above the Gallery's lawn and could be raised or lowered to cover the amphitheatre below. The walled enclosure underneath the canopy functioned as both a café and forum for daily public programmes of live talks, performances and film screenings.

These included the *Serpentine Gallery 24-Hour Interview Marathon: London Dialogues*, which embodied the aims of both the architect and the Serpentine Gallery by creating a context for shared discussion between cultural practitioners, the Gallery and the public. Evolving from Hans Ulrich Obrist's lifelong interview series and ongoing collaborations with Koolhaas, the *24-Hour Interview Marathon* was a unique event in which Koolhaas and Obrist interviewed sixty-six leading architects, artists, philosophers, writers, filmmakers and theorists from 6pm on 28 July to 6pm on 29 July. The *24-Hour Interview Marathon* acted as live research and exposed the hidden and invisible layers of London. Our thanks, first and foremost, go to Koolhaas and Obrist for their outstanding commitment to all aspects of the creation and realisation of this remarkable event.

It was, of course, the illustrious group of speakers, and their acutely perceptive investigation into the intersecting layers of London, that gave the *24-Hour Interview Marathon* its now mythic status. Their energy and commentary, even during the early hours of the morning, created a gripping event. They were, in order of appearance: David Adjaye; Brian Eno; Charles Jencks; Sir Kenneth Adam; Zaha Hadid; Yinka Shonibare; Tim O'Toole; Hanif Kureishi; Ken Loach; Susan Hiller; Jude Kelly; Tim Newburn; Tony Elliott; Tom McCarthy; Scott Lash; Michael Clark; Richard Wentworth with Marcus du Sautoy and Pedro Ferreira; Ron Arad; Jane and Louise Wilson; Cerith Wyn Evans; Squarepusher; Peter Saville; Roger Hiorns; Olivia Plender; Sophie Fiennes; Russell Haswell; Anat Ben-David; Damien Hirst with Ant Genn; Shumon Basar, Markus Miessen and Åbäke; Iain Sinclair; Paul Elliman; Gilbert & George; Adam Caruso St John; Ryan Gander; Julia Peyton-Jones; Eleanor Bron; Giles Deacon; Doreen Massey; Mary Midgley; Mark Cousins and Patrick Keiller; Jonathan Glancey; Gustav Metzger; Isaac Julien; Gautam Malkani; Richard Hamilton; Peter Cook; Chantal Mouffe; Eyal Weizman; Hussein Chalayan; Tariq Ali; Marina Warner; Milan Rai; Doris Lessing. Pre-recorded interviews played during the event were with Eric Hobsbawm, Dame Marjorie Scardino, Denise Scott Brown, Juergen Teller; and others.

The National Lottery, through Arts Council England, gave substantial support for this season of events, without which it would not have been achievable. We are indebted to them, as well as to the Netherlands Architecture Fund and the Royal Netherlands Embassy for their generous assistance, together with Pilsner Urquell, who also made an important contribution.

We are most grateful to the many people involved in *Time Out Park Nights at the Serpentine Gallery* and in particular to Tony Elliot, Founder, and John Luck, Marketing Director, of *Time Out*. The *24-Hour Interview Marathon* was developed with a committed team and we would like to acknowledge the exceptional contribution of Sally Tallant, Head of Education and Public Programmes, and the dedicated Marathon Organisers Kathy Battista, Franceso Manacorda and Emma Ridgway. The project also benefited from the enthusiastic involvement of many volunteers, including Charlotte Bonham-Carter and Tyler Poniatowski.

We are immensely grateful to Rem Koolhaas, Cecil Balmond and their teams for their dedication in realising their ambitious structure. We would like to acknowledge Koolhaas's colleagues at OMA, who worked unstintingly on the project: Clément Blanchet, Karen Crequer, Adam Furman and Karel Wuytack. Arup, as always, worked tirelessly to develop the structural scheme for the Pavilion and our appreciation goes especially to Cecil Balmond for his essential role in the scheme, and to his meticulous team: Carolina Bartram, Chris Carroll, Anthony Ferguson, Andrew Grant, Phil Greenup, Tristan Simmonds and Steve Walker.

Without Lex Fenwick, Sayu Bhojwani and Michelle Rinkoff and their colleagues at Bloomberg, our principal sponsor, the Pavilion could never have been realised, and our immense appreciation is extended to them for their assistance to the Serpentine over many years.

Lord Palumbo, Chairman, Serpentine Gallery, and Chairman of the Jury of the Pritzker Architecture Prize, and Zaha Hadid, Trustee, and 2004 Pritzker Laureate, are crucial to the architectural strand of the Gallery's programming. They continue to advise the Gallery and we are enormously grateful for their commitment.

The involvement of Peter Rogers of Stanhope is also crucial;
he works tirelessly to advise us on all aspects of the project.

We would also like to thank Mark Camley, Chief Executive of the
Royal Parks Agency, and his colleagues, as well as Councillor Angela
Hooper, Chair of the Planning and City Development Committee,
and her colleagues at the City of Westminster Council for their
ongoing support, without whom the Serpentine Gallery Pavilion
commission would not be the groundbreaking project that it is.

There are numerous companies and organisations whose generosity
has been central to the Pavilion's success. The time, money and
resources they have lent to the project have been absolutely
fundamental to its realisation. They are: Stanhope; Bovis Lend
Lease; William Hare; Hightex; Clipfine; Davis Langdon; DP9; John
Doyle Group; Keltbray; Weil, Gotshal & Manges; Knight Frank;
T. Clarke; Asysco; BOC; Hitachi; Lyndon scaffolding; Mark Johnson
Consultants Ltd; SES and Siteco Lighting Systems Definitive
audio visual integration.

We are deeply thankful to Skira, Luca Molinari and Milena Sacchi
for the great collaboration and dialogue that has made this book
possible, and to Stefano Boeri for starting the dialogue with Skira.
Many thanks also to Gigi Gianuzzi of Trolley Books, Simon Brown
from &&& Creative and Mark Irving from Visible Impression Ltd
for their commitment to this project. We are also grateful to Ben
Fergusson, Print and Publications Manager, and Eva McGovern,
Inspire Fellow, at the Serpentine Gallery, for their contributions.

Finally, the role of the Council of the Serpentine is crucial to
the Gallery's success and our scope and breadth of programming
is a result of their commitment and continuing support. Our thanks
and appreciation are extended to them as always.

Julia Peyton-Jones
Director, Serpentine Gallery and
Co-Director, Exhibitions & Programmes

Hans Ulrich Obrist   Before we discuss the Serpentine Pavilion, which you're designing this year with Cecil Balmond, can we talk about your relationship to London? There's no other city, besides maybe New York or Berlin, with which you have such an intense relationship. When did you first come here?

Rem Koolhaas   In 1968. It was a crazy year, because in May, the student riots in Paris happened, in August, the Prague invasion happened. I was still a journalist, so I saw those events. In Prague, I was on an architectural excursion when it happened. Then I came to London, and London at the time was exciting on the one hand, and on the other, so totally British. At the Architectural Association School of Architecture, I was served dinner by ladies in white aprons and it had the atmosphere of a club. But inside there was a degree of radicalism. In a way, what was good about the city was that the contrast was so enormous, and you could clearly tell that both extremes benefited from each other's presence. Peter Cook was there, but next to him there were really old guys snoring in front of the fireplace.

HUO   So it was almost like an oxymoron?

RK   Like an oxymoron, yes. This is basically how society used to be organised: somehow layers co-existed and defined themselves in terms of each other. Anyway, it was also a really grey, cold city. All the things you'd always heard were true: the fog, which was disgusting, the political situation, which was really sad – strikes, coal... It's taken me, frankly, almost thirty years to really like London. That's the interesting thing about the city. It wasn't love at first sight.

HUO   Now, many young artists and architects make London their base. At the time, it wasn't such an obvious choice, was it?

RK   There were two main reasons why I made it mine: one was to learn English, or to learn to write English. The other was that the School at the time was considered the most interesting place to study in Europe. People said I'd be crazy if I didn't go there.

HUO   It's interesting, this mythical aura attached to certain schools at certain moments, like the Black Mountain College in the US. The AA had a very strong moment when you studied there, along with Peter Cook and Cedric Price. What was the AA miracle? What was the secret of this school? We have a grey city, which at the time wasn't particularly exciting, and suddenly this miracle happened.

RK   I think that there were at least three very strong centres of architecture in England during the 1950s and 1960s. Some practitioners were really intellectual, and they were teachers – in Cambridge, there was some fundamental research being undertaken. Some were un-intellectual. There were many people whom you no longer hear about, but who did very, very smart things. There were also James Stirling and James Gowan, the two Smithsons, Cedric Price. That alone is unbelievable. And then, added to that came Archigram. So, it's almost impossible to imagine a similar cluster of talents.

I don't know whether you know Leslie Martin's diagram. It comes into play here. It's very simplistic but it shows that the same substance can either be applied to two towers, or to four or sixteen very low buildings. In a typically English way, they calculated that the whole of Manhattan could also be built on the level of three storeys in the same territory. The point was that density was not necessary. In a way, 'density was not necessary' could be a slogan for London. It's a different model from the concentrated, high-pressure situation (where a tight group of people communicate with each other). Although my relationship with Archigram was critical, it was unbelievably stimulating and polemical. That was the great thing: you were really provoked into polemical positions. Also, it was the time just after Nigel Henderson had taken his almost Situationist photographs of the East End. Denise Scott Brown was involved and the Independent Group, in which the Smithsons were also very involved. Charles Jencks was there in this formative time studying with Reyner Banham, who was himself an incredible influence too. If you think about it, it was really ...

HUO   ... a great constellation.

RK   And they were all English, and 'English' at the time really was a very specific identity and an identity I'd never come across; it was very exotic in terms of what people would show and what they wouldn't show. They would never argue in a traditional 'confidential' way, or discourse in a traditional way! It was much more about feeling 'Celtic'.

HUO I spoke once to Geoffrey Bawa, the Sri Lankan poet and architect, and he told me that the AA was one of the few places in the world where there was a non-Western discourse.

RK There was a tropical department.

HUO Tropical Architecture?

RK Tropical Architecture. It was really related to the Commonwealth, the countries England had 'owned' and that had remained 'friends'; so it had a colonial dimension to it, but in the end that also represented an early way of thinking about sustainable architecture with a focus on the need to build with shade, with natural ventilation, all these things that are currently being addressed, which is pretty impressive. One of the most amazing people was professor Koenigsberger, who was involved in that department. He'd had an accident that had made his head the shape of a hat, with a big dent in it, and he looked like an eccentric German professor, a refugee. But now that I'm looking at situations like Lagos or Singapore, he turns out to have been everywhere as part of UN missions, and basically wrote the plot for all these cities. At that time, somebody in a suit and with reports written in a sober style could influence the entire future of emerging cities. There were also many Arab people; it was a really great, cosmopolitan situation.

HUO Have you ever done any urban research on London, like you did on the Berlin Wall in the 1960s?

RK The one thing we did was the Exodus Project, where we 'scraped' a central zone of old London, but that was more like active criticism. As I said, it took me a very long time to really understand this city, or to like it, so as a Continental European, for a very long time I was simply unable to discover a way in – partly because it wasn't there. If you walked the streets, you could walk for kilometres without seeing any evidence of public life. But now, of course, in retrospect I realise how that impenetrable condition enabled Londoners to cultivate privacy. It's still a city of privacy, but at the time it was even more so; and now, in retrospect, I think that was its unique richness.

I first lived in London in 1968–72. Then I went to America, and came back in the late 1970s as a teacher at the AA: that was supposedly another heyday era. Bernard Tschumi was teaching there, and Léon Krier, and it was like another momentary more international outburst, when the world of architecture seemed as if it could go in many different directions. And Zaha Hadid was our student. In that context, we did a lot on London, as you do as a teacher, but I don't think it was really research. At that point, teaching was strictly setting a subject, and the students would do projects, but simply as design, not research. It was the moment when postmodernism could easily have become the dominant style, so it was quite important to find strategies to avoid that.

HUO   Strategies of resistance?

RK   It really was resistance, yes. So in that context, we took Malevich's Constructivist forms and provoked the students into trying to appropriate them architecturally; that's where Zaha Hadid started. In retrospect it's really embarrassing, but at the time it was reasonably fresh! *[Laughs]*

HUO   The Serpentine Pavilion is going to be your first temporary building and your first building in London. One of the criteria of the Serpentine commission is that the architect should never have realised anything in Britain before, but when we announced this year's project, some people said, 'Rem has already built something in London'. They were speaking about this mysterious agency you built. Is it still around?

RK   I don't know.

HUO   What was it?

RK   It was at the top of the Oasis, a swimming pool, near Shaftesbury Avenue. I was working at the time with a former student, the Italian architect Stefano de Martino; I was asked by Jay Chiat, the same client who commissioned Frank Gehry's Binoculars for his agency in LA, to do an equivalent in London. So we worked on it together initially, but most of the work was eventually done by Stefano. It's an office with some free-floating shapes and a very beautiful sense of materials – lots of polyester and resin. We did it in the late 1970s, 1979 maybe.

HUO   So it wasn't a building, but an interior?

RK   Yes, it was in an existing penthouse.

HUO   You've said that the contents of the Pavilion will be very important. This relates to something we've been discussing for the last ten years: the idea of a discursive space, a space for conversations and interviews.

RK   Yes.

HUO   What's interesting is that this project is a continuation of many things we've done together before, like *Cities on the Move*, the travelling show that I curated with Hou Hanru. When the show came to the Hayward Gallery, London, in 1998–99, you and Ole Scheeren completely changed it, with a new typology and an amazing exhibition design, which recycled the designs of previous shows.

RK   Actually, I consider that my first important project in London, because the beautiful thing about simply living somewhere without any enormous enthusiasm is that you can let its values really soak in, and then you get a very unconscious result. I've been here long enough to change my mind, or to have totally different impressions of the same phenomenon. I remember how completely weird I found the South Bank when it was finished, but how completely beautiful, and increasingly beautiful, it now looks. At that point I felt that some kind of recycling, or some kind of commitment to debris was one of the most fundamental English things; a capacity to live in things that were not new, modern, or perfect. So the approach was to recycle the shows of others.

HUO   You recycled elements from Zaha Hadid's exhibition and a show of Anish Kapoor, which had taken place in the Hayward prior to ours: it became what you called 'an accelerated Merzbau'.

RK   That was, for me, the London coming-out show.

HUO   And then our collaboration continued with many other projects, like *Mutations* in Bordeaux, with architects Stefano Boeri and Sanford Kwinter, and we started to do a lot of interviews together. We interviewed Robert Venturi, Denise Scott Brown, Philip Johnson, Wolfgang Tillmans and Oswald Mathias Ungers, and more recently, the Metabolists in Japan, in a series that attempted to make a portrait of a movement. The next plan is basically that there will be a space for these conversations in the form of the Serpentine Pavilion. Right at the beginning, on your first visit to the site, you started to come up with this incredible project, which was basically a structure of hanging materials.

RK   Yes. Basically, I thought it was very important not so much to reinvent the tradition of the pavilion, but to try to do something that was not about space or about materials. I tried to imagine something that was like Yves Klein's Fire Pavilion, on which he collaborated with Claude Parent and Werner Ruhnau, or the one based on air. That work was never realised and obviously won't be this time, but I've always found it incredibly compelling. When I was still studying architecture, I was really baffled by my inability to be deeply enthusiastic about Archigram's less conceptual domes and inflatables and my unbelievable excitement about Klein's projects. They're two things that seem very similar but have a huge difference in value. To even raise the word 'inflatable' in England now, is either a really radical perversion or a profound irony.

HUO   And what about your collaboration with Cecil Balmond? It's a very special collaboration that goes far beyond the usual relationship between an architect and an engineer. The friendship with Cecil is a crucial part of your own story, isn't it?

RK   Completely. I first got to know Cecil in 1987, the year of our first collaboration, a competition for a bank in Amsterdam. I asked him, 'Can we do a grid of one? Just one column placed in a space'. And it was obviously kind of half a joke, but his reaction was so interesting that we really clicked. What we've worked on for a very long time is achieving beauty. He gave us access to engineering and we gave him access to architecture, and I think our work has benefited from that shared knowledge and also from the conversion between the two disciplines. You know, of course, that Cecil now has his own architectural group, so this collaboration has many phases, ranging from a brotherly intimacy to the current situation, which is not competitive, but is more parallel. The good thing is that we can, at any time when we need to, still revert to our earlier condition.

HUO   Like music?

RK   Yes, like music. And he remains a totally essential part of certain breakthroughs that we've made.

HUO   For the Serpentine, you came to the idea of a floating structure. That could move up and down.

RK   I think the whole thing was partly to do with the fact that this one has to last longer than the others, since it will stay up until October to connect with the Frieze Fair. So the issue of climate is important; we have summer and autumn conditions. For that reason it had to have two identities that would work well either with or without a roof. But equally important was the fact that I've always been baffled as to why the Pavilions have simply been objects in a meadow and have borne no relation to the Serpentine Gallery itself. So that's another excitement; it's independent, but also contextual in a certain way. And another important element is that the artists inside the Serpentine will intervene in our structure with work of their own. So the identity of the author will be completely blurred.

HUO You're going to collaborate with Thomas Demand. He's thinking about projecting a film of his grotto into the pavilion. It's a space that can be used in an interesting way. Because of its transparency, things can be porous; things can spread outside: light can spread outside, speech can spread outside.

RK Yes. And it can absorb anything. The absorbency is the really exciting thing. It can absorb an infinite amount of influences.

HUO And you were also saying that there are going to be videos in the space during the day?

RK Yes, an archive is how we put it. That expands the notion of the interview as a significant form of the transmission of knowledge.

HUO And you're going to do an even bigger project in London afterwards.

RK I'm doing a bank in London, in the City, which is deeply exciting because it's a building situated in such tight conditions that nobody will be able to see it. We've been working on it for almost a year and it looks very good in terms of realisation.

HUO Do you have any unrealised London projects? Things you wanted to build in London?

RK No, because for a very long time, the point of being in London was not to build here, but to have no obligations other than simply to be here.

HUO Was it a retreat?

RK It was a retreat, absolutely. It was really a place of privacy where I could withdraw, and that's still part of its appeal.

* This interview was published in *Art Review*, edited by Mark Rappolt.

David Adjaye

Brian Eno

Charles Jencks

Kenneth Adam

Zaha Hadid

Yinka Shonibare MBE

Tim O'Toole

Hanif Kureishi

Ken Loach

Hans Ulrich Obrist   Thank you so much, David, for joining us. We wanted to ask, in terms of this London Marathon, how you assess the current moment we are living in right now.

David Adjaye   I think it's a moment when there seems to be a lot of potential for new ways of negotiating things to happen. I feel it's a moment when we can maybe start to understand another dimension in our engagement with things.
Sorry! Short answers! *[Laughs]*

HUO   That's good. To extend the question about the current moment to the city, I spoke some weeks ago to J. G. Ballard about the form of a city in the early twenty-first century. He was saying that he thinks it is how it is and we have to accept it and make the best out of it. He thinks that it is unrestricted urban sprawl, it's decentred metropolis, it's transient airport culture, it's gated communities and it's also at the same time the absence of any kind of civic pride. So I was wondering how you would assess it.

DA   I find all that rather refreshing. *[Laughs]* I think I am more fond of the idea of a city that is less formal, more broken-down in terms of its legibility. What's happening to London – you can be critical in terms of a coherence of the city but I think it's about a way that the city can be broken up and remade again in a different way. I think that the boom that is going on, apart from all the congestion it's causing, is a very exciting sort of proposition for the city.

HUO   Can you talk more specifically about London?

DA   The obvious thing of finishing the last quarter of the pie of London is very interesting, the whole Olympic development. Lord knows what that's going to be like! But I am fascinated by the way London has always regenerated itself. If you look at the way the city is looking at itself and the way in which the east has readdressed itself and even how the west is repicturing itself, the sort of bourgeois life that has happened in west London and how it's actually starting to spill right through to north-west London, this is really interesting.

HUO	And you are working on lots of public commissions right now in London.
DA	Three.
HUO	Can you tell us about those?
DA	I'm working on three public commissions, one in the south, one in the east and one in the north; three different types of programmes. The central theme amongst all of them is a notion of bringing forward emerging groups in London's cultural life that up to this moment had voices but didn't have physical homes. So it's about really making cultural centres of a sort in the form of a media performing arts centre in the north, a new arts think tank centre in the east and an education centre in the south.
HUO	Do you have unrealised projects in relation to London, dreams?
DA	Gosh! I think I was just quite shocked by being able to build in London; I am trying to get my head round what that means! *[Laughs]*
HUO	But are there projects which maybe haven't worked out or not yet worked out? The whole notion of the unrealised. What's the percentage in your office of things that are realised and things that are unrealised?
DA	It's interesting. I've never done the statistical test. I don't want to know yet! *[Laughs]* I think that people who do my economics know exactly how much money we've lost on things not realised, but it's not a statistic that I have at the moment. We try to be really careful; we don't make thousands of projects, we work very specifically on things so it's not about that kind of relationship. And I don't have that kind of utopian relationship to London or to the way I practice.
HUO	One project I was curious to hear more about is your Rivington Place project, which is a project for a cultural institution in the twenty-first century. I was wondering if you could tell us a little bit about the vision behind that.
DA	Rivington Place is an organisation that an amazing man called Stuart Hall has been spearheading: two arts organisations, one that's committed to visual arts of the Diaspora and the international community in its widest sense; and Autograph, which is a photo archiving agency. I think in its essence the model for this building is a prototype for the arts now, an agenda that I think is becoming contemporary, one of not a local or

regional scenario but one which has a much more planetary, global scope to it. Rivington Place is really about pushing an international and more planetary agenda. I hope that they are like an incubator for a new model for the arts, really. That's what Iniva [Institute of International Visual Arts] is about.

HUO   And how will it work as a building? It includes exhibitions but it is a knowledge-producing institution.

DA   It's mostly a knowledge-production organisation; it's hardly an exhibition space, actually. The exhibition space is very limited, very small. It's seen as a reactive think tank organisation, so they have a small auditorium for lectures, fast lectures – to be able to bring people in very quickly – and they have a massive data base system, and they publish. Essentially Autograph and Iniva are more famous for their publications and I think that's what they want to expand more, to have this as a place where debate and this sort of things happen.

Rem Koolhaas   [Entering] Have you talked about time?

HUO   No, not yet.

RK   I think that both Hans Ulrich and I are often caricatured as people who have no time, but in your case we are confronted with very stringent deadlines about time. Can you say something about your time, how you use it, and whether you have enough time to do what you want to do, and basically about time today.

DA   About time today! [Laughs] Well, I'm just about to…

RK   I should really say that the reason you are here as people enter the building is that you need to go.

HUO   In a few minutes!

DA   Which time slot would I be in if I wasn't? Time is something one is always negotiating and working with. I don't know what you mean! Is this a personal time discussion, like a diary time discussion? [Laughs]

RK   Well, the beautiful thing is that it's both personal and general.

DA   Yes. Time is a very interesting thing in a way. Time is a kind of engagement issue, so it's about certain kinds of modes of engagement for me. This interview was something I wanted to do but unfortunately I have been planning something that is not just a work thing but a project that I am trying to work on at the moment very much. This unfortunately collided with it. I don't know what to say! I can't miss my flight, so I have to go.

HUO   Your journey leads to Johannesburg. Can you tell us a bit more about this archive project to make photographs of all the capitals in Africa: is it a book?

DA   It might become a book; I think it's going to become a show. I'm very interested in notions of formality, informality and casualness in cities and, in a way, in diarying through that. I'm interested in the fifty-four states of the African continent and using that as a springboard for me to explore certain ideas that I am already interested in. So it's a way of making a diary and bringing eminence to something which I think is a little bit out of focus but also a way of foregrounding my interests and the way in which I work.

HUO   Will it be completed soon?

DA   No, it's on the wall in my studio. *[Laughs]* We are furiously working on it. It's got to be in a show in the spring next year.

HUO   Thank you very much. Have a good trip.

DA   Thank you.

Applause, end of interview

Hans Ulrich Obrist   Many thanks to Brian Eno for joining us. Actually, this is not the first time Rem and I have recorded conversations with Brian, and I think Rem wants to begin.

Rem Koolhaas   We've known each other about twenty years and maybe the largest mystery in all these years is how somebody with such extravagant experiences can be so consistently thoughtful.

Brian Eno   Thoughtful?

RK   Yes.

BE   *[Laughs]*

RK   And in a way I would like to ask you to comment on your own character as stretching from the most baroque to the most minimalist without apparent pain or contradiction.

BE   *[Laughs]* When I was at school I had a very bad science teacher and a very good art teacher, so because of that I think I became an artist. But when I left school I realised that actually it was the sciences that interested me as much as anything else, so I think I spent a lot of time trying to exercise thoughts that came from science in art, somehow or other. I got very interested in systems and cybernetics and in creating conceptual machines of different types to make music for me. I think that, of course, meant that I carried on with my interest in science as well as my interest in art – so they didn't seem difficult to integrate to me; they always were integrated. The other thing, I suppose, is that I studied as a painter and became a musician and when I became a musician I started making music that gradually became more and more like painting in that it was steady state, non-narrative. It wasn't like music normally is structured; it didn't have a teleological quality to it. Then I moved back also into making visual art of some kind but I made that more and more like music, so again I felt these things mapped onto each other very easily; it didn't seem a stretch to make them seem like one activity.

HUO   Maybe it would be interesting to know a little more about the art school you attended. In many conversations we have brought up the necessity for new experimental schools and it is interesting to remember particularly noteworthy experimental moments. There have been so many discussions about the necessity for new Black Mountain Colleges, and when we spoke last time the way you described the Ipswich School of Art and the course run by Roy Ascott it sounded like a very, very interesting moment. It would be great to hear what was so special about this school.

BE It was a very unusual school. In a way it was very much a product of the 1960s, but also it was the product of another person who was as interested in the sciences as in the arts, Roy Ascott. Ascott had become interested in behavioural psychology and also in cybernetics, so the staff at the school included painters, composers, cyberneticians, mathematicians and gallerists, which was very unusual then. There was a guy who ran a gallery in London who used to come in to talk about the business of art, which I don't think was happening at any other art college at the time. It wasn't admitted that there was a business involved. The art school, the first one that I was at, actually only really existed in that form for two years and was then closed down by the Education Committee because it didn't produce many painters. *[Laughs]* It produced people doing all sorts of other things but not many of them were doing painting. So the college had, I think, a very interesting and unusual staff and we all turned up at the age of sixteen or seventeen, I guess, with little boxes of paints which we were immediately told to put away because we wouldn't be needing those for a long time. *[Laughs]* Then the staff proceeded to do things like lock us in cupboards or shout at us or make us paint one hundred and sixty-foot-long pictures on newsprint, all sorts of odd experiments but not without logic in fact. So I had a very good time there; it was a complete liberation for me.

RK Like you, I am a child of that kind of education, whether I wanted to be or not, and I feel very uncomfortable about the wholehearted embrace of painting or architecture now by later generations. What is your kind of relationship with, or attitude to, for example, Brit Art?

BE It sounds very condescending to say it, but I feel I have seen so much of it before. There is a sort of half-hearted conceptualism in so much of what I see around; I think we had a more full-blooded version of it. Conceptualism was very much a movement of the late 1960s and I think we did it very well, in fact. There was no commercial aspect to it then; it wasn't well recognised and people didn't realise that you could sell photographs of it to make a living. They just did it and lost money on it in general. I see a lot of the contemporary forms of conceptualism as being very heavy-footed, leaden, non-humorous, and also non-profound as well.

RK   You and I have talked about architecture and you strike me as somebody with a fundamentally critical attitude to architecture and its inherent authoritarianism. You used to be optimistic about certain figures and their impact: Christopher Alexander was one of them. I have two questions: we live now in an apparent apotheosis of the architectural, not of your kind of architecture but presumably of the more authoritarian type. Are you still optimistic about the potential for those more critical voices? The other question is about the city. More than ever before people live in cities, talk about cities and seem to embrace the monster and the beast that is the city. What is your relationship with this city at this moment?

BE   To answer the second question first, I also embrace the monster and I like doing so. I like living in a city and indeed I like a lot of the structures of cities. I suppose I have been critical of architecture when I felt it contributed neither to the external experience of the city nor to the internal experience. A lot of this criticism I think came from living in New York during a certain period in the late 1970s and early 1980s, when I saw quite a lot of exercise of architecture that seemed to me simply glamorous, actually. Structurally it was totally uninteresting. I'm thinking, for example, of Philip Johnson's AT&T building [now the Sony Building], that big pink building with the sort of scallops on it, which everybody said was such an amazing building but actually it was an amazing choice of marble or whatever it was, but inside it was exactly like any other building I'd seen. So there were no innovations in the place where I thought architects might be making interesting innovations. The innovation was entirely to do with the cladding of the building, and after all, it wasn't that innovative either, even in that respect. I saw a lot of that kind of architecture at the time, though I saw architecture that I very much enjoyed, for instance Renzo Piano's downtown building, where the windows get bigger as it goes higher. It starts with small square windows at the bottom and they become larger and larger so the top of the building is virtually all glass, so it sort of fades off into the sky. That's a very attractive idea.

As regards Christopher Alexander, well I – very unfashionably – am still a believer in him as a theorist though I'm not very interested in his architecture. I still do like the idea of a kind of evolution of building techniques rather than a series of revolutions.

HUO   We have lots of questions for you about London, but before that maybe it would be interesting to talk a little more about the Sonic City. I was wondering to which extent the idea of sounds of the city enters your work, and on the other hand the extent to which sonic interventions in the city play a role right now for you.

BE   It's quite hard to intervene in a city because you generally have to be louder than it and generally you don't want to add noise, so it's difficult to make an intervention in a place that is already noisy. What you can do is choose a place that is already sort of quiet and encourage people to be even quieter there. This is what I have tended to do in terms of interventions like these, but I can't see any point in making a musical installation, as I've been invited to, for example, in Piccadilly Circus. I think it would just raise the general noise level the way that in restaurants people put music on so everybody has to talk louder and then they turn the music up and everybody talks louder still. I don't want to be part of a feedback cycle like that.

In terms of living in the city I think that if you are a composer your sonic surrounding is the context against which you generally rebel. For instance, I made my quietest records when I lived in a very noisy apartment in New York. I lived on the corner of Broom and Broadway and this was a street where the huge trucks on their way to the Holland Tunnel would come by and the whole building would rock. That was where I made very quiet music because that was the place where I wanted to be so desperately. [Laughs] When I lived in the country, in Suffolk, I made my loudest records, so I think I always make the place I would rather be in.

HUO   And in terms of interventions in a more quiet way in the city, maybe your recent project in Beijing is an example.

BE   Yes.

HUO   Can you tell us about that?

BE   That was a very successful project. I was asked to do a piece of music in one of the parks in Beijing and I chose a place called Ritan Park which has a circular wall, so there is a central area which is closed off by this wall. The wall is about three metres high and I suppose the diameter of this space is maybe a hundred and fifty, a hundred and eighty metres. This is, by the way, a place where people go to sit and be quiet and is particularly known as a place where old men fly kites. There are always at least half a dozen old guys in there flying kites. The place is very, very quiet anyway; nobody makes a lot of noise in there. So I started off by making a piece really for these old guys, thinking, 'What would they like to hear?' Plus, 'What would they be able to stand listening to for a month?' Because the installation was due to be on for a month. You have to think of the people who are going to be there every day. I made a piece that was similar to something I did here in the Science Museum; I had sixteen CD players round the edges of this circle and each one had the sound of one bell on it and each bell would ring every so often. The cycles were not synchronised, so sometimes you got clusters of many bells ringing and sometimes individual ones. I treated the sound in such a way that it seemd as though these bell rings were coming from a very long way away, even when you were quite close to them. It was a success in that the kite fliers really loved it and more and more kite fliers started to appear there and they gave very good comments to the park and asked if the piece could be kept there, which it wasn't, in fact.

RK   I want to end with one particular issue: you were a very early optimist about the power of the digital and the promise of the digital as relieving our lives of a lot of substance and a lot of burdens. If you look now with twenty years' experience, do you still maintain that promise?

BE   I still maintain it but I also see that it's a very, very tilted playing field. The promise of digital when it first appeared was suddenly 'everything is possible', or suddenly 'so many things are possible that were never possible before'. But of course, although 'everything' is possible some things are a lot easier than others and those are the ones that you keep doing. So the playing field is very tilted against certain kinds of activities. For example, in music it's very much tilted against the use of the three million years of evolution that went into our muscles and our fine muscle control. Digital inclines you to use that muscle, the one in the index finger, or two more as well if you've got a complicated mouse. What it does not incline you to do is use all the rest of your musculature, and that turns out to be quite an important part of how music is made. Of course you can make perfectly nice music like that, using the index finger, and a lot of us do, but then it's much harder to do something that re-integrates your physical body into the form, and you tend not to do it. So the playing field is tilted against that and that's an interface problem which I think people are starting to solve. The fact is we have very, very, very simplistic interfaces at the moment. We have this very complicated creature here and that very complicated object called the computer and this ridiculously small bottleneck through which you have to communicate with each other. So I think this is the next interesting part of the digital revolution.

HUO   I think it would be really interesting if you could tell us how you see this current moment in the world and also in terms of your work and what is next.

BE   Sometimes I think things are so desperately precarious at the moment that everything else we are doing is utterly irrelevant – sitting here talking or going to my studio and making whatever I make seems increasingly off the point to me. I've always been an optimist until recently and I've become very pessimistic recently, you know; the Lebanon thing is only a simple example of how suddenly it seems that a lot of states are conspiring to have a war because they all think they're going to come out of it best. It's not a little war that they want to have; they want to have a big war. I am saying Israel, America, us, Hezbollah, Iran, Syria, they all see a good reason for a nice big regional conflict and I don't really see anybody who has a strong enough interest in preventing them from doing it at the moment. So that's one type of crisis. The other type of crisis is the really big question, which is about climate change. This, for instance, is the hottest July since 1659 in England; ten of the last fourteen years have been the hottest ten years on record. This seems to me a really difficult problem as well in that even if we suddenly all decide tomorrow that we are going to do everything right, it's a fifty-year ship that's got to turn, you know. It's going in a direction, it's going to be a long time before that direction changes. So I'm kind of pessimistic and I'm looking to my daughters' generation to just burn the lot of us and start again, really. *[Laughs]*

HUO   To come from the pessimistic assessment towards the end of the interview to an optimistic moment, I was wondering about your dreams, if you have any dreams or unrealised projects you would like to see realised.

BE	You asked me that last time.
HUO	I know, but it was a long time ago. It was six years ago.
BE	The embarrassing thing is I think they are still the same ones. *[Laughs]*
HUO	Can you still tell us?
BE	The unrealised projects are still unrealised. I've been developing this idea of something called Generative Music, which is self-creating music. I think I've done that quite successfully but now I want to start to do it at the atomic or molecular level. I want to start at a much deeper level and make it generative. This is kind of hard to explain but it's as if I found how to make motor cars assemble themselves but now I want to find out how to make molecules assemble themselves. That's the only analogy I can make.

RK	Thank you.
HUO	Thank you so much.
BE	Thank you.

Applause, end of interview

Rem Koolhaas	Hello Charles.
Charles Jencks	Hey, Rem. Yo!

RK   Yo, Charles! *[Laughs]* You are the writer of many, many books and we will inevitably talk about them. We want to talk about London in every case, so perhaps the first question I would like to ask you is whether the messiness of London and the incoherence of the city alerted you to the aesthetic and the virtues of the post-modern and was in any way responsible for your insight into the post-modern condition.

CJ   Absolutely. Steen Rasmussen – I guess he's Danish – the architectural historian and urbanist, wrote a book called *London: The Unique City* in the 1930s and London remains unique in a sense because it's a series of villages. And these villages, if you look at them from the air, or you look at them from the point of view of ethnicity, or you look at them in terms of different kinds of consumer groups, or any index of diversity, you get an incredible patchwork quilt that is irreducibly pluralist and very similar, actually, to Los Angeles, where I lived for twenty-five years. Los Angeles has the greatest diversity index of any place, at least it did. New York was supposed to be number one – and you wrote about that in *Delirious New York* – with two thousand and twenty-eight super blocks, and that was called the melting pot. In that image Los Angeles appeared like a kind of pizza with all the extras. London becomes even more diverse, apparently, according to sociologists. If you look up the *Guardian Index of Minorities* in Britain on the web you'll find that London has a shape rather like that which I illustrate in my book, *Heteropolis*, on Los Angeles. It has an incredible amount of ethnic groups, one hundred of them. Now those ethnicities are very strict, down to British categories, which are full of euphemisms, by the way, and false categories, but they still show a hundred different groups. I could start mentioning them from Australians through to Zimbabweans. I'm American as you can probably hear; when I came here there were a hundred thousand Americans in London. Now they don't call us a minority any more; they don't even keep count: we have disappeared. Like you're from London and you're Dutch; you don't appear as a minority either, Rem. So what I am trying to say is that this incredible diversity is, of course, the post-modern condition; the number one part of it that everybody agrees on is pluralism. It seems to me that a city is a mechanism for sustaining difference, and I think you see after 7/7, after 7 July last year, that amazingly sophisticated people in these minorities know that London is a kind of place of diversity: they didn't panic and they didn't turn against each other. That shows that the people of London have very good self-awareness; in the 1960s they used to be called 'the knowing consumer'. I think that Londoners are the most heteropolitan people in the world, so I am really happy to live here and talk about it.

Hans Ulrich Obrist   In preparation for this Marathon Rem and I discussed in particular your book *Meaning in Architecture*, which I think is very interesting in relation to its proposing a different kind of rule of the game for how a book can work. It's a very polyphonic way of dealing with the authors in a book, so I was wondering if you could tell us a little bit about *Meaning in Architecture*.

CJ   That was written in 1969, in a period when meaning was being denied in architecture and George Baird and I, who edited it, had a lot of time between the writing of it – it was written by fourteen people – and the publication. So we decided to send it out to all the contributors and have them comment on each other at the most vulnerable place in a text with a little arrow saying, for instance, 'Reyner Banham, you're completely wrong'. That's what George Baird would say. And then Banham would answer it in another little arrow going against Baird, 'Go back to Canada and learn about architecture', or something. It was very rude hypertext. It was one of the first hypertexts, I think, and it came out of this notion that difference and pluralism make meaning. In other words, people always used to think that what we wanted in culture, the Prince Charles view, the classical view, even the reigning view of modernists, is unanimity, what we want is some kind of consensus. Well, one doesn't have to exaggerate dissensus or disagreement to realise that conversation, which is what you intend to have here, the enjoyable quality of a conversation, is all about difference. If we didn't disagree, have some difference, we couldn't converse. It's like a battery; if you are a plus charge and I am a minus charge we can exchange energy, but if we're both minus charges, where do we go from there? For me the great example is a city like Edinburgh in the eighteenth century; the Enlightenment started at dining tables, conversing, and if you couldn't converse and keep the conversation going then you weren't invited back. I think that's the name of the city.

RK I think your character is, in a way, seemingly smooth but for me there are two recognisable sides: you as an actor and as somebody who converses and is provocative, playful, etc., but I think there is also a you who is more rigorous and, however much you may hate the word, dogmatic. I want to bring this in focus, your two sides, in your preoccupation with the future. I think that nobody has invested so much energy in a career in predicting facts, in predicting trends, in predicting events, basically in predicting the future. None of us would dare to make that such a crucial part of their career. Recently you told me that you actually have very high success rates, between seventy and eighty per cent. So what we all think is a playful game for you to predict the future, is in fact pretty much a life and death situation of almost grim precision. Can you say something about these two sides of you or why it is so important that the futures you predict actually happen?

CJ Well, maybe, as opposed to Brian Eno, I believe in teleology, in unfolding the predictability of events. In January 2003 a group of architects, of which you were one, signed a petition against war and we predicted five things that would happen if Bush took Blair and Blair took some others to Iraq. All five things happened, uncannily almost exactly as we wrote them in that open letter which was published. I think a lot of international relations are predictable.

Again, it's a cliché of our time that with global warming it's a fifty-year super tanker, as Brian Eno said, that can't be turned around. It takes fifty years to turn it around, if it's ever going to turn. We have apocalypse fatigue at the moment because there are so many negatives that are both happening and predicted for our future. Since you and I Rem – not you, Hans Ulrich, you're too young – are people from the 1960s when, in a sense, the apocalypse started at home, we've been predicting this meltdown for such a long time that we have apocalypse fatigue. I do believe we've got to invent humorous, enjoyable, funny metaphors for getting over that fatigue. I see globalisation like John Gray, the philosopher here in London, who says whatever you think about globalisation, don't be fooled. In global meltdowns there is going to be an incredible difference in the outcomes, just as there are five or six capitalisms around the world, struggling, competing, there is not a single way it's going. So we have to predict what the five possible outcomes could be, which ones are likely to occur, and be critical of them. So I see prediction as a critical tool in order to get a fulcrum on politics and the future. The best predictions wouldn't be true because they would be countered by our actions if we were effective politically. So I see prediction and intervention as two parts of the same coin.

That figure of getting it right eighty per cent of the time, of course, is ridiculous and made up by me. I wrote a book on the year 2000 in 1969 and I re-wrote it in the year 2000 to see what had come true. According to my score eighty per cent had come true, but I'm sure if you ask Ken Frampton, about five per cent came true. So never judge by the author!

RK   You're primarily an intellectual, I would say, a writer, but recently you've also become a designer, or, you have been a designer for a very long time but design seems to become more important as part of your repertoire. Can you say something about your emergence as a designer and why it is happening and what you think you can contribute fundamentally which you cannot contribute as a writer?

CJ   Well Rem, I started off designing and writing like you did and I think they are again two sides of the same thing. Although my designing has always been marginal, I am a writer who architects if you like, who designs, rather than a designer who writes. But I think that you gain insight if you struggle with design and you face things that you wouldn't face if you were just a writer. Le Corbusier is my model of a man who developed different parts of his character, of his brain and his activities through painting and all the rest of it. I think that it's multi-modal and the writing and design have to inform each other because the design has to be predictive of the future, it has to in a certain sense be utopian, in a certain sense ideal, in a certain sense critical. My design is very dogmatic, as you would say, and it has to do with the necessity of having iconography. I think one of the most evasive things of our time is our inability to come up with content (something you talk about) which is inter-subjective and fought over and believed in. So I am dogmatically committed to seeing if there are things that you can really have design about, and of course I've come up with all these ideas about nature and the universe. So I'm a dogmatist about cosmogenic art, which I'm happy to bore you with if you keep asking me. *[Laughs]*

HUO Can you give us an example in terms of your house? Rem has told me a lot about your house.

CJ I'm a bit embarrassed to talk about my house. Again experimenting on myself, it's a cosmic house. You enter the door; there are twenty-eight themes as you come in, each one is written. It starts off over your head with a bang and then the universe evolves around you. This was designed in 1979–84 and it was designed when the Steady State theory and the Big Bang and the Crunch were all competing, to a degree. So I hedged my bets at the end of the universe. Below that is a cultural story about pluralism which starts with the Willendorf *Venus* and ends with E. H. Gombrich, who disappears. He came once to the house and said, 'Oh, I always put people to sleep when I talk', which is rather nice, anyway. It's thematic: it's designed around themes and themes are mostly to do with nature and the cosmos, mostly the cosmos. That has been my interest from the beginning and still is.

HUO Can we talk a little bit more about London, a recurring theme of this Marathon? Is there such a thing as a theory of London? Certain cities have been consistently referred to with definitions; but is it possible to define London?

RK And I would like to complicate the question by asking whether you think the shapelessness of London, which is about to undergo a huge transformation with a lot of architectural additions by major, presumably iconic architects, will be enhanced or threatened by this future.

CJ Oh dear! That's kind of an impossible question. Anyway, in regard to impossible questions one always has a kind of escape. First of all, my belief about design in cities and theories about cities is that cities, in a way, are by-products of economy, like perspiration: when you run you perspire and when you have an economy you have the city. We should never forget that. So a city is a parasite on the countryside to a degree; ninety-five per cent of the energy and food comes from outside, eats up the countryside and pollutes everything. So it's this kind of unconscious process of economy and people are drawn to it for cultural, economic and social reasons. And then after it gets a consciousness of itself and survives various catastrophes, the city keeps restructuring itself, from the very beginning. So it's re-design and you get a mayor, for example Livingstone, or the mayor of Barcelona, who says we must grip the congestion or X or Y and then you get a burst of plans and re-design and then it sinks back into the perspiration mode. So I think a city is sometimes design and sometimes letting go and it's never been totally controlled, just as the economy has never been.

Architects have a completely false view of this, for very good reasons: they want to make work, they want to convince society they are in charge of the city and they can do something, and they maybe design three per cent of it or two per cent, maybe influence thirty to forty per cent, but it's always out of control. We are always trying to make it better. I'm not against design at all; I'm all in favour of it but I think we have a false consciousness when talking about it. One of the iconic buildings – and I have in my pocket here the most iconic building ever designed in the last fifteen minutes – which is the Tate Modern. It's just appeared. And it's amazing it's made it onto the front page. Anyone who hasn't seen this hasn't been reading the papers or watching television *[waves newspaper around]*. Now that's incredible for architects to find that from an unselfconscious background Herzog & De Meuron have suddenly jumped onto the iconic bandwagon with Nick Serota and managed to convince ninety per cent of the elite critics that we really need this kind of Frank Gehry icon. Frank designed one of these cubic buildings for Nîmes in 1985 and was beaten by Norman Foster. It's that kind of building, which Herzog said is freaky on the one hand and then he said it's very much designed from the inside out, a series of cubes. He didn't say, but there are fifty cubes there. Now fifty white cubes on the outside and eighty white cubes on the inside of his former Tate Modern makes a hundred and thirty white cubes. If you read the theory of the white cube in art – read Brian O'Doherty, Patrick Ireland on the white cube – modernism stuck a white cube into art and more or less killed the art object by putting it into a de-contextualised Protestant chapel. Having a hundred and thirty of them is maybe over-white-cubism, it's white cubism cubed. This is not to criticise it, because as Serota says, why can't art – finally the cathedral of our time, the cliché since the 1980s – why can't it be an icon rather than just commercial buildings? Absolutely right! I think that the argument from content is that if you are having an icon, let's have it there. And it's certainly a typical iconic building because it's completely enigmatic and not a pyramid. It's a non-pyramid – that famous phrase about the nude descending a staircase and an explosion in a shingle factory – it's a series of little white cubes that are exploding over each other and made out of this amazing Herzog glass. So, well…! *[Laughter]*

HUO	Maybe that's a nice conclusion. We have one more question. I was wondering if you have any dreams for London, any projects you dream of?
RK	Or whether you yourself have an unrealised project.
HUO	Yes, projects which you tried to realise, which for all sorts of reasons have been unrealised, so they could also be realisable.
CJ	Rem accused me of being dogmatic, and I am dogmatic about the cosmogenic and the universe project, which is what I am committed to. How about that as a project? – *The Unfinished Project* (to quote Habermas project about modernity), the unfinished project of the universe, 13.7 billion years old, and still running. It is really the ultimate referent; I think of it as a collective project of designing an appropriate iconography to understand and appreciate it. I'm interested in working with all sorts of different kinds of people, scientists and artists, craftsmen, designers, architects, builders, to re-route our culture in an understanding, as Gauguin painted, of "where we come from, who we are and where we are going". In that universe project it seems to me it's fundamental that cosmogenesis, like the Genesis myth, is the operating manual for our local solar system. So yes, that's an unfinished project that I'm very committed to.
HUO	Many thanks to Charles Jencks. Thank you.
CJ	Thank you.

Applause, end of interview

Hans Ulrich Obrist Rem Koolhaas	It's a great pleasure to welcome Ken Adam. And we will start with a five to six minute compilation of his work as a set designer to refamiliarise each of you. *[Audio-visual film shown on ten monitors situated around the inside of the Pavilion]*
HUO	We are very happy to start the interview with Kenneth Adam after the introductory images. We'll ask some questions about these ground-breaking production designs but also about his architectural projects and about spy movies. To begin at the beginning, it would be interesting, having seen the document on the screens, if you could tell us a little bit about the great moment of your Oscar.
Kenneth Adam	Well, the first nomination I had was in 1956 for the original *Around the World in Eighty Days* and my first Oscar I got for a film called *Barry Lyndon*, which Stanley Kubrick directed. Actually the film was not one of my happiest experiences, but you know *[Laughs]*, I was very happy to get the Academy Award. Then I had a second Oscar for a film from the same period, strangely enough, as *Barry Lyndon*, which we shot in England in 1995; it was called *The Madness of King George* and it is a film which we did for ten million dollars and shot in ten weeks before it came on the screen, so I was very proud of that. I was responsible for doing the first seven Bond films with the exception of *From Russia With Love* and I've always been asked why I never received an Academy Award for the Bond films. I think in a way at the time when I designed those Bond films, which was mainly in the 1960s and the 1970s, they were so successful that the producers or United Artists never thought of trying to sell them for Academy Award nomination. In fact I was nominated for one Bond film, which was *The Spy Who Loved Me* and I didn't get it. I lost it to *Star Wars*, well deserved at the time. *[Laughs]*
RK	If you see all your work then the spaces that you designed for evil people or for evil processes stand out as by far the most memorable and intense. How do you explain your ability to design environments for evil?
KA	I don't know. *[Laughter]*

I have been asked that question, Rem, many times and critics feel it may have had something to do with my past; I was born in Germany, I left Germany as a refugee in 1934. But I don't think so, really, because my sets of evil are always with a tongue in cheek attitude. I always tried to get a little bit of humour into it and they appealed to me. I don't know. To mix dark modernism with antiques and sort of juxtapose one thing against the other and at the same time, hopefully, treat it with a sense of humour.

RK   I think that is certainly evident but there is also a really exceptional intelligence. Do you realise, for instance, how much influence some of your sets have had on contemporary architecture, or do you realise how envious many of us are that you can realise with relatively simple means what some of us are doing with incredible effort and less success?

KA   Well, thank you very much. You've made my evening. *[Laughs]* *[Laughter]*
Frankly I did not realise until the Serpentine had their first exhibition.

RK   In 1999.

KA   Yes, an exhibition of a film designer in a fine arts gallery.

HUO   It could be very interesting to hear a little bit more about this Serpentine exhibition, which was actually curated by the late David Sylvester.

KA   Absolutely.

HUO   He is the great inspiration for our whole interview project because we probably wouldn't have started it without his groundbreaking book of interviews with Francis Bacon, which was a trigger for me to start doing interviews. Could you tell us about your dialogue with David Sylvester and how this exhibition here at the Serpentine happened and how it worked?

KA   Yes. I had known David when I went to prep school in London. It was called Vernon House School and he was – you wouldn't believe it – but a weed of a scholar and I didn't respect him very much because he was collected by his parents after school. He was a little bit, we thought, of a sissy. Little did we know! But then eventually I lost touch with David. Obviously I heard about his work as a curator and so on but I met him again when the Royal College granted me an honorary doctorate and he was in the audience. He then approached me and we started our contact again after so many years. He said, 'One thing I absolutely want to do before I die is to launch an exhibition of your work'. And he did. It was for me unbelievably exciting because, you see, as a film designer my main purpose of a sketch or doodle, or whatever it is, is the set or scene I design, it's not how I get there. So to suddenly find out that my sketches or concepts were considered art came as a big surprise to me and again I felt very proud and very flattered. David in many ways became my mentor because he spent hours at my home looking through my work, throwing stuff away and saying if something would appeal to him and we became very close. In fact I think ten days or twelve days before he died I gave one of the last interviews to him at his home, which is part of his autobiography, published posthumously in 2003.

HUO   Rem mentioned the incredible influence of your work on the world of architecture and that made me think it would be interesting to ask if you had had architectural projects, if there was ever the idea of you going into the world of architecture and actually building.

KA   I started off that way. I studied at the Bartlett School of Architecture, London University, prior to the Second World War but I really never wanted to be an architect. I was advised by a very famous film designer called Vincent Corda that if I wanted to get into film or theatre design he thought an architectural background was very useful, rather than the background of a painter like he had. So I never finished my architectural studies, also because of the outbreak of the Second World War, but it no doubt had an important influence on all my work. On the one hand I liked drawing with T-square and set square and I liked the history of architecture styles and periods but eventually I had to liberate myself from the restrictions of architecture and free myself as a film designer. But I'm very grateful I had that background.

RK   Do you continue to watch movies?
KA   Yes, I do.

RK   And what is your opinion about the fact that larger and larger parts of what used to be sets are now digital environments that have no physical reality and that seem to have, increasingly, an effect on the reality, as you named it, of movies in general?
KA   I think it's a very important question, Rem, and I've thought about it. I think CGIs, computer generated images, are an incredible advance in technology but they should be treated as such and not as a means of

making whole films, for several reasons. I think first of all the director, who is the prime artistic element in making a film; well, if he feels everything is possible I think this limits his artistic input. Whereas we knew that if you, to give an example, have an attack on some fortress or something you can only have a thousand extras, now you can have a hundred thousand extras, so everything is possible. I think that in the long term this is not good. The other thing I feel is that the technique of film acting has completely changed because you no longer have the surroundings of a setting or a location which inspired many of the great actors I had the privilege of working with. You stand in front of a green screen and you might on a monitor see an object or something you are playing against – but it is a completely different technique. So my feeling is it is a fabulous tool and it should be used as such but I think there are limitations to it.

HUO   I have a last question, a recurring question in all the interviews of the London Marathon. I was wondering if you had any dreams, projects which are yet unrealised, projects you dream of realising.

KA   I always dream but you know, I think lately my dreams are becoming less dreamy, somehow, because one has to face reality. Unfortunately one has to face the fact that one isn't any longer maybe in the prime of one's artistic life or activity. Maybe one day I would like to have a go at something like this at the Serpentine. *[Laughs]*
[Applause]

HUO   Many, many thanks.

KA   Thank you.

RK   Thank you. Impressive!

Applause, end of interview

Rem Koolhaas	Our next guest is Zaha Hadid.
Zaha Hadid	Hello.

Hans Ulrich Obrist   We are thrilled to welcome Zaha Hadid to the London Interview Marathon. To begin, we wanted to ask you about London. Some years ago you were telling me that for you London, as a city, could almost be viewed as an unrealised project; I was wondering what would be your assessment of London now in 2006.

ZH   I think it is still an unrealised project for me, and I still feel it is a very exciting city because it is so unpredictable. Maybe it is more predictable than before but every time you think you know it well, something comes along and surprises you. And I think that also shifts your opinion about what you might do there, constantly. So in that sense, it's still a kind of educational situation for me.

RK   There is a problem, that we know each other very well.

ZH   Too well for comfort, yes?
[Laughter]

RK   And I follow your career very closely, so I think the questions I would like to ask you are more intimate in a way. So if you don't want to answer I would completely understand.

ZH   That's OK.

RK   I think your career is at a very interesting moment that actually very few people reach, where you have to decide whether to repeat things or whether to continue to innovate.

ZH   I think I am in a position now where I can do both. As you know from your own work, there are things you can use as a generic project, but there's still an excitement about inventing things. So I don't think one precludes the other.

RK   Can you be specific there? Can you give an example of a generic thing you have built?

ZH Let's take the MAXXI [Museum of Art for the XXI Century] project in Rome as an example. We are trying to turn space into linear lines and show how they separate and connect. You can look at that diagram in a variety of ways and you can apply it to Rome or you can apply it to the BMW production facilities, because that line has to do with that kind of site. The image could be generic – not only in terms of programme, but also formal language. On the other hand, the years of endless work not winning a single competition gave us an incredible opportunity providing us with an enormous repertoire that allowed us to invent. It allowed us to rely on our own experience and previous inventions to move on to the next project. I don't think you have to reinvent the wheel all the time.

RK I have another question and it's not really related. I am totally fascinated because I am now, for the first time, working in the Arab world and my entry there follows yours, maybe by a year. You're Iraqi, of course; you are not working in Iraq but you are now working in Abu Dhabi, in Dubai and in other places there. What is your feeling about entering, as an Arab, the Arab world at the moment of its maximum Westernisation?

ZH I think it is very interesting. I entered the Arab world many years ago with a bridge in Abu Dhabi, which has taken a long time to make because they are literally knitting the steel as it comes along because it is so expensive; it is a knitting job. I don't want to be critical of the Arab world: they always favoured foreigners, non-Arabs, because there was always a feeling that those people are better informed than their own people – which I don't think has always been the case. Just look at the poor planning work done in Kuwait or in Iraq in the 1960s and the 1970s. The same applies to Saudi Arabia. The work done in Lebanon on the downtown, which is a very relevant story right now, is also problematic. I think there has been a shift recently that you could describe as a combination of extreme Westernisation and a pride in Arab identity. I think that I have entered the Arab world during that moment. Nowadays I have the impression that they tend to hire an Arab because they want to associate with someone who is 'successful' in the eyes of the world. I think it is very interesting. I was in Dubai and met with the ruling family, and I didn't have the same feeling as before. Suddenly things are possible that weren't necessarily possible before.

RK And do you notice that there is some effect of Arabness in your work there?

ZH   I think that the effect of Arabness, as you call it, *[Laughter]* coincides with certain interests right now in terms of the whole landscape project, which is related with dunes and stuff like that. There is also interest in Aldus pixelation and geometry which relates a great deal to the Arab identity in terms of algebra, geometry and mathematics. It's suddenly possible to connect in terms of materials and ideas. So, yes, there is a connection, not only for me, but there is also an interest abroad in these ideas. Not forgetting the whole idea of the courtyard; I think that could be reinvented again.

RK   I think that Dubai is usually caricatured, in the same way that Singapore was caricatured maybe ten years ago, in a way, as a place of excess, 'Disneyfication', etc. Do you think there is a deeper and more creative background?

ZH   There are some extreme ideas that could be very interesting and I think it is possible to do them there. The more extreme the idea, the more it is welcomed, not because you want to make a kind of freak show, but because you want to create things which could actually make other places look at Dubai or build up the work. I think it depends on the ambition of individuals in the office. Ambition means pushing boundaries and I think Dubai is the place where pushing boundaries is possible at the moment.

HUO   Can you tell us about some examples of projects you are doing right now in Dubai or in the region in terms of your own practice, and projects which are not possible here but would be possible there?

ZH   I think they are possible in many places. I just say that the scale of the work is not always possible everywhere. It is possible in China; maybe it is possible in parts of America. Take for example these towers we are doing in Dubai, which Rem is also working on. The scheme grew; it was already enormous, now it includes a bridge and a stock exchange and museums. The scale, I think, is intriguing – it is an idealist skyline, which is interesting. People demean the Arabs and in the West they are always going to think there is something funny about them; that they are running around with dresses and they wear funny clothes, they are covered. But there is a spirit there which I think is used in an interesting way in terms of the urban fabric and architecture. We are also supposed to be doing the opera house in Dubai, which is an island. We don't know about that yet. I was also doing work in downtown Beirut, but I think now with the situation there, it is really the least of their problems.

HUO   Can you tell us about this project? Was it an urban scheme for part of Beirut?

ZH   No, it's not. One is a bank headquarters and the other one is a building for the AUB [American University of Beirut], where I studied many years ago. I don't think they meant to insult me, but they adapted the idea of a perimeter block, which is really not appropriate for the city because Beirut is not Berlin. Instead of making a thousand blocks they made five, so the scale is weird. I think they started off wanting to do an American downtown like Atlanta and then they shifted to Berlin. By doing that, they made Beirut into a *tabula rasa* – into one flat plane – even though the city was much more layered. And they did not have common discourses about complexity and different ways of dealing with urban renewal.

RK   If I look at your career, I think that there is a first phase where your own signature, your own work, your own hand, you own rush, is incredibly imaginative, inventive and crucial to every single project. If you look at the firm now, and also at how the firm presents itself, it is a firm dedicated to digital production and, according to rumour, awesomely efficient in terms of working on enormous projects with relatively few people. Very few people I know have succeeded in making this transition from being almost a miniaturist to a kind of hypermodern and contemporary organisation. Has it been as seamless as it seems and have you lost something, or, what have you lost and what have you gained?

ZH   I resisted digitisation for a very long time. The fascinating thing is that with three-dimensional work, it was not so complicated because the computing almost imitated the way we worked. So it was an interesting transition. Now it is less complex, it's less transparent and it's much more opaque and, let's say, real. I still think the work that was done in graphical presentation was originally more complex and less predictable. On the other hand, when we were ten people, we were doing the work of thirty because we worked three shifts. We are now one hundred and fifty people doing the work of four hundred and fifty people. It's very interesting, not because people work extremely hard but because, as I said earlier, during the days and the years when we were locked up in Bowling Green Lane with nobody paying attention to us, we all did a tremendous amount of research and this gave us tremendous ability to reinvent and to work on things. And – although it's hard to generalise – it was also exciting to see that young people who came in with no experience, I think if you gave them enough confidence, they actually could be as good as someone who had twenty or even thirty years experience if there are the right people around to guide them. As you well know, the most important trick is to be able to delegate. You know from early on that you can't do everything yourself; you can do bits of it yourself, you can make people do things the way you want them done, but you have to rely also on their own invention and their own challenge and abilities. I think that teamwork has been very important to me for a long time. I have always believed in it and that is why it is manageable.

RK   And yet there are things that only you can do. What would you say you concentrate on now?

ZH   Well, I was in a car with somebody from my office and he said, 'You're too fast. I can't write everything you are saying and I can't do whatever you are telling me to do'. I said, 'I'm on a roll'. I don't think I can do anything better than others particularly; but I can see things when I focus very clearly, with no confusion. Put another way, I can confuse people but I don't confuse myself. That is the great advantage I have. So I might send you off in a haze of confusion, but I am quite focused. I can plan and organise very well; I still am very good at that. And thinking of things which are not always predictable in terms of what I would do with a project; I still think I do that well. And I can now also be charming. *[Laughter]* People always used to think I couldn't.

RK   Talking about charming. *[Laughter]*

ZH   I have never tried it with you.

RK   There are, equally, two periods in your life; one, now, when you are honoured and a previous life when you were neglected, not to say insulted. Are there parts of that current condition that you find painful and of the previous life that you relished?

ZH   When I was neglected or ignored I always thought that it would be a passing phase. There were moments, when I felt extremely down, but my depression never lasts very long. I am fundamentally an optimist and I knew I would eventually come out of that situation. I don't take the acclaim terribly seriously though – perhaps unfortunately. I think it is fantastic and I am very grateful for it, but I don't take it so seriously that it affects my life. I believe when there are good moments you have to recognise them and enjoy them, and that's it.

HUO That leads to a more general question. Rem was asking you about the current moment in relation to your whole practice. I wanted to extend the question and ask how you assess the current moment right now in the world and how you see it.

ZH For me it's a very interesting moment. However, it's still very difficult for women to operate as professionals. There are still worlds you have no access to. In practice, I still offer resistance all the time, and I think that keeps you on the go. It's not that I am there and everybody says 'yes' to me; it's still a struggle, despite having gone through it a hundred times. It's not necessarily always great but I think it keeps you in place, and it also makes you think about things in a different way.

HUO To come back to London, it would be interesting to hear from you if there is such a thing as a theory about London and what it would be.

ZH The old theory about London is always about a city which is made of many villages that merged and created areas of density and a metropolitan condition. We did a project, which was very interesting, more than twenty years ago at the AA [Architectural Association]. We drew lines through the city and we travelled on these lines. That was a very interesting project because, first of all, it showed certain things aligned with each other and certain things, when you jump from one level to the other, were tremendously varied. I think that it has become much more homogenised, but there are still major gaps in the city that would allow for a major urban intervention of an interesting scale. But nobody seems to have taken on the challenge. They either want to look at all of the South Bank as one project or to look at larger areas where you can intervene, but not a way that would allow a degree of lightness to come into the city. I think all the new development is very heavy-handed and not as light as it could be. It is still a fortified city. I feel that the main focus is still on the urban perimeter block, and this is also something that could be changed.

HUO When you spoke about London and the unrealised projects, you announced you are now designing a project in London in terms of a permanent building. Can you tell us about this?

ZH We are doing the Architecture Foundation Building. I wouldn't call that a major project; it's a very small thing behind the Tate and I'm not saying that against the Tate or against anything but it's a very tiny intervention. It's maybe the size of a pavilion, which is nice. Another project is the Aquatic Centre.

RK In the space of one week there have been two pyramids launched: yours for the Architecture Foundation and a pyramid for the Tate.

ZH Mine is an upside-down pyramid.

RK That's what I wanted to talk about; do you know the Fountain Head? In the Fountain Head they have a sign of a genius and I think that is a genius of the set designer. The sign of genius is to design an inverted pyramid and this is your first inverted pyramid.

ZH For the Foundation building, we had to make major changes and simplify the project because Land Securities could not afford the original idea. I always felt like I was in front of three projects which are three very large, corporate boxes behind the Tate, and the only thing you could do is something looking like a flower, in a way, in front of these boxes. So it came out as an inverted pyramid. Now people are saying, 'What do you think about the Tate project? Another sign of genius'.
[Laughter]

RK Evidence of genius.

ZH Evidence. OK.

HUO I was wondering if you have any dream projects for London or any unrealised projects you would like to see happen.

ZH London always inspires projects that are unpredictable. Look at the site for the Olympics. This was done more than fifteen years ago in a drawing about how London should be developed eastward. I still think these projects are possible. How do deal with the site between the Festival Hall and all the projects farther east? There are still all these quirky situations. There is an obsession here about making everything look nice or feel nice, but niceness is not appropriate in London because the city relies on a slight messiness. If it were possible to do a project which is not so even and clear, it would be more interesting than this idea of rectifying everything to make it more manageable.

HUO   Many, many thanks to Zaha Hadid.

RK   Thank you very much.   .

Applause, end of interview

Hans Ulrich Obrist   We have now the great pleasure of introducing our next guest, Yinka Shonibare. Welcome.
[Applause]

Rem Koolhaas   I think your work is very beautiful and it's also very generous. I would like to ask you about that generosity because although you work with African, but in fact Dutch, textiles, your subject is very English. You work on the dandy, you work on the Victorian age and in your work there seems to be an absolute absence of reproach, which is actually quite rare. In a sort of way instead of criticising England you seem to want to preserve some of its values. Can you say something about that?

Yinka Shonibare MBE   Well, it's interesting you should say that. When I started work in the mid-1980s, really identity issues were the main things that people were working on. After the period of the Civil Rights Movement there has been feminist art and post-colonial practice, and from the earlier generation I could see that there was actually a lot of anger. But I realised that the anger wasn't really taking people anywhere. Of course I understand that the anger was very important in terms of an identity discourse, in terms of visibility as an artist of African origin, and I really felt that a Trojan horse strategy would be more effective; a strategy of parody, I thought, would be more interesting. Of course talking in terms of parody and disguise, well I'm sure many of you know this, I was awarded an MBE and I am a member of the British Empire. I was actually ambivalent because, as you know, Benjamin Zephaniah, a poet of Caribbean origin, refused this award because of the history of colonialism. But I chose to adopt the MBE as my artist's name because of some of the issues in your question, really; I thought this would make a few people ask questions about the legacy, if you like, of the empire and the question of equality and visibility within society generally and the art world. Of course I also primarily consider myself an idealist. I think the idealism that made me want to become an artist in a sense remains with me into my career. When I talk about idealism what I am really talking about is the issue of actually questioning representation and questioning visibility within society.

HUO In relation to Rem's question it would be interesting to hear from you how you work within London and to which extent a strategy of infiltration or subversion would work within the city. I have heard a lot in the last couple of months about the project you did in the Underground, which was a sort of underground infiltration, so it would be good to hear about your work and the city.

YS What you are talking about is a project called *Diary of a Victorian Dandy* [1998] in which I basically was in a stately home, I suppose, a very grand place. I enjoy trying different clothes – I have a kind of a fetish, if you like, for Oscar Wilde – so with a number of actors, about ten of us, every day we just got dressed and replayed this Victorian period. I wanted to challenge people's view of representation with this; so, on about forty sites on the London Underground I had these huge posters and the poster of a day in the life of a Victorian dandy. But of course if you look at historical painting, at Hogarth, in the images of Africans you would see they were generally in a more subservient position, like valets. Basically I put this image of an African more or less in the front of the piece. The good thing about those posters was that I didn't really indicate whether they were for a film or for anything. The images caught a lot of people's attention. In terms of public art, I felt that in the context of the London Underground possibly four to five million Londoners were able to engage with the work without actually having to go into the gallery, whereas with a gallery exhibition you probably have your mother and a couple of friends. *[Laughs]* In terms of actually engaging people directly, I thought that was, in a way, quite effective in terms of the response that I got.

RK I have some questions about your biography. If I calculate correctly you went from London to Lagos in the 1970s and you came back to London in the late 1980s or early 1990s.

YS Yes.

RK And that means that you lived in Lagos in a very fundamental and critical moment. In the 1970s it was an incredibly active city where in a way the future of Africa was being worked out, and in the 1980s and 1990s it was a city in a situation of profound crisis and dysfunctionality. What is your conscious memory of Lagos and what is the influence of Lagos on your whole thinking?

YS   It's very interesting you should talk about Lagos and also, actually, the issue of colonialism as well, because my parents belonged to a very optimistic generation. My father studied law in England, where I was born, then I went back to Nigeria with my parents when I was three. This was a period of independence in Nigeria; there was a lot of optimism and of course the pan-African movement happened, people challenged Western ideas of colonialism and the administration was subsequently handed over to Africans. But of course the feeling of utopia didn't lead to the kind of riches for the society that were hoped for. There was a civil war, I remember, when I was growing up in Nigeria; it was a Biafra civil war. Some of you probably know about this. So the early sense of optimism that my parents had about creating an ideal, democratic, African society evolved more or less into military dictatorship. Most of the time that I was living in Nigeria there was a military dictatorship. You have probably heard about people like Fela Kuti and Wole Soyinka and some of the pioneering Nigerian artists; an artist at that time could actually be thrown into gaol for being political. The change of context for me and the freedom that I see it's possible to enjoy in the West are important. So for me freedom of artistic expression is more than it might be, say, for people who haven't experienced or do not understand a regime who will try to stop you from having it. This is rather unfortunate but that's the situation in which I had to make the decision to develop my career elsewhere.

HUO   We started the evening with a conversation with David Adjaye, who was on his way to Johannesburg. He is working more and more in Africa and is making a sort of portrait of all African capitals, but he is also starting to build there. I was wondering if you have any activities or projects or exhibitions planned in Lagos.

YS   I have not, as yet. I haven't been invited to make projects in Lagos, although there are quite a few people talking about that right now. I've shown in Ghana and in South Africa as well, but not as yet in Lagos.

RK   Have you been in Lagos recently?

YS   Well, the rather strange thing is that I have not been in Lagos for, I would say, probably twenty-six years, so I have not been there for a long time although I've had ongoing contacts.

RK One of your works I find particularly striking, because it's so complete-ly seemingly unrelated to anything, is *Space Walk* [2002]. Perhaps you can establish a relationship for me.

YS *[Laughs]* Again, I did that work because I was actually thinking about the idea of utopia, but also I was thinking about colonialism and the dis-covery of undiscovered places, about the space exploration as the new kind of frontier, the next 'heart of darkness', if you like, to follow Con-rad. But I thought it was interesting to bring the African textiles into that because there is another aspect of African-American funk which actual-ly looks at space travel as the alternative to a world in which racism ex-ists, and so on. So it's kind of a thought dimension.

HUO I interviewed the musician George Clinton a few years ago and he re-ferred to Afro Futurism as a movement or an idea. Is there a link?

YS Yes, but in terms of the current debate about the environment and the various failures of NASA, in a way it's a failed mission, a failed project.

HUO You have mentioned on two or three occasions the word 'utopia'. I was wondering if you could talk a little bit more about what you mean by that notion of utopia in your work.

RK The interesting thing is that every speaker has mentioned utopia and has been provoked by it.

HUO There are so many notions around utopia. Ernst Bloch, when he was pushed against the wall by Adorno in a heated conversation to say what he really meant by utopia, said, 'something is missing'. I am curious as to what your idea of utopia would be.

YS I don't know if that situation will ever exist but it would be a world in which you could actually look at people who are different from you and somehow acknowledge the difference but be comfortable with it. If such a thing should happen I imagine perpetual art-ness, a world in which we could perpetually become artists and we would perpetually be creative and we would actually be able to not see the difference of others and we would become one. It sounds very hippy but in a way I actually still be-lieve in this notion of idealism which can somehow remove global con-flict: I believe art is a unique platform. This is why I love art so much, because it does transcend prejudice. It is the true space in which preju-dice can actually be transcended: this is my feeling about it.

HUO   That leads to another question which is about your own utopias or projects which have been too big to be realised, dreams, or also projects which for whatever reasons have not happened, censored projects. Could you tell us a little about the yet-unrealised in your work?

YS   There was a project in France that I was going to realise and it didn't really happen because I wanted the local government to give me a lot of money to expose French colonial practices in the nineteenth century. The work was very expensive to produce and I wanted the government money to do it. The administrators got a bit nervous about this and it didn't happen.

HUO   Where was this? In which city?

YS   I don't want to be too specific at the moment. *[Laughs]* *[Laughter]*

RK   It's very moving to hear you speak about art as a space of generosity, but if you look around you at the English art scene and the almost industrial dimension and importance of art in London, do you recognise some of that, do you feel engaged with that or do you worry about it? You were part of *Sensation* [*Sensation: Young British Artists from the Saatchi Collection*, Royal Academy of the Arts, London, 1997] and you seem to have chosen a different way.

YS   Again, I would like to think that I retain my madness as an artist. By my madness I mean not giving in to economy. In my view money should always follow culture, culture should never follow money. Don't get me wrong, I love money as much as the next person but my frustration about this scene you talk about is that, sadly, we are reaching a stage in which it's the other way round: culture is following money and I think that money is stupid and that artists should never be a slave to this. I believe strongly in that. I believe that basically the art scene that we have now is not challenging capital enough. I think capital should be challenged by the artists.

RK   I would like to end on that note. Thank you very much.

HUO   Thank you so much.

Applause, end of interview

Rem Koolhaas   America is not known for its management of public infrastructure, so your appointment as Managing Director of London Underground has been a surprise in some quarters. What does the fact that you are an American bring in terms of special expertise?

Tim O'Toole   I met with some employees once and asked them if they had any questions. One of them said, 'There are sixty-five million people on this island. What the hell did we need you for?' So I know there is some scepticism of my coming over here but actually I don't come from public operation of railways. I operated a freight railway in the United States. It ran from New York to Chicago and down to St. Louis and up to Montreal. So I actually had never run a metro before but they came to me because I had a background in finance that they thought might be useful in trying to deal with the rebuilding of the Underground.

RK   One of the themes of this series of interviews is reinvention and you mentioned the rebuilding of the Underground. What does the Underground need beyond repair and maintenance? What can be new about an Underground?

TO   Just about everything's got to be new. It was really mortgaged over the last thirty years to build the JLE and no real money went into it. New York went through the exact same thing. It was in a far worse state than London; New York used to have one derailment a day before they put about $27 billion into the system.

The same thing has to happen here, so it really means you've got to rebuild all the track, you've got to buy new trains, you have to put in new signal systems. What's different about London is the tunnels are so small and so deep underground that it's unique. If you think of any metro in the world there are great, large tunnels very close to the surface; but these London tunnels are just eleven feet eight and a half inches in diameter and there's only fifteen centimetres between the tunnel wall and the train. You can't make the tunnels bigger so you've got to put in new signal systems so you can fire more trains down the pipe.

RK	And that's what's going to happen?
TO	Yes, that will happen. It will take a while. People won't believe it until they see it, I know. You will see the first completely new signal system in on the Jubilee Line in 2009 and in the meantime we'll be rebuilding track and the like. And then it comes about every year after that you'll get a new line; so then it will be the Northern Line, then the Victoria Line. Then ultimately the thing that will make believers out of everyone is we will have a rebuilt sub-surface, so the Circle Line and the Metropolitan and the District, and people will be pleased to know that at that time those trains will be air-conditioned.

[Laughter and applause]

Hans Ulrich Obrist	We spoke to Marjorie Scardino. Marjorie mentioned the urgent necessity of reinvention and this seems an important issue in relation to the London Underground. We were wondering if you could give us the bigger picture of how you imagine this reinvention to happen and also what role globalisation plays in this. I heard that you are making links between the London Underground and China.
TO	Yes, I spent some time, at their invitation, with friends in Shanghai. It's an interesting connection to make because we are the oldest system in the world trying to rebuild and they are the newest system building at a furious pace. They have a system about half our size; by 2010 it will be our size and by 2015 it will be twice our size. That's an example of what happens if you don't have to secure a lot of planning powers; you can just build what you want as quickly as you can muster the resources. But there is an important subject you touch on, invention and re-invention, related to the great challenges we face in the world – for example, this year or next will be the first year ever that more people live in cities than not. The world is coming together and we need new machines, we need machines that move people around to still allow growth, machines that deal with our great thirst for energy. And it is frustrating because if you look at the solutions we are applying to this today, they are mostly solutions that come from planners and lawyers, like the congestion charge. The questions you ask yourself are, Where are the Brunels of today? Where are the great engineers? Why don't we have lighter, faster, more energy-efficient trains instead of really just bespoke variations on some very old technology? That's where we are now. And if you look at the great challenge we face,

which is heat, we need completely new solutions that are available to us right now.

HUO   As a part of this reinvention I was told that you met every single person who works for the London Underground. Can you tell us about this plan?

TO   Well, 'met' is a little generous but actually I did think that we had to bring people together and so in November I hosted meetings for every single employee. I would meet with them three to five hundred at a time. I did it over fourteen days, some twenty-five meetings, three a day often, and I would explain to them where I thought we were taking this place and then also would just stand for questions. It was an exhausting experience but it was something they'd not done before. It was a good time to do it because I was trying to capitalise on the way they felt about themselves coming out of 7/7, in that it was the first time in a long time when Londoners really accorded them the respect they deserved and they felt good about themselves. I wanted to remind them that it is easier to get through the day if you work really hard and please someone than if you spend your time fighting the job and fighting the very people you're trying to serve.

HUO   Earlier on this evening we had Yinka Shonibare here in a conversation and he told us about the projects for the London Underground that he realised some years ago. There is something highly specific about the London Underground, which is very strong work with contemporary artists. Could you tell us about how the platform for the arts works and what the plans are for this?

TO   I always think the secret to running a company isn't to bring some new-fangled solutions, but you have to look into it and you have to find the answers in the business. When you look into the London Underground all the elements are there, you just have to bring them out. One of these elements is the respect for the complete product and it was really born out of the work that Frank Pick did many, many years ago [Publicity Manager 1908, Joint MD 1928, CE to 1940]. He was a visionary Managing Director because he knew it wasn't just about running trains, although that comes first of course. It was also about the precision of design and being sure that every single element of the passengers' experience is critical. It was under him that Harry Beck's iconic map was created. It was under him that the new Johnston typeface was created so

62

you had the best signage in the world; he really gave greater energy to this whole concept of poster art and advertising on the Underground, mostly because he wanted to distract the people as they waited for trains. We also have to stay connected with that and show that we have some respect for the ways we develop ambience, and platform art is one of these ways. It started out somewhat modestly but you can see now the exhibits we run at Gloucester Road, Piccadilly Circus and other places; we want to expand this. As we re-build the stations, and we will re-build every single station before the Olympics, we want to find more spaces where we can put in public art. So we kind of stay true to this whole heritage of design that Frank Pick really gave birth to on the Underground.

RK   I want to pick up the thread of engineering because I think it's very interesting that you were asking where the new engineering is for this very ancient industry. Do you have a theory why people are not interested in engineering or why the talent doesn't seem to go there?

TO   Well I think it's that the innovation follows the money and the money went into aircraft and whole other areas that didn't even exist. You have to remember that in the 1830s to 1860s, when the rail industry was being born, if you went into a bookshop it was like going into a store now and seeing computer magazines. There were countless periodicals on railways; think about Brunel and his father and all the genius that was brought into this industry. When the money left the railways post-1950s and everyone was more excited about building cars and highways than trains, the technology kind of stopped. What really re-energised it somewhat is the investment that's occurred in the Far East and the new train systems there.

RK   Is the magnetic train one of them?
TO   Well…

RK   The most evident one.
TO   Yes. The magnetic levitation train is in Shanghai. It was in Germany and they bought it lock, stock and barrel. It's a fascinating thing; you ride on it and it goes about three hundred miles an hour but it's a very wide train. I don't know if you'd want it here, though, because it also requires building a massive concrete structure from here to that wall its entire length. It would cut a city in half pretty dramatically.

RK	So new but not desirable.
TO	Yes. I don't think you're going to see a whole lot of those.

RK	Where do you think it could be re-invented? Just wait?
TO	It is about waiting, it's about new materials. For us in London it's about finding new ways of ventilation, finding trains.

RK	Could air pressure play a role, could you put vacuums and pull trains through the tubes?
TO	They tried that, you know. On the original lines here in London they tried pneumatic railways and in fact they built a pneumatic railway to move goods. It was over near Paddington and some of the dandies of the day insisted they were all going to ride it one night. About sixty of them insisted on getting on this little pneumatic railway and they sent it down the line. When they all came out the other end blood was coming out of their ears and they had to carry them out, so I don't think they're going to be repeating that experiment!

HUO	It reminds me of experiments of the, now very old, American futurist, Jack Fresco, who dreamed about these subway and air train scenarios for the future. I was wondering what your dream is for the London Underground for the years to come.
TO	Well I believe it is like Blake: the world falls apart if the centre will not hold. I think the Underground is the centre but it will never be brand new. Even with all the investment the tunnels will still be too small and too deep, so it is about capitalising on the heritage that's there. What's different about the London Underground compared to any other metro system is the number of employees that are on the stations. That's completely unique. If you go to New York or you go to Paris they have a different business model and the business model is 'the public will figure it out'. London, because it is so deep, needs people to make up for the physical shortcomings. What I'm hoping is that once we get an absolutely reliable train service – that's every two minutes through the centre on every line – and after we get ventilation so it's not like running a convection oven on days like today, we'll also have this continuing environment where we care for the people who use it. Some day in the future when people ask, 'What's the best system in the world?' they are likely to say, 'London Underground'. And when asked, 'How can you say

that with modern systems in the Far East?' the answer will be, 'I don't know; it felt safe, the place was clean, people always helped me when I got confused and it takes me to the most wonderful places in the world'. That's my dream.

[Applause]

RK   What is your relationship with politics?

TO   Well I work for the Mayor, which is a fascinating experience.

[Laughter]

He is absolutely determined to make this the greatest city in the world and especially the one that uses the most public transport. It's the only major city in the entire world where there has actually been a modal shift to public transport: four per cent during his term. That doesn't exist anywhere else.

RK   What is the total percentage of people using the Underground now?

TO   The people using public transport who come into the centre, where we serve, is between sixty-five and eighty percent, depending on the season. Especially where I come from, that's absolutely unheard of. One good thing about Mayor Livingstone, I have to say, he hires professionals and he just lets them get on with it. He never, ever, tells me what to do in terms of operations. He's really a perfect boss in that respect.

RK   How much stability do you need? Are these very long-term ambitions?

TO   How much time will it take?

RK   Whatever time it takes they are very long-term ambitions and we live in a very short-term political framework; four years, three years is a kind of maximum stability for any ambition to survive.

TO   That is a problem. It's one of the reasons they created this otherwise diabolical financing structure, the PPP, for thirty years because it's so hard to change; that also becomes a straight-jacket. But that is also why, in my opinion, the Paris Metro is so good. Politicians in Paris don't have to be brave; there is a Transport Tax that is in place, it has been there for years and just automatically funnels money to the RATP so that they are constantly rebuilding, constantly rebuilding. The problem we face here is when you have long-life capital assets it's very easy to kid yourself 'live off them, they don't break for a while'; but when the belt comes off the machine you pay hell. And that's what's happened here in London. The belt came off the machine a couple of years ago and now we have to spend a fortune to bring it back.

HUO   That's actually a great conclusion. Thanks so much.

Applause, end of interview

Hans Ulrich Obrist   It's a great pleasure to welcome our next guest. Welcome, Hanif Kureishi.

Rem Koolhaas   Hi! With *My Beautiful Laundrette* you were maybe one of the first people to depict a glamorous and exciting way in which the co-existence of different races could work in London and could multiply and give new dimensions to sexual relations. In other words, you could be seen as one of the first advocates of that notion. That was more than twenty years ago; what do you think has happened in the meantime and do you recognise the description?

Hanif Kureishi   I think I was aware when I first began to write that I was a Pakki. I had grown up in south London in the 1950s and through the 1960s and we were quite an isolated, I guess, Asian family. My mother was English, my father was from India/Pakistan and I grew up in an entirely white world. And I grew up in a world that was also incredibly racist. I think we thought we were going to be deported, we were going to be sent home on the next boat. After all, there had been many precedents in Europe in the twentieth century for racism. So when I began to write, I think I began to write in order to save my life; I wrote because I thought I was going mad. If you are the victim of racism and you are living in a white society, you don't see yourself anywhere; there is nobody like you in the world, in the media, and so I began to write, in order, I think, to keep myself together, to keep all the bits in the same place. So for me to write was to make myself and also, like most people, I wanted to tell my story, I wanted to say, 'Look, we are here. There are Pakistani people living in south London and this is our life'. So when I started work in the theatre, and later with *My Beautiful Laundrette*, I think I became aware that I was telling stories which hadn't been told, really, in Europe before, which were about immigration from the former colonies, from Pakistan, India, Sri Lanka and so on. So I wanted to say something that hadn't been said before and I wanted to put Asian people on the screen. I think I had to prove with *My Beautiful Laundrette* particularly, which I made with Stephen Frears, that it was possible to make films about these people, about this subject; a film with an Asian person in it, not only that, a gay Asian person kissing a skinhead. What more would you want from a film? But it was very hard to convince people that they needed this. Eventually the door sort of opened. I think *My Beautiful Laundrette* sort of opened the door and it then became possible to make films about these communities.

HUO   One of the things about this London Marathon is to address the notion of memory of the city. While preparing the Marathon we spoke to Eric Hobsbawm and he said that this Marathon could be the form of a protest against forgetting. Yesterday we read your introduction to the script of the film *My Beautiful Laundrette* and there was one very interesting thing which was unexpected and we wanted to ask you about. There is a very long paragraph where you talk about the seminal importance of the Riverside Studios as a space for tolerance, for scepticism and for intelligence. It really sounds like a very interesting model for a cultural institution. You talk about your dialogues with David Gothard that led to you meeting the director of the film. We are speaking here a lot about different moments of the past in London which resonate or which can be toolboxes for today. I am mainly thinking about what the future of cultural institutions can be. It would be interesting to hear from you why you think that moment of the Riverside Studios was so particularly interesting. You even said that it functioned like a university to some extent.

HK   Well I came from the suburbs and the biggest event for me coming from the suburbs was when we crossed the river. In the 1960s we used to go up the Kings Road; on Saturday everybody would walk up and down the Kings Road and kids from Bromley, from the suburbs where I was from, would get the train and cross the river. When you crossed the river you knew you were free and you knew you were in the city, and I still think of London, of the city, as being full of excitement for me as a kid from the suburbs. It's partly to do with race. One of the ways in which any culture is going to develop, the only way a culture expands, the only way a culture remains alive, is by letting new people into it, you know. And you've got to let people into the culture who haven't spoken before and when you hear them speaking you know that there is new life in the system. So for me London is a place where people can speak more freely: they speak to each other and there are more people and they are from more places, so the possibility of being with people who are talented, who are artistic, but also who worked in a number of fields, is considerable. When I went to Riverside I met poets, I met dancers, I met playwrights,

I met actors, etc. I am very much against segregation in the media. I love the idea that architects, painters, writers and musicians might meet and talk together. I've never met an architect before, actually. It's fantastic.
[Laughter]
I was looking for someone to do my house, actually, as well.
[Laughter]

RK   Later we will hear from Doreen Massey and although she is also impressed by London's ability to absorb many different cultures and to actually coexist and live with many different strangers, she is also more critical and points out the dark side of that to the extent that in order to sustain its current level of civilization, let's say, it needs to import many people from abroad. For instance, English hospitals are unthinkable without a constant importation of Sri Lankans or Ghanaians, people from poor countries who survive here under difficult circumstances. She also comments on the fact that we import educated people from poor countries. So could you comment on that dark side?

HK   That's how immigration works. That's how capitalism works; capitalism works by using labour from the Third World, either in the Third World or bringing labour, people like my father and his family, from the Third World to the First World. We are not here because we make plays or make paintings or do architecture; we are really here to work. Most Pakistanis came to Britain to work in the mills. What's always interesting is the next generation and the generation after that. My father wanted us to be English. He said to me that if I was going to be successful in England I should change my name to Kevin. He thought that was a great idea.
[Laughter]
I've always been very attached to the name Kevin, which you might know is a very English, rather clunky, name. He thought we had to disappear in England in order to survive. One of the things that have happened is that there has been a celebration, as you say, of ethnicity and different voices. You say the city is dark. Well, a city is going to be dark. It's the darkness that makes the city interesting. It's the darkness that makes anything interesting. If you're a writer or an artist of any sort it's the darkness you're looking for, it's the interesting bit of our lives; you can't move that bit out, that's just going to go somewhere else and turn up worse.

RK   I think this is very interesting. In previous conversations with architects and with artists we had to introduce the whole notion of darkness because it seems to have disappeared from their domains.

HK   When I go to a city the bit I want to see is the dirty bit. I want to see the ports, I want to see where the dealers are, I want to see where the whores are, where the bad people are, because you really get a flavour, you get a sense of what the place is really like. There are whole areas of London where you can see London much more authentically than you can in places like Covent Garden, for instance.

HUO   When I spoke to Orhan Pamuk in Istanbul some months ago he said he thinks it is very often literature which invents cities. He mentioned the idea of Gerard de Nerval inventing Istanbul to some extent. One of the things we wanted, hopefully, to achieve with this Marathon was to ask if there is such a thing as a theory of London. We were wondering how you, in 2006, see London.

HK   Well, there are stories, I guess. I think stories is a better word than theory; there are the stories people tell about this city in order to make the city and in order to live in it. I guess as a writer I'm just excited by describing what goes on here. What I want to do is be surprised by what goes on. I want to walk on the street and I want to talk to someone or see something that I haven't seen before. For me it is a city of infinite possibilities; you're never going to run out of bits of it to see, people to talk to and so on. Is that a theory? Is that theoretical enough? I think just being interested and walking around, seeing what's going on, that kind of engagement seems to make a city alive by the way you engage with it, by the way you use it, by the way you look at it. I think theories are too narrow, too constricting. They are good for some things but not good for other things. You can't dance to a theory.

HUO   Do you have any dreams related to London, or any unrealised ideas or projects you would like to see realised?

HK   I think what I want to do is just to tell stories about the city, stories that just occur to me as I wander around in a rather random way. I think being a writer is such a random project. I don't know how you guys work but when I get up in the morning I don't want to know what I'm going to do that day or how it's going to turn out. I want to have a dream or tell a story or find something that seems to surprise me or shock me, I guess. And that's when I'm interested. If I know what I'm going to do – it's bad enough getting up as it is – if I know what I'm going to do it would be even worse.

RK   I want to talk about critics. I have witnessed your career and anyone witnessing your career is confronted with somebody who is received sometimes very critically and sometimes with a lot of adulation. I have seen very few writers who are so inconsistently described. What has that done for your life? Has it kept you alert?

HK   I'm sure you feel like this: I think in the end you just go your own way. You are going to do your work. There are certain subjects, certain areas of your life, certain bits of your psyche that you are particularly interested in. It's like you're painting the wall blue and you think, 'Blue is a great colour today' and a critic comes along and says, 'I think green would be better'. But if you are into the blue, it's going to be the blue. People can say what they like. You can't control, fortunately and unfortunately, what goes on in other people's minds or what they say about you. The thing about me is my work's cheap. I just need a bit of paper and a pen and maybe someone will publish it. Your stuff costs millions of pounds. I can see that you get much more pressure than I do. When I do something nobody really bothers me because they think, 'Well, who gives a damn anyway?' Whereas your stuff is really expensive, so you must have lots of people saying, 'Those windows are too small or the windows are too big or why aren't the windows on the top?' and so on. But I don't have that. I really work quite freely, I guess, which is the virtue and the freedom of being a writer to invent freely. I think sometimes it might be a good idea if there was more criticism, you might feel there was more response to what you do. It seems to me that in England if you are a writer there is a general indifference. Anywhere else if you are a writer they kill you and torture you but in England they take no notice of you. [Laughter]
Which is probably better.

RK   Does your background and your history make you somebody with a particular insight into 7/7?

HK   I became very interested in what's become known as Muslim fundamentalism in the 1980s, particularly after going to Pakistan to stay with my family for the first time in the early 1980s. My uncles were sort of middle class intellectuals, liberals and so on and they said to me that they were being crushed. They were being crushed between the fundamentalists on the one hand and the United States on the other. And they realised it was all over. Then in 1989 my friend Salman Rushdie had a *fatwah* put on him by the Iranians, so in the 1990s I began to hang around with young kids who were called fundamentalists. I went to the colleges and the mosques and began to talk to these kids. I wrote a novel called *The Black Album* [1995] and then a film called *My Son the Fanatic* [1997], which was concerned with some of these things. But I became very aware that all over the Muslim world young people had become deeply disillusioned with the Muslim regimes, right. And the most significant post-war event, really I would say, is the Iranian revolution, when it occurred to the Muslim masses that they could overthrow people like the Shah and establish a Muslim ideology. If you're living in a Muslim world, a Muslim ideology is far more liberating, far purer, far better in every way than the corruption of people like the Shah. So radical Islam began as a kind of liberation movement. It's hard to believe that but this was where the people organised, on the street, in the mosques, in order to overthrow people like the Shah. But it became deeply corrupt and after the fall of the Berlin Wall it became implicated with the West. Bush and Blair need radical Islam in order to keep the West militarised, let's say. Do I have any insight into it? Well, lots of people all over the Muslim world feel enormous resentment, firstly about what's happening in their own countries and secondly about what's happening to the Muslim world because of the enormous efforts of Bush and Blair to kill them. There are real resentments here, there are deep resentments. You could psychologise these kids and say these kids are fucked up because of X, Y and Z and I have done that, but it seems to me that what we have to do now with the young people who have a resentment is engage with them and see what their resentments are. That doesn't mean we turn London into a Muslim city – it's already a great Muslim city – but that we have to engage with these people. One of the interesting things about you having these conversations is that you value the art of conversation, i.e., that people speak to each other for a long time before they kill each other. It seems to me to be a good idea.

HUO   In terms of conversation, a lot has been written about your ongoing conversations with Salman Rushdie. I was wondering if you could tell us a little about this dialogue.

HK   Rushdie is an Indian writer. The first time I went to Pakistan one of my uncles said to me – he looked at me rather oddly as if I were a curiosity – 'The thing is we're Pakistanis, aren't we? But you're just a Pakki and you'll always be a Pakki'. That really shocked me because I thought I was going home to Pakistan, this was my home, my family, the bosom, I would be welcomed here, I belong here. I realised I was living in a fascist Muslim state and I hated every minute of it. So I realised I was an English kid and I didn't have, really, the same connection with the sub-continent that somebody like Rushdie had. I think as artists there may be connections between Rushdie or Zadie Smith or Monica Ali or any of the other so-called post-colonialists; we are all artists who go our own way and do our own thing. But I think the publication of *Midnight's Children* in the 1980s was a huge breakthrough in British writing. It suddenly showed – and I showed later on with *My Beautiful Laundrette* – the door opened. It wasn't provincial, insular England; it was a new world coming in through the door and I think British culture really perked up after that.

HUO   You have mentioned that your working process is quite spontaneous. I was wondering what you are working on at the moment.

HK   As I've got older one of the things I notice is you are young for a very long time and then suddenly the clock chimes and you're old and I became very interested in older people. I made a film called *The Mother* [2003] which was about an older woman who begins a sexual relationship with James Bond.

[Laughter]

And I've recently made a film with Roger Michell called *Venus*, which is about two old blokes and a minger. A minger is a street girl. And I just became interested in these two old blokes, played by Peter O'Toole and Leslie Phillips, and suddenly you just throw a girl into the middle. One of the things I noticed – I watch a lot of television, I know I should be reading Proust but I watch a lot of television – I noticed that you are no longer allowed to make jokes about Pakistanis or Jews or other ethnic groups but you could make jokes about white working class girls, mingers. And I noticed watching Catherine Tate and *Little Britain* and so on, that white working class girls were scapegoats; you know, these lazy, fat slags who never worked, had lots of babies with black men and so on, 'weren't they mingers!'. So I wrote a film about mingers. Do you have mingers in Holland? Do you know the concept of the minger?

[Laughter]

RK I live here.

HK OK. Then the concept of the minger won't have escaped you.

RK So we are stuck for time. Thank you very much.

[Laughter]

Applause, end of interview

Rem Koolhaas   It's my pleasure now to introduce Ken Loach. As you must have noticed, we have not prepared this interview beforehand. There is a slight change of script. We were supposed to meet him outside but now he is here, so we have to kind of improvise a little bit.

Hans Ulrich Obrist   I have a first question: the 1965 film *Up the Junction* is a story of three women in Clapham and is one of your earliest movies and one of the few times, actually, you have worked in the metropolis, in London. I wanted to ask you why you seem to prefer to work in northern England rather than London and if there are a certain set of professional difficulties in terms of filming in London.

Ken Loach   Yes. I think there are. [To RK] Hello, anyway! We met in surreal circumstances in Tokyo many years ago.

RK   Let's not go into them! *[Laughter]*

KL   Yes, I've always found it easier to work in communities that are quite compact and London is actually big and amorphous. When you are, for example, finding people to be in films, when the area and the community is quite circumscribed it's much tighter, you don't have such a big choice, so it's easier to find people. In London it's a real needle in a haystack; because the choice is so huge it is therefore more difficult. But I always work with a writer and where the writer writes and the idiom the writer writes in is always critical. For example, I have been working with a Scottish writer so we have been working in Glasgow. Before that I was working with a writer from south Yorkshire, so we worked a lot in south Yorkshire.

HUO   Can you tell us a little about this early *Up the Junction*, which took place in London?

KL   Yes, it was a book written by a writer called Nell Dunn, who is a very fine writer. She lived for a time in Battersea and the book is a little vignette, little incidents, anecdotes of this group of people and they are partly funny and they are partly sad. The anecdotes all put together make a kind of mosaic, make a picture of life at the time, which was the mid-1960s, not quite the swinging London of cliché but rather tougher than that.

RK   I believe there is an interesting thing about your career: you are incredibly consistent and yet you are successful.

KL   *[Laughs]*

RK   Can you comment on that? And were there times when you thought your consistency would undo you?

KL   I hope by consistency you don't mean repetitious. *[Laughter]* I take it in its most favourable light. I suppose you try to work according to the way you see the world. You try to tell stories and relationships and descriptions that fit your view of the world, whatever that is. You try to articulate that and you try to work it out in conjunction with the writers, so the biggest question is always, 'What film shall we do next? What story shall we do next?' That's something you discuss a great lot and argue about and consider. I suppose that if you try to reflect a consistent view, then there will be that consistency. I do hope so. But it should be sometimes surprising at the time, then maybe consistent in retrospect.

RK   Your most recent film is an historical film.

KL   Yes.

RK   Of course your perspective remains very critical of England, a leftist perspective. At the same time there are currently issues in the world that are so unbelievably urgent and drastic. You address them in many letters and there is no doubting your involvement in current events; but how do you explain the preoccupation with an historical subject at the moment that the world seems to be going up in flames?

KL   As you say, the world does seem to be going up in flames and it is an alarming time. The Irish story is one we've wanted to tell for many years because the events we tried to describe are really a classic story of an imperial power removing itself, or being forced to remove itself, from its colony but nevertheless doing everything it can to safeguard its interests. And in the process screwing up the people that it's apparently granting independence to, screwing it up so that there's been trouble in the north of that country for the last eighty years. But I hope it says something about what happens to an army of occupation when it's surrounded by a civilian population which doesn't want it. It says something about empire. It says something about resistance and the divisions that can be hidden when there is a common enemy but which come to the fore once that common enemy is no longer there. All of which has something reflected in some way.

RK   Has a resonance.

KL   Yes, has a resonance with what is going on now.

RK   I had the privilege of being the neighbour of Lindsay Anderson for a long time and looking at your work I recognise something quintessentially English about it, and also an enormous preoccupation with English issues. How does the fact that England is now, let's say, unrecognisable from the England of fifteen years ago affect your work and your subjects?

KL   That's interesting. Superficially I think it is quite different. Essentially I think it is very similar. We are very used to, for example, leaders of the Labour party who are voted in as left-wingers and who become intensely men of the right. This is a familiar pattern that stretches back to the last century. But in other respects you're right; it is very different. The drive to privatisation has transformed the very way our society is organised. I was interested to listen to Tim [O'Toole] and I was waiting for him to talk about the privatisation of the Tube or the return to public ownership and I don't think he talked about it. I was quite sad about that, actually.

RK   We'll have to ask him about that.

KL   If there's opportunity. The landscape does change but in a sense the skeleton underneath is the same, I think.

RK   Is a filmmaker concerned about the skeleton or the landscape?

KL   About both. Because if you don't know about the bones underneath, you don't know which bits are important, really. I think the structure of society tells you how to evaluate the events you see around you.

RK   But, for instance, if I were a filmmaker in England I would be absolutely fascinated by the co-existence. Muslim world radicalisation, etc. Is that something where we could ever imagine you doing a movie?

KL   I did one, actually, Rem, a couple of years ago. [Laughter] It was called Ae Fond Kiss. It was about a family in the Pakistani community in Glasgow. The young man is a DJ, he is very contemporary, he has one foot in the modern, Western world and one foot in the traditional world. It was about his situation: he has a relationship with an Irish girl, who is in fact an immigrant to Scotland, while he is in fact native. But he is treated as an immigrant and she, because she is white, is treated as not. So it's about the situation of that second-generation family and it was a very interesting, very extraordinary subject to explore, really.

HUO   Rem's question leads us to a question about the present moment and your work. At this time of protest and mass demonstration (we think about the big anti-war demonstration which still resonates) it is reminiscent of the 1960s. Your methods of cinema seem very apt for that moment right now. I was wondering if you were tempted to turn your lens to the present.

KL   Well, it is very tempting but I think, in a way, if you do fiction then you want to reflect on the way the world is and reflect that, or refract those ideas on that, through character and character developments and relationships. The way that would be fascinating to deal with the present is through documentary.

RK   Yes.

KL   And that is very tempting. It's something that we have talked about doing, but the world is changing so fast. Who would have believed that we would be sitting listening to our Prime Minister saying, in effect, carry on bombing, carry on killing? Who would have believed we would listen to that? Who would have believed we would be selling arms like pouring petrol on the flames? It is unbelievable. So keeping up with the treachery would be one of the problems in any documentary now.

RK   Yes.

HUO   We spoke about a lot of your realised films, about realised projects. I was wondering about the whole unrealised cinema, if you had any unrealised projects coming to your mind which you would like to see happen.

KL   Well, stacks, really. They still might happen one day. I had been wanting to make the Irish film for nearly thirty years and, finally, working with Paul Laverty, we managed to do it. We tried it a couple of times. We were once turned down by Channel 4 to do virtually a similar story to this. Jeremy Isaacs, the Director at the time, turned us down. He said he did not want to import Sam Peckinpah into the politics of Northern Ireland, which I thought was a little ungenerous of him really! There are lots, but they are tucked away in a drawer and they might reappear one day.

HUO   I had a question about improvisation because Rem and I have been preparing the script for this Marathon and yet there is quite a big space for improvisation. I was wondering what kind of emphasis you put on improvisation. I read in some cinema magazines that, actually, you often do not give actors the entire script, so I was curious to hear more about that.

KL   *[Laughs]* Well, in the end the only thing that matters is what you see on the screen. It's like asking Rem about the mechanism for constructing this really nice pavilion. What matters is that it is a really nice pavilion; the mechanism is secondary. One of the things we try and do in a film is that when you watch it you have the impression that really these things are just happening. So how do you do that? One part of the method is that we shoot in sequence and then take the actors and cast through the events so that they know everything about themselves, they know everything about who they are in the film. But they don't know what the acts of God will be in the course of the story, so that when a surprise happens it is a surprise. We try to find actors who, as they reveal themselves, will reveal something about the character they are playing in the film. So for that reason we hold back some of the story. It keeps it alive, you know. And maybe some people are going to die and they are usually running a book on who is going to face death before the end of the film. *[Laughter]* It keeps a certain kind of tension in the process, which can be quite creative.

RK   Globalisation has a huge effect in films. There is a particular kind of film that is global but without particular features. What has been its effect on your conception of movie making? I would also like to ask if there are particular influences that are less than self-evident that you could talk about.

KL   Yes, everybody always has influences, particularly when you are growing up and forming your ideas. The things that influenced me, well the cinema influences, were the obvious ones, I guess the Italian neo-realists, the French filmmaker Robert Bresson, the Czech filmmakers of the 1960s. The other things that I think were very much part of the culture as I was growing up were the musical, you know, the variety, and then comedians, the names that probably won't mean very much now to people under fifty; the comics of the time, people like George Formby or Frank Randall, the raucous working class comics that we used to go and see in the 1940s and 1950s. And a theatre director called Joan Littlewood, who was one of the most creative individuals that I think have ever worked in the theatre and had this brilliant theatre in east London, Stratford East, which she described as a palace of fun.

HUO   That was the project she had with Cedric Price, wasn't it, the Fun Palace.

KL   Yes, yes. Very big influence on all of us. I think those were the main things.

RK   One of the strong effects of globalisation is that it doesn't seem to enable somebody to stay with a particular mentality or stay with a particular sophistication, but it forces every one of us to constantly adjust. Does it have the same effect on you or your way of making films?

KL   Not really. Perhaps it should, but it hasn't. I suppose we experience globalisation in the cinema in the fact that most of the cinemas that we all go to, the multiplexes, have a very standardised product. It's always referred to as product, rather dismally, which I find rather depressing, but it is seen as product and it tends to be rather standardised and it's aimed at the global market. But there is a strong European film culture, which is supported particularly by the French and by the Italians and by the Spanish and sometimes by the Germans and the protection of that cinema identity is seen as very important. I and other filmmakers from here have got support from those audiences.

RK   From that area.

KL   Yes. Not much support from Britain I have to say. We tend to produce bureaucracies but we tend not to actually do much, but the French put their money where their mouth is.

HUO   Maybe it's interesting towards the end of the conversation to bring it back to London because one of the ideas of this Marathon is to have different views on London. We wonder how you see London now and if you have any dreams for London.

KL   The last few days I've been getting the North London line (I don't know
      if anyone else here gets it), the North London line that goes from my bit
      in NW5 round to Stratford, though Hackney, Homerton and Dalston and
      the rest, round to the docks. When you go on that line, you do see the
      back side of London a lot of the time and you realise the vast expanses
      of the city that are really just battered and left and sad in some ways,
      and wonderful buildings caught in isolation. What would be a great vi-
      sion for the city would be to really regenerate it from the backside in,
      rather than always starting in the centre. To really, really clean that part
      and to cherish the good things that are there and to bring the inspira-
      tion of new architecture to those parts of the city that you just see when
      you travel on that line and other lines like it. The truth of the city is of-
      ten seen on those railway lines that go round the edge of the city rather
      than on the set pieces in the centre. I think it is those areas that we could
      really polish up, cherish and renew.

HUO   Many thanks to Ken Loach. Thank you very much indeed.

      Applause, end of interview

Susan Hiller
Jude Kelly
Tim Newburn
Tony Elliott
Tom McCarthy
Scott Lash
Michael Clark

Hans Ulrich Obrist We are very happy to begin the second round of the Marathon with Susan Hiller. Welcome, Susan Hiller. I want to ask you when you decided to move to London and why and also if you consider yourself a Londoner now after all these years here.

Susan Hiller Yes, I'll answer the last part first. One can never really become English but you can become a Londoner. Yes, I am a Londoner, I hope; I have lived here now since the end of the 1960s. And why did I come to London? Well in those days London was the only place to go if you were an artist and you didn't have any money; if you wanted to live some place really cheaply you came to London. Of course that's not true any more. When I got here I discovered that it really was the most exciting place because everything was coming together. You've all heard this a million times, but politics and music and art and fashion and design and theory, literature, poetry, there was no real separation between the people participating in those kinds of activities and it was absolutely wonderful to be here then.

HUO Can you tell us more about your relationship to the city and particularly about its unconscious and its memory? One of the first people we spoke to when preparing this Marathon was Eric Hobsbawm; he was saying that we must ask about memory because he thinks that in view of the amnesia it is necessary to organise what he calls 'a protest against forgetting'. So what are your notions of the unconscious city and the memory of the city?

SH It's interesting, isn't it? Somebody recently sent me something about a show that they were organising called *Ghostbusting* and it was sort of attacking what I'm interested in. These people accused me of being interested in ghosts, me and a lot of other artists actually, and they said in the blurb for the show that in order to go forward into the future you had to abandon the ghosts of the past. Of course we know that is completely ridiculous, that you are just doomed to repeat, endlessly, the past if you don't know anything about it. But in a city like London, and in fact in most great cities, there is so much change all the time that the memories, even recent memories, only exist for people who have actually lived through

85

those moments. I was thinking when you were talking about that, how is memory, other than personal memory, preserved? Of course it's preserved in buildings and in photographs and in archives and it's preserved in conversations. I don't think in London you ever really get away from the past. I'm contrasting it with the United States now. I think the street names and the whole layout of London is really about the past. For example, the problem with the buses. The problem with the buses is that the streets of London were never meant for these huge buses so you can't get away from the fact that the problems of life here have to do with the history of the city. I find that quite fascinating; it's part of everyday experience, not registered in any kind of special monument or memorial.

Rem Koolhaas	Did you train as an anthropologist or is that a myth?
SH	Oh God! OK.
RK	I love to pose the 'Oh God!' questions.
SH	[Laughs] Being from the United States originally, I can honestly say that American universities and colleges don't produce specialists, so if you are going to be an artist in the States and you go to a university, which most people do because there are very few specialised art schools, you take art courses alongside history, physics, languages, everything. You have to take everything and you only get to specialise in your last couple of years. I was always, in a sense, wanting to be an artist but I didn't know how one did that. I had no idea how you could be an artist. You probably don't want to get into the whole gender thing but it had to do with the fact that when I was growing up there were very few women artists of note and the ones that I knew about, people were always saying they were second-rate or their work was derived from some man, blah, blah, blah, all that stuff. I never wanted to be second-rate, who does? I read a booklet by Margaret Mead, who was a very famous American anthropologist, and in fact many first-generation American anthropologists were women. They had all started off as poets, actually, and then they switched to anthropology. Anyway, I read this book by Margaret Mead called *Anthropology as a Career for Women* and I thought this was amazing because nobody had ever proposed anything to me as a woman. Imagine! *Anthropology as a Career for Women* and all about adventure and travel. So that's what I did. But after doing post-graduate work in anthropology I realised that it really wasn't for me and then I struggled again to figure out how to be an artist.

RK   Did you ever do any fieldwork?

SH   Yes, I did.

RK   And do you consider some of the work you are doing now is fieldwork, or is the metaphor of fieldwork still interesting for you?

SH   I don't want to be negative about everything but that's another problem. There are a lot of people doing fieldwork-oriented art and I'm not sure that I'm doing that, really. I'm interested more in the unconscious structures rather than what you might call the sociological. Everybody always thinks that I'm doing anthropology but I think that may be because they don't know much about anthropology. I honestly believe that art is a first-order practice; it is as important in terms of creating knowledge as any academic discipline, so I'm always very upset when people try to justify art practice with, as it were, a hyphen, like saying political art or feminist art or gay art or identity art. I think this is totally wrong. Art is art and art is productive of knowledge as much as any other kind of discipline.

HUO   In previous interviews you have spoken a lot about notions of collecting and archiving. I was wondering if we could talk about this but with a different angle, the angle of the city. One recurring topic is the idea of how to map the city and the whole impossibility of having a synthetic image of something so complex as a city. I was wondering if you could tell us about your archive practice and mapping practice in relation to the city. Rem and I were looking with admiration through your book, *The J. Street Project* [2005] this afternoon, which hasn't to do with London, but it definitely has to do with mapping an aspect of a city.

SH   I guess I have a lot of problems with abstractions like 'the city'. To me there are specific cities and particular personal experiences of different cities. The *J. Street Project* came about because I was in Germany and had a reaction to a street sign there.

RK   Can you describe the project? We can show it.

HUO   It is here, yes.

RK   Can you explain what the project is?

SH   OK. This book documents a project that I worked on for three years in Germany and the 'J' that is referred to there is the Jewish population of Germany. Actually, to be honest I think it's a very difficult time to be discussing this, given what's happening in the Middle East. I have to be very specific and talk about this in terms of Germany. Anyway, in Berlin I came across a street that was called – and Hans Ulrich please correct my pronunciation – it was called Judenstraße, Jew Street. Actually we have a couple of streets in London of the same name and from the same period. We have Old Jewry in the city and there is also a Jew Street in Brighton and there are a couple of others, not many. I was very shocked by the street sign occurring in Germany and couldn't understand whether retaining the sign nowadays was meant as a respectful commemoration or what. And if it was, then how ironic it was because what, in fact, this was commemorating was a history of racism and segregation. So it had many levels. To make a long story short, I then discovered there were five streets in Berlin that have the same signifier and I thought if they were in Berlin they must be in other places. I felt literally compelled to visit all these places in Germany and make work about them.

HUO   Have you done projects in relation to London you could tell us about in terms of mapping?

SH   No, I have never done mapping and archive projects in London. In the 1970s I did a project called *Street Ceremonies* which took place around the Portobello Road area where I was living, which mapped the neighbourhood in terms of the Equinox, when day and night are of equal length and people measured the boundaries of the neighbourhood based on traditional British boundary-walking ceremonies that still occur in towns and villages in the countryside. But I've never done an archive in that way in this country, no. This was a very particular project, sort of one of those projects that perhaps you engage in as an artist, that you feel you are compelled to do, that you have a responsibility to do – maybe you don't even want to do it but you have to.
[All lights suddenly go out]
That's stopped everyone! *[Laughs]*

HUO   No, not at all. Actually, it's getting dark and I can't read my notes any more. *[Laughter]*
That is the real reason. Anyway, maybe that is good; it will lead us away from the script and further into improvisation. One of the things we wanted to ask you is if you had any kind of dreams or unrealised projects. The unbuilt roads of Susan Hiller: projects which have been too big to be realised, too small, censored projects, forgotten projects.

SH   Yes, I do. I have a lot of projects but I have a superstition that if you talk about something and you use it up in talking about it then you'll never use it. I don't know if other people feel that. It was very strange for me when I was making the film of *The J. Street Project*, which is probably the biggest project I have ever done, and I had to sell this idea to people.

RK   A pitch.

SH   Yes, you have to go and talk to people and convince them and go through everything before you've even done the thing; I thought that was immensely difficult. It takes a special kind of persistence to do that and I almost felt I made the film before I started it. I have been trying to get a project off the ground that I have so far failed to do; it's called *International Dreaming* and it would involve dreams from one part of the world being sent on the Internet in real time to a place twelve hours away, so that you could sleep, say in Japan, and then use the brainwaves and things which could be sent on the Internet to trigger off an environment. I've talked about this to several – it seems like several hundred people so far – *[Laughs]* and nobody seems interested in it. So that's a project I'd like to do.

HUO   That leads to one of the things I'd like to ask you in relation to dreams. One of my favourite exhibitions is *Dream Machines* [2000], which I think you curated.

SH   Yes.

HUO   You acted as an artist/curator in this case and it's something I've always wanted to ask you about. Could tell us a little about this project? The show took place at Camden and toured; it was something you worked on for many years and was somehow a survey on dream machines.

SH   It wasn't a survey. I realised afterwards that if I'd had some funding or possibly a research assistant I wouldn't have insulted so many of my friends by leaving them out of the show. *[Laughs]* I did the best I could on the basis of faulty memory. I am very interested in the idea of what art is and what it does and what possible function it can have. I am particularly interested in artworks that destabilise, give a notion of the real in all sorts of ways. *Dream Machines*, the title, comes from that rather famous Brion Gysin's *Dream Machine*, which is a magnificent device made very crudely by Ian Somerville in the 1960s. It's a thirty-three and a third record turntable with a cardboard cylinder on top of it and some holes cut in it. You look at this thing and if you are lucky you hallucinate and you see wonderful pictures. It's the simplest thing; there are lots of plans on the Internet for drawing it out. I was looking for other artworks where artists used themselves as experimental subjects. My selection was cross-generational; it ranged between, I suppose, artists like Jane and Louise Wilson and the hypnosis piece to older artists like Henri Michaux, whose estate was actually delighted to lend work because they said he would have loved being in a show with young contemporary artists. What I was amazed by was that I was allowed to do this show because there were a lot of references to drugs and hallucinations and visions and the whole visionary tradition in European art, which I am very fascinated by. It was particularly interesting to see teachers bringing crowds of kids in to see the show and I wondered if that meant that the work was all harmless, that it wasn't actually going to do anything. But it did get an absolutely dreadful review by Brian Sewell, who gave me 'nil points' and referred to me as a mad woman. *[Laughs]*

[Laughter] So it did succeed in some quarters.

HUO   I thought it would be interesting to hear from you about speech and sound because you have used that a lot as a medium of your practice.

SH   Yes, I am very interested in sound. Someone pointed out to me recently that even in my video installations the work is carried on the soundtrack, which I hadn't been fully aware of. I'm interested in the human voice primarily, and this conversational thing that you're going through is an interesting example of that because don't you think that – am I allowed to ask a question?

RK   Yes.

SH   Don't you think that more comes through a voice than the words, that you get more meaning than the words alone convey?

RK   Of course.

SH   That interests me a lot. In some of my pieces, like *Witness* [2000], the piece that uses three hundred people talking about their visions of UFOs and other related elements, there is something about a room full of three hundred voices that is just absolutely compelling. The human being is conveyed through the voice.

RK   I wanted to ask you about drugs just before you started talking about them. You clearly have a lot of sympathies for some ways of interacting which date from the 1960s, a kind of generosity and open-endedness and absence of boundaries. Do you also have a particular interest in, and do you still believe in the relevance of, experiments like Leary's?

SH   It's interesting, isn't it! Some of us can remember back to those days when it seemed – and it included things like the student revolutions, it went across all the fields – that Western society was making some kind of breakthrough and possibly a breakdown of fixed notions of the personality and what the potential of the human being could be. Being anthropological about it for a minute, I would say that all cultures are prisons in a sense but in different ways, and all languages constrain us within that language and set of meanings and so forth. Human beings have always wanted an exit from that. I am interested in the way art can be that kind of exit for people. I don't know if that's very much a generational commitment or if it's a kind of yearning that poetry and art can provide sudden insights that can shift your perception and actually change the way you see your life. Yes, Leary was a very interesting person. Ultimately a failure, but don't you think he was fascinating?

RK   Yes. And we believe in failure also.

SH   Yes. But the whole thing was a failure. The whole ten years, twelve years. It's interesting though because people are reinventing it all. This event tonight in a way has made me think about those days and here you are providing a structure which everyone experiences very differently. Not everybody is actually listening to the conversations. Some people are just lying on the grass, having a beer, whatever, but the structure is here for them to relate to however they wish. That kind of open-endedness is what I liked about those thinkers of the time.

HUO   Open-endedness is a marvellous way to end. It has only just begun. Many thanks to Susan Hiller.

SH   Thank you.

Applause, end of interview

Hans Ulrich Obrist It's a pleasure to introduce our next speaker, Jude Kelly.
Rem Koolhaas   Welcome.

RK   I would like to start with something really blatant. You are the cultural
      commissioner of the Olympics.
Jude Kelly Am I?
RK   Are you?
JK   No.

RK   What is your relationship with the Olympics?
JK   I'm the chair of something called the Advisory Committee for Ceremonies,
      Education and Culture for the London Olympics. That's not my day job
      but it's very relevant to this event. When you say 'cultural commission-
      er' I'd have to start a way back, and I will, if that's OK with you.

RK   Yes, OK.
JK   I got involved in the Olympics a long, long time ago, not to do with the
      sport of the Olympics but just to investigate, really, what democracy had
      been built around and why the Greeks used the Olympics as their mo-
      ment in time to consider the amazingness of humans. I was interested
      as to why they chose to use poetry and music and sport. And then I was
      interested in the reality in the Greek civilization of running a torch
      through every war-torn state and saying, 'Don't have war today; we're
      having the Olympics'. So when I heard we were bidding for the Olympics
      I got curious to know whether this idea of culture, education and sport
      and this notion of falling in love with mankind for the purpose of peace
      would be something the Olympic Games could still deal with. I made a
      film suggesting that under current government, probably any govern-
      ment at the moment, democracy had fallen to pieces and that it was un-
      likely that young people were going to look for idealism via politics, by
      any form of official politics. So I was wondering if it was possible to re-
      capture the idea of this ludicrous ambition that Pierre de Coubertin had,
      which was that every single nation would walk through one door together
      at the same time (and could you just imagine inventing that when he

did, in 1884, without emails, without any way of doing it?). I wanted to know if we could reclaim that scale of ambition. Could young people then respond, 'Alright, I'll buy into the universe for the next fifty years'. Well, we did win the bid for the 2012 Olympics and part of the reason why I think we did was because we had no chance of winning by being well-behaved and, thank goodness, finally we weren't well-behaved. There's a big gap between what you say you'll do and what you'll ever do. But the final realisation was that the thing that London had, if London was prepared to say it, was that it had always been a nation of mongrels and with any luck we'll always be a nation of mongrels, made up of immigrant after immigrant after immigrant. Actually, instead of going, 'Look. We're English', you go, 'Look. I don't know where we're all from but the world's here'. The Cultural Commission, as it were, is about getting the Olympic Movement to recognise that finally yes, sport happens inside the games time, but the way that humans express joy and belief is through the arts. And that's what I'm doing, if I can.

HUO   The Olympics brings us very much to the future and your other projects. You are currently Artistic Director of the South Bank and that obviously has also to do with the future of London. Before we speak about the different projects, could you tell us in a more global way what your dream is for the future of London?

JK   Well I've had a different set of relationships with London. I'm not from London, I'm from Liverpool and you can tell that gradually as you listen to my vowels. Of course like most people from the regions I had a very hazy idea of my capital city most of the time while growing up. In the main I loved growing up in Liverpool but when I came to London it was to start Battersea Art Centre in the 1980s and the thing I was really horrified by in London, which I hadn't noticed in Liverpool, was it seemed to be quite possible for the gentry to live absolutely side by side with a ghetto and for it to be apparently a matter of total indifference. That did not seem like good example-setting for a capital city. So I have a number of dreams for London: one would be that we would look at the UK map flat, and that the tributaries that go backwards and forwards on the map are like a flatland as opposed to the way people currently think and talk about the UK. They talk about going up to London or down to London and so there is always a geography which is to do with the map standing like that [upright]. Of course if you are in Scotland you want to turn it upside down. I think it would be interesting if you just said it's flat and so if you took the same idea for London as you do for canals and rivers and said it's backwards and forward, flowing out to the sea all around it, you'd get a much more loving and mentally prosperous UK.

HUO   Thinking about that plan for the future it's maybe also interesting to think about the past. I quote Eric Hobsbawm again and the need to protest against forgetting.

JK   True.

HUO   I was wondering what your toolboxes from the past are. One of the previous speakers, Ken Loach, mentioned Joan Littlewood as a great pioneer; we spoke to Hanif Kureishi about Riverside. There are models from the past which may be interesting for us to learn from, so I was wondering what were your models or – heroes is a big word.

JK   Well, one person who stood out for me when I was at university was Charles Parker. I'm talking about the person who made the *Radio Ballads*. He recorded the voices and the thoughts of fishermen, travelling communities, a range of people who I suppose you would think of as the unheralded, the less central communities.

HUO   He made interviews.

JK   He made interviews with them all and he captured them forever. And as Susan was saying, it wasn't just what they said, it was the actual tonal quality of their voices, so they were like the equivalent of geology projects; you could feel on the rock face of their voice these qualities that contained not just their memory but their ancestors' memories. For me that was very affecting.

The other thing was a gradual understanding of why people went to war. I have thought a lot about the Second World War because my father fought in it. I realised it was the only time that a huge proportion of the world went to fight against fascism on all fronts and at the same time housed refugees from all of those places. That combination of the world going out to fight for freedom and refugees being housed is something which, although I didn't do, my family did, and now I feel it's a memory I want to find a way of preserving, not in the sentimental way that people tend to do, quick documentaries about the war, but actually investigate what did it mean that people went and fought for freedom. This directly relates to what I'm doing now because the Festival of Britain site, which is what the South Bank is on, was twenty-seven acres carved out after the war called The Landscape of the Imagination. I think during the war a social revolution happened. They say Britain never had a revolution; I don't think that's true because I know that people went to the war with one class system and came back with another. I think it was only because there was so much fighting and death and destruction happening that you didn't notice that there was also a revolution. So coming back and creating all these social policies of health and housing and welfare and education, and at the same time saying: this twenty-seven acres is for the imagination – can you imagine doing that now? We wouldn't do it in that way and I wish we did. The memory of the Festival of Britain, when you ask people about it, is that all of the imagination that went into the Bauhaus movement, all the imagination that went into Black Mountain College, all the aesthetic investigation, also met this notion of the right for beauty and the right for playfulness for everyone. That combination of incredible aesthetic standards and total commitment to democracy was what that site was for. It's forgotten, so how do you revive its memory?

RK   Do you think you will be able to resurrect some of it in the Olympics? Is that your plan?

JK   I wasn't really putting the two projects together in that way.

RK   In the current cynical moment about politics particularly, do you think that a poetic vision like that through the intermediary of somebody like you can be realised?

JK   The interesting thing about the Festival of Britain is that it was obviously an absolute jewel in a crowd of belief systems and within eighteen months it was demolished, it was pulled to pieces, because a Conservative government came in and took it down deliberately, although the good thing is the memory stays. I wouldn't begin to imagine that there is going to be a great big consistent sweep of wonderfully joined-up good things because that would be hubris anyway. The Olympics is a metaphor, isn't it, for extending yourself beyond your normal capacity. I do think those of us who want to can choose the Olympics or not to be a moment when you say, 'I'll do something even more difficult than I was going to do in the first place'.

But I want to pick up on something that was said earlier about big projects. I think there's a contradiction between great big projects or even medium-scale projects, of which people say it would be nice if it was all tidied up and sorted out and made consistent, and the fact that real energy comes out of mavericks. If you want great cultural institutions you need to keep destroying their institutionalness. So if you try, architecturally, to tidy everything up so it looks as if it all belongs to the same story, you stop people who are artists coming along and putting their own personality into it and you force the cultural institutions to become barren landscapes. So I'm for messing things up, actually, rather than tidying them up.

RK   You currently run the South Bank and the South Bank clearly is established in the remnants of the Festival of Britain. It's been an incredibly contested project for a very long time; very few people have said good words about it, there have been decades of trying to tamper with it, physically almost every component has been given up at some point. Can you say what your intentions with it are, to the extent that they depend on you?

JK   Well, I think first of all to remember what it was, as I have just been talking about, and the things that inspire me about what it was, and therefore what it could be, is that originally – well, eighty muralists were on the site, there were a hundred and twenty-seven sculptors, there were fountain projects, there were horticulturalists working there. They took a slogan, 'Women and children first' because they didn't believe it should be a machismo space. I think it's about being interested in returning to some of those principles of the landscape. I think it's also about recognising that there are points in history when people provide new energy. So I personally like the idea that next to the Festival Hall, which by the late 1960s had probably become a bit middle-aged and complacent and spreading, you get this teenager going, 'Screw you' with elbows everywhere, which is how I think of the Hayward, and that's why I love the Hayward, because it doesn't care. And then you've got this weird thing of the Queen Elizabeth Hall where the scripts to the architects (who are unnamed; they were six young architects in the GLC, I think) said, 'Whatever you do, build it inside a concrete bunker because we're worried about the helicopter noises'. These are all amazing anomalies and you could say that's not consistent so we'll tidy it up. I would say no, that's its history, let's go with it. It's like a family, isn't it, you inherit your family or you have your family; some of them are different shapes and sizes, just love them all. So my aim is either actually or metaphorically to put a great big ring road of flags around everything that the South Bank is responsible for, which is now twenty-one acres, and then get going and make it wonderful. I don't think it needs a great master plan or a wavy line. Cedric Price, who was a great friend of mine, always said the trouble is with a lot of buildings, people are building them because they really want a divorce but they haven't got the nerve to approach their partner so they go off and build a building instead. I don't think we need a major project there. We need good art and great ideas to be a landscape for artists.

HUO   It's very nice that you mention Cedric Price. When we prepared the Marathon and went through questions, the moment we saw so many elements recurring in relation to Situationism and urban debriefs and all of that, Rem asked if one looked at what Guy Debord was to France whether that would be what Cedric Price was to England. I thought that was a very interesting point. One of the first things I read in the newspaper when I moved to London this spring was a kind of homage you wrote to Cedric Price and I wondered if you could talk a little bit more about Cedric Price, Joan Littlewood and the Fun Palace, and to which extent that whole idea of energy you mentioned is related to them.

JK   Joan Littlewood was the person that all of the women directors you ever met, and there were very few of them, wanted to be. There was a reason for that, actually. Not only was she so amazing, as the male lecturer said to me when I said I would like to be a director, 'Well there's Joan Knight who's a lesbian, Buzz Goodbody who's dead or there's Joan Littlewood who's retired. Which would you like to be of those three?' Susan was saying earlier that you really knew that there were some battles to be fought and Joan Littlewood fought all of them at the same time.

I met Cedric because I was directing Eleanor Bron, who was his partner, in a play and he came up to stay for the weekend with me. I didn't realise the commitment that he and Joan Littlewood had made to this Fun Palace had lasted for so long. In fact almost everything they said about the Fun Palace on the River Lea, a sort of transparent playground full of technology and possibility for talking, is all still there to be done. Nobody's quite done it yet. So that in itself was very inspiring. Cedric was also the first person who tried to do a master plan for the South Bank and it was a really wonderful, amazing one. But I met him because in as much as I have been interested in creating big institutions because they are influential, I think they should be matched by little tiny institutions that explore intimacy. So I developed this project called Metal, which I am still doing as well, and Cedric helped me design this railway station. He basically said one thing, which was 'design a space by light'. And I thought he didn't just mean the practical.

RK   Thank you. We need to move to the next person, but thank you.
HUO   Many thanks to Jude Kelly. Thank you very much.

Applause, end of interview

Rem Koolhaas Welcome to Tim Newburn, the Director of the Mannheim Centre for Criminology at the London School of Economics. I'm extremely happy that you're here because we have been talking in very idealistic terms about London but I think there is also a very dark side. For me one of the darkest sides of London is its complete surrender, and our complicity in that surrender, to the whole notion of policing. I think it is perhaps of all the cities in the world the one where there is not only the highest density of CCTV cameras but where also, if you read the ground as a script, it is full of traps and points where you can betray yourself, one that really imposes an incredible amount of behaviour on the citizens. I am wondering whether you can explain this enthusiasm for policing that we feel and why it doesn't affect our sense of the city.

Tim Newburn I'm intrigued by the question. When you started and you were talking about what was the underbelly of the city I thought it was going to be a question about crime but actually it's a question about social control and policing. It's an intriguing issue. It's possibly particularly visible in London but is characteristic of Britain generally, and something which separates us, I think, from most other nations. How is it that we find ourselves, as you put it, watched constantly, with cameras almost everywhere, including here? You wake up in the morning and once you leave your home and walk down the street, go to work or wherever it is, you go from railway station to bus, through the city, possibly to your place of work and all the way at least there is the potential that you are watched.

RK In addition you buy newspapers that are crying out for more police, more security and in which crime plays a huge and disproportionate role.

TN We are part, I think, though we may be at the more egregious end of it, of a worldwide movement, really, certainly in liberal democracies, in which people are increasingly buying into the idea that we are surrounded by crime, that things are always getting worse, and that the only solution to it is more control. I don't know whether it's a reasonable thing to do but perhaps we can just involve the audience for a second. Can I ask people to put their hands in the air? I would like to ask people whether they think crime is going up or going down. If you think crime is going up, over the period of, say, the last ten years, in England generally or in London, please put your hands in the air. We've got a frighteningly intelligent audience, obviously. I do it with students all the time and the general popular perception is that crime is going up, that somehow year on year, month on month, crime rises. The reality is crime has been going down now pretty steadily on most categories for a decade or more and yet we buy in most of the time, as you are implying Rem, to the notion that what we need is more control, more prisons, more police and so forth. It is a largely politically-driven conceit and the reason for it, if you are looking for a single reason for it, is that ten to fifteen years ago politicians on the Left persuaded themselves that if they presented themselves publicly any way other than tough on crime, that was electoral suicide. The same would be true in the United States, the same is true in Australia and many continental European countries, that parties on the Right and now parties on the Left find themselves joined in a really nasty marriage of penal populism, of having to be tough on crime.

Hans Ulrich Obrist And that is something you have explored a lot in a book you've edited with Trevor Jones called *Plural Policing* [2006]. I was wondering if you could tell us the key ideas of plural policing.

TN It's related to what we are talking about. For a short period, maybe forty or fifty years ago in England – I look around to see what age people are here – there existed the assumption that there was 'a thin blue line' between us and disorderliness and that thin blue line was the police. It was the employees of the State who wore blue uniforms and funny pointed helmets, who walked the streets in those days, and who were epitomised initially in the 1950s in an Ealing film called *The Blue Lamp*, and then subsequently in a television series called *Dixon of Dock Green*. That was the high point, if you like, of the legitimacy of policing in the UK. Now, at the heart of that notion, amongst other things, was the idea that policing was done by the police, and this goes back to your first question. Actually, in practice policing has always been done by a whole array of organisations. The idea in the book and what underpins it is the sense that it's now impossible to deny that all around us there are policing organisations of various hues wearing outfits and uniforms of various different colours or maybe not uniforms at all, or systems of control appearing in other guises like Closed Circuit Television and so forth. So the central questions in the book are how do these organisations work, how do they relate to each other, how many people are employed doing things like security, and more importantly, to what extent does this vary if you look across the developed world, to what extent are these arrangements the same in every place or different?

RK And what do you find?

TN You find that there are some differences culturally and so to go back to our starting point, it's Britain that's most besotted with Closed Circuit Television. You won't find that in the United States, or indeed in Canada, or in continental Europe to the extent that we find it here, though we are beginning to move in that direction in some other countries. But in terms of the general trends, in terms of using things like prison much more extensively than we have in the past, in employing more and more police officers, more and more private security guards, to go down the whole road of formalising social control, is essentially the pattern that you will find in most liberal democracies now.

HUO How do you see the future development of these tendencies? Earlier this evening we had Charles Jencks here, who amongst many other things is a futurist and, as Rem said, with an eighty per cent accuracy of prediction. It would be interesting to hear how you see the future development of plural policing.

TN Well I'm an optimist, which means that generally I'm wrong.
[Laughter]
Not all that regularly, but from time to time, I write futurology pieces about what policing is going to look like in ten years or what the prison system is going to look like in ten years and it is almost always wrong because it is almost always worse. Though constitutionally an optimist, I'm actually desperately pessimistic about everything that's happening in the crime, justice, social order arena. We now have 78,000 people in prison in Britain, where ten years ago we had 45,000. In the United States – why not use the most egregious example of this, and forgive me those who already know these figures – there are currently somewhere in the region of 2.2 million people in prison. If you add onto that the numbers of people on parole and probation and electronic tagging and so forth, there are somewhere in the region of 7 million people in the United States – this is a country of two hundred and fifty, two hundred and sixty million – under the control of the criminal justice system. And it continues

to expand, whilst, let me say, crime is going down. Am I optimistic? No, I'm desperately pessimistic: no matter where you look in our political system, Republicans, Democrats, Conservatives or Labour Party, we are locked into the assumption that what we need is more. It doesn't matter what's happening, it doesn't matter whether the crime trends are more or less positive, what politicians say to us continually is 'Let us spend more of your taxpayers' money on prisons' (we've had that announcement this week), 'let's spend more of your taxpayers' money on Closed Circuit Television, on policing' and so forth. Where I see it going is more formalisation of social control so that increasingly every aspect of our lives becomes governed by subtle rules about how we can behave, where we can go, what we must do, whether we can step on the grass, how much we can drink, whether we can smoke and so forth. Those rules appear less and less like policing yet they are actually more and more insidious as a form of social control.

RK So can you combine your observations with the highly idealistic tones that you have heard before in this meeting?

TN Well…

RK … in other words, are we being incredibly naïve living under this regime and still maintaining all our fictions of freedom?

TN I think coming back to the optimistic bit of me and trying to feed into the feel-good arguments, I think the history of crime and justice tells you there comes a time when people will say, 'no more'. In the 1850s and 1860s, when we had been transporting tens of thousands of people, originally to America and then to Australia, there came a time when actually enough was enough. There came a time when we no longer hanged people in public and so forth. My sense is that there will come a moment when voters, citizens will say to politicians, 'We don't buy this as a story any more. This narrative that you've been feeding us of more and more control just doesn't sit comfortably with the way in which we want to live our lives'. The difficulty is in identifying where the tipping point is in all this. What is going to bring the moment when people in sufficient numbers say, 'No. We vote for you on different terms'?

HUO When we read your text this afternoon we also discussed how strange it is there is no protest at the elimination of freedom. It seems somewhat surprising.

TN I think that there's a kind of 'other' that's used the whole time. I don't want to make it sound too apocalyptic, but in a sense it is used to scare us away from that sense of resistance. Traditionally that 'other' has been the street mugger, the person who is going to attack you on the street late at night. Now the 'other' has become the international terrorist.

RK It's never-ending.

TN There's a kind of never-ending accretion of threat. Obviously many of these threats are real and yet, as Londoners, and in a sense bringing it back a) to London and b) to optimism, that's the moment when you begin to put some of those things together. Actually Londoners every day, post 7 July last year, post 11 July last year, have gone about their everyday lives, actually haven't clammered for new anti-terrorist legislation, haven't been asking the Mayor week after week for more police officers or Closed Circuit Television. Actually the bulk of Londoners have gone about their lives in very ordinary ways. I think that, in a sense, is very important to hang on to in thinking about the future of policing and the future of justice.

HUO As this leads to a more optimistic note, I wanted to ask you if you have any dreams or unrealised projects.

TN Probably unrealised projects. Dreams – I will stick with London and with my area: I'm a criminologist, so for good or ill and sad life though that may be, I spend my time thinking and writing about crime and criminality and so on. If people ask difficult questions like, 'What do you do about this and what are the causes and why is there this amount of crime and not less?', the things that you would really want to change and therefore the dreams about London would be threefold. First of all, I think, democracy; actually what you need more of in any capital city, or actually in any jurisdiction, is more democracy. You need to link people to the democratic process and it's linking people to the democratic process and linking this process to policing that educates people and actually brings about more coherent, more just, more enlightened criminal justice policies. Secondly I'd say that – this will sound desperately bleeding hearts – there is something very important about social inequality. What we know, I think, about trends in crime is that when things go badly wrong they go badly wrong because the gap between the richest and the poorest gets unfeasibly big. So in terms of the capital city, the real worry and the thing that one needs to guard against, is that unrealistically big gap between the wealthiest and the poorest, particularly in juxtaposition. Doing something about that is crucial. Finally, if I may, I think it's the political thing. The dream, and it feels like the thing that is most dream-like almost, and to a degree I absolve our Mayor from this one because I think he is one of our more realistic politicians in this regard is to get our politicians to talk sensibly about crime.

RK   Thank you.

HUO   Thank you very much.

Applause, end of interview

Hans Ulrich Obrist	We are very happy to welcome our next speaker. Welcome Tony Elliott.
Tony Elliott	Hello.

Rem Koolhaas — Tony, if anyone has invented modern London it is you. Do you agree?

TE — No. *[Laughs]* I think we reflect modern London and certainly one of the things I'm proudest about is that *Time Out* has enabled a lot of things to happen because of the sheer fact that it's free to get listed, that we take an interest in people and we particularly take an interest in things that are new, young, often under-funded, and fresh.

RK — I think it's really nice to be so modest but without *Time Out* a certain experience of the city has become impossible and I think that you pioneered a product in this city which brought something that was totally fragmented together and I think that device has now become a model for metropolitan life in many other places. I think you, compared to, for instance, architectural thinking, are perhaps the one with the most impact on the urban condition worldwide. Would you recognise that?

TE — I kind of know what you're getting at but I'm slightly embarrassed by it.

HUO — I have a question in relation to that. Some years ago I had a conversation with Swiss artists Peter Fischli and David Weiss and they had done a magnificent sculpture in the 1980s of Albert Hoffman, the Swiss scientist who is now in his hundred and first year, at the very moment when he invented LSD in his laboratory. Out of this conversation came the idea that it could be interesting to talk to people who made major inventions about when and where they made them. I fully agree with Rem that your invention is very significant for London and many other cities, and travelling around I feel that there are now cities with *Time Out* and there are cities without *Time Out*. For cities without *Time Out*, one can only say something is missing. So I was curious when and where and how you made this invention.

TE — I was a student in the 1960s; I was at Keele University and Keele was a very lively place. Those people in the audience who are old enough will remember that from about 1964 through to 1972 the most extraordinary expansion of culture took place. To some degree it was a consumer change with all the things that you take for granted, like in music the Pink Floyd and the Rolling Stones, in theatre people like Peter Brook and the Living Theatre, fringe theatre even. We coined the name Fringe Theatre but we didn't invent it; anyway it was starting then. I was interested in all those things and it was very hard to find out about them. There was an environment of underground, alternative or fringe papers then, some of which were political papers, which sadly you don't have now, and very lively publications devoted to art and culture and so on. People were going around looking for new things that told them something important and I pulled it all together in one place. Also, I think significantly, we told people what was worth going to and what to expect when they got there.

RK   So what is the new thing? I think in Paris there are these magazines that tell you what is going on. Is the new thing about *Time Out* that it doesn't make a distinction, or rather includes anything alternative or not mainstream?

TE   We started off with a mission to be comprehensive. When I first started the magazine, partly because it was smaller and there was less space, I for example wouldn't list some things – the equivalent today would be not listing Andrew Lloyd Webber's musicals because the important thing was to give space to plays that were good and well written and acted. Now obviously we are obliged to provide a comprehensive service. The emphasis always is, and I hope seen to be, on what's good.

HUO   We are very interested in this idea of mapping the city and the impossibility of having a synthetic map of the city; something is always missing. How did the mapping through *Time Out* operate? Working on the different categories for the Marathon, Rem made many drawings with different colour schemes. It was very related to the *Time Out* categories.

TE   The mapping, in a sense, is clearly done basically by the journalists and I think a lot of people don't realise, but it's obvious when you think about it, that *Time Out* is a series of mini-magazines all bolted together. I don't think there's a single member of staff who works in any other area than the one they're employed in. People think they can do magazines like us by just getting a bunch of journalists and they go: 'You can write about theatre and dance and comedy because it's all on a stage'. We don't do that. You employ people to be really experts in their area. Sometimes they screw up. An example was – I am very embarrassed to say – *Time Out* virtually missed Punk in London and the reason was that the music editor at the time was very focused on what was important then, which was Pub Rock, because all the pubs were having all these bands, but in a quiet little corner this amazing thing was happening. Also the magazine had a very politically focused staff then, who rather dismissed these young people as decadent and irrelevant, and we really nearly screwed up. We caught up later. I have to say that particular music editor didn't stay on.

HUO   Obviously *Time Out* now exists in many different cities, so we also wanted to ask you about globalisation and the impact of globalisation. Édouard Glissant always says that there is the risk of homogenising forces taking over through globalisation. I was wondering to which extent there is a change when *Time Out* happens in other cultures, in other cities, in other geographies, in other contexts.

TE   Do you mean that changes things in some way?

HUO   Yes, if there are local transformations or adaptations.

TE   Yes, we have a lot of people who come to us. And we also look for people to do local magazines. One of the things that's fantastic is that they tend to get it right because they are passionate about doing it and the local international *Time Out* magazines work because they are a reflection of what goes on in those cities. They are all not the same. They are not dominated by international advertisements from Starbucks, Gap, whatever. The people there are looking for the aspects of cities that are full of character and are good.

RK   How does it work if another city wants a *Time Out*? What do they do?

TE   Basically when somebody comes along there is a publishing activity called Licensing Titles and it works very simply that they do a business plan projecting the number of copy sales and likely advertising and against that we work out what we will be paid and it's normally a percentage of their revenue in the region of eight per cent. Then we give them a format, which is basically the design, and they recruit the staff and start producing it. We carefully monitor that they are producing a magazine that fulfils what it ought to be.

RK   Can you revoke it?

TE   Yes. We haven't pulled out any yet.

RK   They get a license for a number of years?

TE   Yes, they are licenses that are three or five years and the plan is that they would always renew. One of the areas where there was a problem at the beginning, it's been rectified now, for example, was China and a lot of that was to do with the fact that the people they wanted to employ were young and, compared to Western people, relatively undeveloped and less experienced, I suppose. And so it was a struggle to get it right, but they have now got it right, with some real direction from us.

HUO   Are there unrealised *Time Out* projects? Cities where you always wanted to go and where it didn't happen?

TE   The places we'd really like to go substantially are the major European cities like Paris, Rome, Barcelona, Madrid, and the problem there is that there are existing very established magazines and they are more like glorified classified advertising; they don't really have editorial. They are useful and the local audience is completely used to them and they are normally very cheap. The trouble with *Time Out* is because you need to employ a lot of people to get it right, the cover price is expensive. So if you launch a magazine, for example in Paris, that's the equivalent of what we do here in London, it would be five or six times the price of say, *ParisScope* and the French would say that's far too expensive.

RK   Do you think the time is ripe to do something on Europe, that you should leap to a bigger scale, not to a city but a continent?

TE   No, I don't think so. *[Laughs]*

RK   I think it would be so unbelievably interesting to buy a directory every week of what is going on in Europe. You could be a political genius if you did that.

TE   We can do elements of that on-line because you flip through an on-line version of *Time Out* and look at art across all the European cities, or music or whatever.

HUO   One of the things we want to achieve with the Marathon is to get a picture of London, obviously a very incomplete portrait. Can we hear from you how you feel that London has changed, how you see London in 2006 and if you have any dreams for London?

TE   London is fantastically exciting. I go to America once a month because we have a magazine in Chicago and one in New York and I am always very happy and excited when I come back into London and I come through the elevated highway in West London called Westway, which I think is one of the best roads in the city. For those of you who don't know, there was a plan years ago to build a whole box all the way around London which would have been like Westway but all the way. A lot of people, including us, completely opposed it and it's a pity in a sense now it does not exist.

London is incredibly sophisticated now compared to what it was even fifteen years ago in terms of cafes and bars, a fantastic number of art galleries and, really significantly, the way there's a formula that as London pushes out into other areas people expect to have a fairly sophisticated environment. Then there is generation after generation of people who come through the whole time doing things. I think we are more entrepreneurial, frankly, than the Americans, whom I spend a lot of time with.

RK   The only critique I would dare to voice, I think sometimes *Time Out*, particularly in countries like Dubai, becomes the kind of voice of the expats. Where does an ex-pat go to? All the intricacy of the London *Time Out* is completely lost and it suddenly becomes a magazine for say Australians to survive in a foreign locale.

TE   Dubai is a special case. I don't know how many people have been to Dubai, but there are a lot of ex-pats there and to some degree it's produced for that group of people. Where else do you think it doesn't work as it should?

RK   Maybe in China. There is some of the same thing, that you would like more Chineseness.

TE   Let me tell you what our most successful current title is, and it's in Almaty. I wonder how many people here know where Almaty is.
        [Member of audience calls 'Kazakhstan']
        Right! We weren't looking to do a magazine in Almaty but some people

came along and they are now licensed and it's fantastically successful. It's amazing.

RK In terms of content.

TE It works. There's enough going on there and it's great.

RK Thank you very much.

HUO Thanks a lot.

Applause, end of interview

Hans Ulrich Obrist	It's a great pleasure to introduce our next speaker, Tom McCarthy.
Tom McCarthy	Hi!

HUO   Before talking with you about your recent novels, I want to ask you a bit about your practice in relation to the city. You've been involved in a society called the International Necronautical Society, which has a lot to do with urban research. Could you tell us about your organisation, how it works and how it relates to the city?

TM   Well, I guess the best way of describing the International Necronautical Society is that it's a construct. It's a construct in the same way as the IMF is a construct or the World Bank or the Catholic Church or the Mafia. It's a sort of network, part of which is public and part of which is more propositional. I guess the difference with the INS is that it very self-consciously appropriates and repeats previous cultural histories and particularly the modes and procedures of early twentieth century avant-gardes like the Futurists. We release manifestos and proclamations and denunciations and so on in a quite self-conscious, almost plagiaristic way. One of those cultural moments that figures very strongly is Situationism, which had a very strong sense of the relation to the city and the way that ideology and identity are played out in a sort of urban context. So we've done projects like having a London-wide radio broadcasting station where we broadcast a whole bunch of coded messages, very much trying to turn London's symbolic or technological space into a sort of crypted space, turn London into a technologically mediated tomb or crypt.

Rem Koolhaas   We have been working together in preparing this event and we were really struck by how many figures on our list were referring to Debord and to the Situationists and it seems that maybe forty years after the fact there is an incredible, flourishing Situationism in England. I, as a Continental, would ask what the interest in Situationism is here. In Paris, through its formality, there is an incredible amount of destabilisation that you can imagine, but in the total chaotic formlessness of London the effort of destabilisation seems to have a totally different thrust.

TM   Yes.

RK   So two questions: what is unique about Situationism and why the need to introduce this issue in this city at this moment?

TM   I don't know. Kafka used to say that he wrote in order to affirm and re-affirm that he had absolutely nothing to say, he had nothing to tell the world, he had no analysis to make, and I very much concur with that. I don't know if I'd be comfortable saying something answering your question. Maybe in the same way as the writings of Marx really provided a good codex for understanding industrial culture, maybe somewhere in the writings of Debord there is the codex for understanding post-industrial culture. Of course he'd have hated that but it's what you get!

RK   Why now in England?

TM   I don't know. I suppose there's been a sort of rumbling through the work of people like the London Psychogeographical Association and Stewart Home and more latterly the Association of Autonomous Astronauts and these cross-over organisations where political activism met avant-garde art practice and a sort of public playfulness that sort of developed quite indigenously in England. It's a paradox because it's the most un-French place you could imagine; but there has been this late flourishing of Situationist ideas in this new environment.

RK   That's exactly my point and I was asking you to answer why. I have never seen somebody in such a short time take such grandiose prototypes as IMF and the Catholic Church; it seems appropriation on a scale unimagined before.

TM   Yes, but it's like Marlon Brando says, 'What have you got?' If that's what's there to appropriate, those are the best things to appropriate; it's better than appropriating the church flower-arranging committee or something. [Laughs] I can't answer your question. This is my point. I don't know if I can answer why, I can just agree with you that this seems to be something that's happening.

RK   OK.

TM   It's interesting to note that. I don't know if I'm the person to say why. I just like the symptom.

HUO Before we move on to your other life as a writer, could you give us other examples of events and mappings the International Necronautical Society has organised? I wonder if they have to do with infiltration of the existing city.

TM   Totally. Another big influence would be William Burroughs, the American novelist, so lots of the sort of propaganda we put out is very much about viral infiltration using information networks and somehow poisonously infiltrating these. We are lucky enough to have a woman called – I can name her now – she's called Rachel Baker; she was an artist working at the BBC writing their web pages as a day job. She read an interview where we said we wanted to find moles in important media organisations; so she contacted our propaganda department and said, 'Would you like me to insert your propaganda into the source code of the BBC?' If you click 'view' and then 'source' you get all this *html* but if you don't know where to click you just see the normal news page. So we were outsourcing; we were getting writers and artists to send in propaganda which she would hide in the source code and move it around every day. Again, I don't think the content itself was particularly interesting; it was more about the process and about creating this air of general paranoia because we announced that we'd infiltrated a major news organisation, but we didn't say which one. We were tracking it on Google and quite a lot of people were writing, 'I'm clicking "view" and "source" on ABC, CBS and I can't find it'. In a way that's more interesting: the panic – well I wouldn't call it panic, that's pretentious, but the paranoia is more interesting than the actual content.

HUO Are there projects in relation to such urban interventions or infiltrations which have not yet been realised, which were maybe too extreme to be realised, or censored?

TM   Well, we're working at the moment on Berlin, which our chief philosopher, Simon Critchley, has announced is the world capital of death following close readings of Hegel and Nietzsche that are quite elaborate, too elaborate to go into here. Basically we're looking again at the idea of encryption and the idea of a crypt as a psychoanalytical model that emerges from some of the writings of Freud on mourning and particularly on the failure to mourn and how this might be played out through the neurotic surfaces of a post-traumatic city. And so we're moving into Berlin. We're going to establish a set of found crypts, of found tombs; we won't actually do anything, we'll just designate certain sites as sites of mourning or failed mourning. That's an ongoing project.

HUO It would be interesting to hear from you a little bit more about London. Earlier we spoke with Tim Newburn; that was a quite, in parts, gloomy picture about surveillance. When I interviewed J. G. Ballard, who is also a reference of yours, about that whole surveillance notion in the city he said that he thought London is being turned into a kind of Orwellian nightmare disguised as a public service. At the same time we've had very optimistic assessments about the incredible new experiments happening in London, so there were both gloomy moments and optimistic moments. I am very curious to hear your assessment of London now.

TM I think I agree with Ballard. I think it's empirically the case, correct me if I'm wrong, that London is the most surveyed city on earth, it's got the most CCTV cameras per square mile or whatever, so one could be very pessimistic about that. But then the Death Star in *Star Wars* is where the main scene of rebellion has to take place, so maybe that's a good thing ultimately. *[Laughs]*

RK Why are you laughing?

TM I don't know. It just seems a bit sort of funny, really.

RK Funny because it is so earnest or because you are so earnest? Or because we are so earnest?

TM I just think it's funny to find the contours of a contemporary politics through this sort of right-wing American film. It just seems a bit odd but appropriate.

HUO It would be interesting to hear about your parallel activity as a novelist and I'm also interested in hearing how this strange transition has happened: quite recently you were published by a small publishing house which is in the art world, Metronome Press, in a tiny edition, in an environment where no big publisher would publish your book. Within a few months then your first novel, *Remainder*, got published by a mainstream publishing house. It would be interesting to hear about the publishing dimension and then about your book.

TM Yes, it was interesting to find those contours as well, between art and writing. In the last decade as publishing has gone more sort of mainstream and corporate and dumb, basically, the art world has become almost like a haven, a refuge for literary activity. You go to a publishing party and nobody's read Kafka or Beckett or Joyce or any of these people whereas all my friends who are artists have read Faulkner, they are doing work based on the novels of Alain Robbe-Grillet and so on. Paradoxically, art had become the place where literary ideas and processes are creatively discussed and transformed and realised. That's certainly my experience: I wrote this novel and none of the mainstream houses would touch it and then this art project, Metronome Press, brought it out and I was lucky to get some good reviews and then suddenly all of the same ones did want to publish it.

HUO   Rem, do you have more questions?

RK   Yes, I have one more question, maybe more. You wrote about Tintin and there again it's described as connected to the way people like Roland Barthes or Jacques Derrida would look at it. Can you talk about that book?

TM   Yes. I wouldn't call it a piece of criticism, I'd call it an essay like Roland Barthes wrote essays; it's a sort of eighteenth-century format and it's called *Tintin and the Secret of Literature*. I guess I just always loved Tintin when I was a kid and when I read it for the first time I thought it was brilliant; the thing to be in life is Tintin. And then as I grew up and started studying literature and was beginning to write, I couldn't help noticing that Hergé's plots are incredibly classical; they always revolve around the host–guest relationship gone bad, very much like Shakespeare's plays. They are about anxieties around forgery and simulacra and a condition of fakeness, and so again you have this paradox that he never considers himself a writer. It's not something that has a highbrow cachet and yet it's got these incredibly complex processes being played out. In France Michel Serres writes about Tintin but in England the distinction between highbrow and lowbrow is too strong, so I thought it would be very interesting to examine this and I was lucky enough that Granta Books approached me and said, 'Do you want to write something about Derrida?' I said, 'No, I want to write about Tintin and Derrida, it would be more interesting'. So that's how it came about.

HUO   Frederic Tuten, the American novelist, wrote a book about the dark side of Tintin. Does this play a role in your book?

RK   In general in your life?

TM   In my life! *[Laughs]*

RK   You seem relentlessly cheerful. Is there something dark?

TM   No. It's all a front. *[Laughs]* I mentioned William Burroughs earlier; the weird thing about Tintin is that it's almost like a sort of super-erogated, as Freud would say, a potty-trained version, of William Burroughs. You've got all the drugs, all the homoeroticism, all the dark, boiling sexuality underneath but it's all contained, whereas in Burroughs it's ripping through the page. Interestingly, Andy Warhol actually credited Hergé with being the person who influenced him most after Disney.

HUO   So did Lichtenstein. Lichtenstein loved him.

TM   Lichtenstein was a huge fan and Hergé collected Lichtenstein, yes.

HUO   What's your next book?

TM   Well, next year the same publishers who are doing the new edition of *Remainder*, Alma Books, are putting out the book that I wrote before *Remainder*, which is called *Men in Space*, which is a novel about disintegration set in an Eastern Europe in the early 1990s falling apart after the collapse of Communism and it's got a very picaresque, disparate cast. It's a bit like Thomas Pynchon's *V.* or something, all these people running around after an illusive set of ideals. Anyhow I'm working on a new one, which is again to do with mourning – and incest; I'm very interested in incest, incest and technology. It seems to be something that keeps coming up in modernist literature in people like Joyce, Kafka. I'm trying to look into that a bit.

HUO   Many, many thanks to Tom McCarthy.

TM   Thank you for having me.

Applause, end of interview

Hans Ulrich Obrist	Welcome, Scott Lash. Scott, we discussed many topics which could come up tonight and you mentioned that it could be really interesting to discuss urban form and you also mentioned that the senses, taste, hearing, balance, orientation, smell, sight, touch would be significant for you in relation to a portrait of London. Maybe it would be interesting to start with the senses.
Scott Lash	I meant to bring that up with the other interviewees.
Rem Koolhaas	You can.
HUO	We thought it would be good to bring it up with you first.
SL	People talk about the city as a soundscape a lot, don't they, groups like Sonic Youth way in the past in New York City were trying to pick up urban sounds, so there is the whole idea of the city as a soundscape. I think in that sort of context you also want to look at the city as a scape of gestures: we're going to have Michael Clark and others later whose work involves dance and gesture but also the visual, of course. The city and calligraphy, writing the city. There are a number of senses: proprioception, balance. When you stand looking at the architecture you are balancing, but you are also doing that in the city. What sort of confusion, disorientation, etc. will you have in the city? What other senses are there? Touch, smell. London – is it London that smells more like pigeons or is it Paris? I can't remember. But London has a smell. The Paris Metro has a smell. I think the senses are really important in terms of a sense of orientation in the city. We'll come back to this later maybe with some of the other interviewees. On the one hand you've got this idea of scape, obviously from landscape or cityscape, but on the other hand I think this is something that also relates to your work, Hans, and to Rem's, the idea of experimentation. So they are a kind of metaphor – not metaphor, wrong word – a metonymy or whatever else, of laboratory on the one hand and studio on the other. I think that's going to come up, too.
HUO	Can you tell us more about that idea of urban form which you wanted to bring into the discussion?
SL	I don't remember this but fair enough! Wow! I thought you were going to ask me some personal questions, which I was ready to answer.

RK   Shall we ask you some personal questions?

SL   Please, yes.

HUO   We can come back to that later. That's perfect.

RK   I have been very impressed by a recent development in your life, that holding a former position of an academic authority you put yourself in a position of weakness by going to China to learn Chinese. I would like you to talk about that experience of weakness but also what you hope to achieve by it and what China is doing to you.

SL   That's interesting. China is disorienting me but the thing about the Chinese experience is not so much the disorientation but the new mode of logic, really, a new mode of order out of chaos. I guess a lot of the interviewees later in the evening are thinking about various modes of putting order on the chaos, including cosmology and all sorts of other things. I think the Chinese have a really different mode of putting order on the chaos, and it is an order. Yet in a lot of ways, if you are looking at Guangzhou or Shenzhen or Shanghai, or even Beijing, China is so out of control, in our eyes chaotic. I think Shanghai, Guangzhou and Shenzhen specifically are what might be called mega-cities. The scale of immigration, the scale of disorientation, is something the European city has never experienced.

My London experience is a very strange double experience; I was here as a graduate student at the London School of Economics starting in the mid-1970s, like a century ago. I came back at the end of the 1990s after being away in places like Berlin, Paris, São Paulo and China for a number of years and the extraordinary thing is that London has become that much more out of control. In 1973, 1975 it was English people that lived in London, basically, with some minorities; there was just no comparison to now. The rate of migration in London is twenty-five per thousand per year, twice New York's rate of migration. So the kind of confusion and the kind of rapid input from outside that we associate much more with places like Mumbai or Shanghai, Shenzhen and Guangzhou is something that is happening right here, I think, now. I'm not sure that's a very good answer.

RK   It's a very good answer but I am more interested in the personal. You wanted a personal question. How has the experience of putting yourself in the position of somebody who learns something and somebody who doesn't exercise authority, but on the contrary undergoes authority, been transforming you at this age and how? And what do you hope to learn beyond learning to speak Chinese?

SL   I want to talk to people in China. There are two things that have transformed London between 1975 and 2006; on the one hand it's the migration and on the other it's finance, it's money. Because London, in between those times, has become the financial capital of the world very much and it's the money flows as much as anything else. It has also set up gross inequalities that weren't there thirty years ago but are there now. I'm doing work on financial markets in China and we're doing work on the construction of financial markets in China. I've always been a sociologist of the future even though I'm now an old sociologist of the future! The kind of stuff that was going on in London in certain ways is going on there now in terms of the cutting edge of finance but it's a totally different set up and I don't think I'm going to be in any kind of position to understand it – and we're going to be doing a lot of work on that in the next three years – unless I've got Chinese. I want to get out into the localities and see what credit cards mean to people; I want to see how people relate to finance in a day-to-day way; I want to understand how financial markets are transforming the space of Shanghai in particular.

HUO   And to bring it back to London, being a sociologist of the future, how do you see the future of London?

SL   I'm probably too optimistic.

RK   Interestingly enough, that is something that everybody has been saying this evening.

HUO   It is the sentence which has been said most often.

SL   The reason the three of us have become friends over the years is because of our ridiculous optimism. But nobody else is optimistic; everybody else is pessimistic and they're probably right. I don't know. I think, quite rightly, for artists and people like that, of course London is becoming ridiculously overpriced. That's the third factor, of course: migration, finance and then art. All completely transformed in the last thirty years and I'm sure others have said this already. But London is being completely overpriced. The gross inequalities you can only imagine getting worse. As a university academic at Goldsmiths, and as Rem calls it an authority, although I suppose you've got authorities in architecture and art and all sorts of other places as well as academic life, what I found completely different in London is something I couldn't do in New York and I couldn't do in Los Angeles and I couldn't do elsewhere and that's move over right into working with people in art, in architecture, in the general cultural sector. You can't cross those boundaries in New York City. None of my friends at Columbia University or NYU are doing it. You can't do it in Paris, which is so incredibly gridded. I think there is the chance to do that here.

RK   Shapeless.

SL   The shapelessness, the boundarylessness. That's almost saying London is chaos and it will be chaos and I thrive on chaos but a lot of people don't.

RK   I want to talk about you as a writer and there is one particular invention that I really admire or enjoy without necessarily understanding it. I think it is in *Critique of Information* [2002], where as a counterpart to 'goods' you introduce the word 'bads'. I would like you to elaborate on that word 'bads' because without entirely understanding it, I think there are a lot of bads these days.

SL   I think that's right. It's in the context of globalisation.

RK   I think you should first explain the concept of bads.

SL   What are bads? People talk about goods; globalisation is about the circulation, the movement, of all sorts of goods like cultural goods, economic goods, capital goods, consumption goods, service goods, media goods, etc. But what about the bads? Obviously things like the environment, pollution, things like that. There is also this incredible globalisation of bads and to a certain extent the bads are the unintended consequences of the goods. On the one hand we've got this amazingly productive, and fantastic in a lot of ways, finance sector here, which is on the one hand bloody good; it employs two hundred and fifty or three hundred thousand people including another hundred and fifty thousand outsourced jobs to Glasgow. (Get on any flight to Glasgow any morning and it's just full of bankers.) On the other hand it's produced the most unsustainable levels of inequality with the bonuses, with everything else that's going on. Now with pension funds being invested in hedge funds, being invested in what are supposedly security markets, markets that are supposed to pump up security, all sorts of people are being put at incredible risk in the worst possible ways. So the other side of the goods is, I'm afraid, bads. I want to be optimistic, you know.

Hans, you must have another question.

HUO   Rem was saying earlier it was difficult to address questions to Zaha Hadid because he knew her so well; it seems similar in this interview. One of the things which has come up a lot, which I think would be interesting to follow up here, is what you called a permanent state of exception as opposed to rules, which obviously has to do with a Carl Schmitt moment. I think it could be interesting to explore that here in relation to the Marathon about the city, about London, and it's something which will definitely play a role tomorrow in the conversation with Chantal Mouffe.

SL   Yes, I think that's right. I think that London is clearly much less rule-bound than the classical modern city in advanced countries. If you compare it to New York City, well, New York City is gridded, Manhattan's got a grid. London hasn't got a grid. Paris is incredibly structured, Paris inside the Périphérique. We saw what happened outside of the walls of Paris; outside of Paris was the *banlieu*, outside of the walls of Paris is the riots. London isn't so clear. In Paris the walls are the *périphérique*. In London you don't know where the walls are. Is it the Circular? Where is the inner city and where are the walls? In Paris and New York the chaos is banished beyond the walls of the city. The order of the centre city, and here we are talking about urban form, right Hans, is banishing the chaos to the edges. Well, London's got a lot of chaos right inside; we haven't got the walls, it's a concoction of villages and in that sense there is a sort of permanent state of exception. Chantal Mouffe will refer to this tomorrow but Carl Schmitt was Adolf Hitler's favourite political theorist, at least of the Nazi party, and of course his state of exception was partly used to justify the *Führerprinzip*. The *Führerprinzip* held that because things are in a state of exception you can no longer go under the rules of Parliament. Subsequently, of course, a state of exception has been understood in terms of invention. I'm afraid in London we've got both sides of it. We have a magnificent state of exception but not for everybody. For a lot of people, OK it's not a *Führerprinzip* but it's a lot of suffering and people living on a level that's really unacceptable. Having said all that, I think that what's amazing in London is the way the chaos is taken inside the city walls instead of just being expelled outside so there is kind of a wonderful, but at the same time horrible, permanent state of exception here.

HUO   Carl Schmitt brings us to the past and we have discussed in many previous interviews notions of dynamic memory. Are there any philosophers or sociologists who you think provide toolboxes for today?

SL   These are really hard questions. Dynamic memories. Can you think of anybody? Getting back to your first question, which I've just started to register a little bit, the question of urban form, one person I would definitely recommend to everybody is Rem's friend Sanford Kwinter, who wrote a wonderful book called *Architectures of Time* [2002]. For Sanford the city is temporal: urban form should be understood in a time sense and not just in a space sense. The city should be seen as almost partly a self-generating form, but just as importantly, obviously, for any kind of quasi-Darwinian, what is the environment, what is London relating to? Clearly global finance is one thing. But I think London as urban form, even though it's kind of an out of control form, what kind of form is here at stake?

In terms of memory London is a very strange place; Walter Benjamin said that in Paris – and I lived in Paris and Berlin before I came to London properly in 1998 – you had the ancient and the modern, whereas Berlin was just the modern: it was cleaned out, cleaned up, no ancient at all. What about London? People come from China and the first thing they say about London is it's so old. In a weird way the history does not inform it in the way history is always under the ground informing everything in Paris. We act as though the history wasn't there in London, as if it were some kind of *tabula rasa* that came about in the 1990s or late 1980s or something like that. On the one hand I think that the history is all there but on the other hand the history is not there at all.

HUO   Thank you very much, Scott Lash. This is not the end of our time with Scott because he is going to stay with us for the next few hours.

SL   Thank you.

Applause, end of interview

Rem Koolhaas   Hi! Welcome to Michael Clark.
Michael Clark   Hello. How are you going to keep this up for twenty-four hours?
Hans Ulrich Obrist   It has only just begun!

RK   We will see! As somebody who saw your beginnings, because I live in London and follow them, I am very surprised by your current involvement in the classical. You are doing two Stravinsky programmes in the Barbican.

MC   Yes.

RK   And I would like to know how that works, somebody who from the beginning of his career was able to create a continuum between the street and the stage. I am not in any way objecting to it, I am just interested in how that works for you.

MC   Yes, it's a very different kind of dialogue; very often when there is a relationship between dance and music, there's a dialogue going on between them as well. With a lot of music that I've chosen to work with in the past, the music has been more simple, maybe even deceptively simple and with more complex lyrics, like the lyrics by Mark E. Smith from *The Fall*, for example. Obviously with Stravinsky's music there's a complexity that needs a different kind of dialogue. I work with music in lots of different ways, but Stravinsky's music has a different kind of sophistication, I guess.

RK   It's not only the music, because obviously if you work with Stravinsky you are also competing with Balanchine and basically engaging the whole history of ballet in the twentieth century.

MC   Maybe not too many people know here, but certainly from my perspective, the three pieces I will create to the music Stravinsky wrote for dance, are seminal works in themselves. It's almost sacrilege to touch them, so I guess, that's part of the challenge for me.

HUO   The city is less a topic than a catalyst for us in this Marathon. Could you talk about the city in your work and how the stage relates to the city, to the pedestrian? I am particularly interested to which extent Trisha

123

Brown and the ways she related to the city in *Trio A* would have been an influence.

MC   Certainly a work like *Trio A* was an influence, but it was only something I had read about. These notebooks of Yvonne Rainer were quite influential to me as a book, [*Yvonne Rainer Work 1961–73*]. I had never actually seen any of the work, but I found the ideas that she was able to explore in context with dance, were something I hadn't come across before and realised were actually possible. I remember when I saw some of her work much later on, I was surprised by how human the work was, I guess because the book was printed all in black and white and had some quite serious texts. I just didn't realise there would be that much humour and humanness about it. That was kind of interesting.

RK   Was that a disappointment, or not?

MC   Maybe initially it was a disappointment but not for long. It made me realise something about the written word and dance and how different they are.

HUO   Can you tell us how the space of the performance relates to the street in your work, how that negotiation functioned in the past but also now and if that's changed?

MC   Personally I take a great deal of pleasure in street performance, not in a busking type of way, but I like trying things out in normal, everyday situations, usually for my own amusement. Of course there's a very different expectation when people have paid to come and see something, but I would still like to embrace both. There is always a complexity in the way things are structured. I would love to take my work to the least suspecting audience; that would be great. I think that's what you are touching on with some of Trisha Brown's stuff, where the work happened on floating platforms or on rooftops, that sort of thing. I think that's what you were referring to.

HUO   Yes. So both/and would be the answer. Related to that, a lot has been written about not only Trisha Brown's influence on your work, but your early dialogue with Merce Cunningham and John Cage. I was wondering in terms of memory and toolboxes from the past if there have been any things in terms of London or the UK which were important for you at the beginning of your work.

MC   Before I go on to London, I'd like to say that Yvonne Rainer's note-books were a key influence, definitely, really, because of the sophistication of ideas she showed could be possible in dance and that was something I was never really taught. Maybe it's not something that you are taught, but find out. In London more specifically, what was going on in other fields and other things that interested me outside of my training were influences. It took some time for me to realise that I could actually bring those influences together. Cerith Wyn Evans, whom I met...

HUO   ... he is going to come here in a few hours.

MC   Yes. I met him when I was sixteen and he was doing something similar through film at that time and I guess, we had similar interests in terms of music. There were various friends working in different ways finding basic support in each other's work. We've collaborated together on many different levels and this will continue. The most obvious thing would be to say, that I was studying at the Royal Ballet School in a very rigorous, classical way and at the same time Punk was going on, so there were those two things. I was very focused during the day on my dance training and this practice was something that gave me a great deal of satisfaction and pleasure. But also there was this other completely different thing going on, which was very exciting too and it just took me a while to realise those things could actually feed one another.

HUO   You mentioned Cerith Wyn Evans; there was also collaboration with Leigh Bowery. Can you talk about this?

MC   I guess a lot of what was considered serious New Dance, I think it might have been called that at the time, stripped away the notion of costume. There was that whole manifesto of Yvonne Rainer saying no to this and no to virtuosity. I don't know if she would agree with this herself today, but at the time, this was her manifesto. To me dance was a visual art form and the way in which dance was presented was pretty important to me. I was surrounded by people whose only means of expression was how they dressed. Leigh is a very good example of that. When Leigh and I started working together initially, he simply wanted to make us look like him as much as possible. *[Laughs]* This was quite a challenge. That changed over time. It changed when he became a member of my dance company and saw and experienced the work on a daily basis as well as being physically involved. His understanding of our practice became a much more integrated one and I think this was reflected in the costumes that he then started to design for the work.

RK   If I were you I would think that a moment like that one would be a moment that would never come back again.

MC   Yes.

RK   Or that a moment of similar intensity or affinity or mutual reinforcement would never come back again. Do you think it will or do you live in the expectation that you will find similar moments of convergence? Or do you think that was something that would happen only in that period?

MC   That was something very special and unique. Something I have certainly learnt from this is that my best working relationships are the ones that evolve over time. The first time I work with somebody isn't always the best; when I'm collaborating with somebody they'll generally do their best work, if I let them do exactly what they're interested in doing at that moment in time. Part of the reason I was drawn to people with very strong ideas, was that I hated the idea of a costume designer fulfilling a brief. That just didn't interest me. Cunningham and Cage had a different approach, similar but different in that they had decided on no interaction between the design, music and the choreography, there was to be no discussion about it – maybe they would discuss the length of the piece. With me there has always been a lot of interaction but, as I said, I chose to work with people who have very strong ideas of their own who are not going to do what I tell them.

Scott Lash   You work on Stravinsky, you can think of Stravinsky's Paris and all the amazing amounts of high culture that were around the time, Picasso and so on, and you talked about Leigh Bowery. I am obviously older than you but I came to London at the exact same moment as you did, pretty much, 1975, and also the thing that really struck me was people whose mode of expression was how they dressed. It's like some kind of popular street design broke through, something that was quite fixed and not dynamic at all, it just broke through and opened up so much space. Now you have gone back to the classics a little bit but have you followed up your experience in 1975, 1977?

MC I was fascinated by those characters. I was amazed the first time I saw somebody cry because they couldn't get their hair the way they wanted it, before they went out; that was a shock to me. I know that Leigh spent his entire flight from Australia to London in the toilet re-doing his hair. *[Laughs]* Which I thought was quite an amazing achievement! But I have never been someone who gets that personally involved. I guess part of preparing for a performance can be like that. I'm not like that. There are rituals.

SL It was almost as if street was being performed here. I'm sure it was happening in other places, too, but it was almost as if the breakthroughs that later tipped over into visual art and pop music started with dress.

MC I do remember at that time it was pretty straightforward in lots of ways. If you had your hair shaved off, you basically could get away with not paying your tube fare; it was really that simple. You could just walk through at the other end and not have to pay. It's not quite like that now. But it meant something different then. I'm not being nostalgic. *[Laughs]*

RK I have a question which may be totally off the wall. When you started, I think bodies were different than they are now and the discrepancy between an athletic ballet dancer's body and the kind of average body was huge. I think you are now surrounded, on the whole, by more athletic, more beautiful, more perfect bodies.

MC It's interesting you say that. It depends in what circles you mix!

RK Yes, I know.

MC On the one hand people do a lot less with their bodies; quite a lot of people sit at computers all day. I'd love more extremes, but I can see what you mean. Just within the field that I work in, in the sort of dance that I make, it was unusual when I began making work for somebody who had recognisable technique. That was still strange then; it's not any longer. I guess there was a period when technique was rejected, when more pedestrian movement was being embraced. I tried to do that through working with people like Leigh. Usually people who weren't trained and doing my work were people who I was close to in some way – my Mum.

HUO	I wanted to ask you about your yet-unbuilt roads, projects which have been unrealised or too big to be realised or too difficult or censored, or dreams.
MC	Yes, there are quite a few of those.
HUO	Can you tell us some? It could be a book.
MC	There is a book. I'm sure everyone has a kind of file. *[Laughs]*
HUO	Maybe you could give us an example of something particularly urgent?
MC	I can't think of one immediately off the top of my head. There's a book and I'll put it in there later.
HUO	Great. Thanks a lot.

Applause, end of interview

3

Richard Wentworth

Marcus du Sautoy

Pedro Ferreira

Ron Arad

Jane and Louise Wilson

Cerith Wyn Evans

Squarepusher (aka Tom Jenkins)

Peter Saville

Roger Hiorns

Olivia Plender

RICHARD WENTWORTH with **MARCUS DU SAUTOY** and **PEDRO FERREIRA**
[with Scott Lash]

Hans Ulrich Obrist	I am very happy to introduce the first three guests of the third part of the Marathon. Welcome Richard Wentworth, Marcus du Sautoy and Pedro Ferreira.

[Applause]

This session has a lot to do with self-organisation as well as organisation. As is often the case with more complex conferences, we believe in the idea of not only inviting but inviting to invite, and in conversations with Richard Wentworth we found out about the work of Marcus du Sautoy and Pedro Ferreira. So we are delighted to have this extraordinary constellation here tonight.

I want to start with a specific question for Richard, and I am incredibly thrilled that we can have this conversation tonight because really everything in relation to London started for me with meeting Richard Wentworth on my very first trip here.

Richard Wentworth   When was that?

HUO   I think it was 1987 or 1988.

RW   Before the war.

HUO   *[Laughs]* It was before I had started to organise exhibitions. Richard participated in my very first exhibition, the *Kitchen Show* [1991], and at that time you said that London is a city you still do not understand, but you explained it to me through your ongoing photographic research, *Making Do and Getting By*. Could you tell us about how this project started and where it stands now, and also how it changed in time?

RW   I don't quite know how to say this, but I really dislike photography.

[Laughter]

I think it's a very feeble medium. But we use it and I don't suppose there's anybody here that hasn't taken a photograph. I'm not even quite sure how it came about that I took some photographs. I mean, I did and I've always done it, but I'm not a photographer. It took me a long time to realise that the photographs have a kind of subject matter and that subject matter is a little bit like the top of this table: it's quite modest, it's how things get put down, how things get arranged, how I've got my ass organised on this block. Over a long period that turned into a kind of grammar or a syntax. But I am talking about an amount of time which is longer than a lot of people's age in this space, maybe thirty years. What's odd to me is why would I go on doing that and I think it's probably a little bit of an illness. It might be a bit autistic but I do still do it. I think the subjects are at the edge of the really formal things that architects often intend cities to be, so they are the way cities don't quite function or don't quite do what they're told to do or do something in a different way. Of course cities don't do that, it's us, it's people. So it's about the way things get bullied, knocked about, a little bit loved, a little bit loathed; that's probably the centre of what I do. Is that a reasonable description?

HUO   Yes. I'd like to know more. How does it change over time? It is a series which has been ongoing for such a long time. It's an archive and also a piece.

RW   Well, I can tell you how much it's not an archive because they're still slides and unfortunately people have those as digital images and they send them to other people and say, 'This is available or you could buy this or publish this', then they ask me for the original one and I don't know where it is. So it's not an archive in the sense that a lot of people here would run a very organised and beautifully categorised system. I haven't mastered that yet and it's a bit late in my life to worry about it.

Rem Koolhaas   Over these thirty years, has what you have found changed? In other words, you kept different things that existed. London has been famous for its informality and shapelessness but I think it is currently undergoing a rush to design, almost a regime of organisation. Has that affected your work?

RW   Yes.

RK   How?

RW   I can't do it! It's a very good point. I think this is a city that is extremely loose – I was going to say irregular – but with lots of soft edges, lots of things bumping into other things, and it's somehow just working but always working in a very approximate way. Now it's becoming a regulated city and it's also becoming a really owned city; the sense of the proprietorial, which is often them not us, which is an emotional remark, is much stronger. So actually the sorts of things I am more likely to be drawn to are probably more institutional, they are probably more the smell of how institutions can't quite function but try to keep their authority up. I think they are less affectionate.

RK   Less affectionate?
RW   Yes.

RK   Interesting.
RW   Not necessarily crueller yet, but I wouldn't be surprised if they went that way.

RK   We had an interesting conversation earlier about the policing of London with Tim Newburn, a criminologist. When you started maybe the things you captured were captured for the first time. I think currently London is highly policed and ubiquitously filmed with CCTV. Does that affect your work? There is probably not a corner of London that you can photograph that isn't permanently recorded by other devices.

RW   I would expand that into something else, which is that I really like my privacy. I don't want to be recognised and as you get older you know more people so perhaps you meet more people whom you know. But I think being able to move around a city privately is a really special thing. I probably live in a city because I need that emotionally; I need the comfort of friendship but I don't want to be constantly stroked. I think that there's a funny hybrid between that sense that the city is vigilant and there is less privacy. Somebody knows I am here. I know I had dinner and I know I paid for it and for sure that means somebody could work out I am here or not very far away. I haven't made a telephone call this evening but that would be another method. So all of those things that describe where I might be have somehow diminished my sense of being the lost child.

HUO   Maybe it would be great to open it up now. Richard, nobody could give a better introduction to Marcus du Sautoy and Pedro Ferreira than you.
RW   Oh, I think other people could do it much better! There are lots of unsung people here tonight and I have a set of friendships that mostly goes back to a kind of cult called Artangel. They always seem to be women and they always seem to be exceptionally interesting and generous personalities. Two, particularly, who worked with me three or four years

ago are Kathy Batista and Tracey Ferguson, who are both here tonight. Kathy, I think, might explain why at least half this room is here, because she has been, with everyone else, joining things together. So she said 'It's all getting a bit artsy. Do you know any scientists?' I, of course, being in the art tribe had to say, 'Oh no, no. I don't know any'. And then an hour later I thought, 'Actually, yes I do'. Of course I don't actually think it is interesting to think of people as 'the man I know who does maths' and 'the man I know who does astrophysics', because that would be like a horrible address book. But I have a growing friendship with this man who is called Pedro Ferreira, who is an astrophysicist and I don't even really know how we get on; we don't talk about astrophysics. I don't know Marcus so well but I think I said, rather crudely, to Kathy, 'Marcus does good radio'. That's an incredibly difficult thing to do. You are amazingly articulate, Marcus, when you are doing that stuff and you are very unpatronising and generous. I have to say, really importantly, you are both quite funny and I think funny in English, of course, can go from weird to humorous. Anyway, welcome.

[Laughter]

I need a drink!

Scott Lash	But is there a way in which ideas…
RW	… I'm sorry, I don't know your name.

SL	Scott Lash.
RW	You're Scott Lash. Hi! That's nice.

SL	I'm also curious about your kind of early Goldsmiths days because I came here at the end of the 1990s, having just met John Thompson, to teach at Goldsmiths. Perhaps you could talk about what you saw in terms of the cityscape at that moment which might have worked into your work and how stuff might have changed now, thirty years down the line.
RW	Not to spoil your question, but some people here might not know who John Thompson is. John Thompson is an artist who, I think aged thirty-one or thirty-two, became head of the Fine Art Department at Goldsmiths in 1970 or 1971 and he immediately did an incredibly obvious thing, which was that he just employed eight or nine people who were about twenty-four years old, and I was one of them. That probably sounds rather odd now but at the time it didn't seem like such an odd thing to

do; it was a generous and imaginative thing to do, and it was like, 'Why don't you get some people to work in a school who don't know what they're doing but are interested?' The point I was going to make was that actually came out of John's social intelligence and his kind of generosity and I think that's a fantastic quality. I think if you get that in a school you've got everything anyway. Maybe this is a school. How boring to have everybody in an art school and find out they all went to art school. It's not interesting!

SL   I was trying to think of ways in which certain kinds of assumptions in your work, Pedro, or your work, Marcus, have kind of cycled through Richard's art. I want to ask Marcus a question. I was really interested in your theory of prime numbers. This is coming from a position of total ignorance. I think in something I saw on the web you cite Leibniz as distinct from Newton on something. Leibniz really saw mathematics in terms of an ontology and not just controlling and running but also being, which probably opens much more onto art than the straight Newton thing. The other thing about Leibniz that is less known is that he (like Madonna, though I think Madonna has left the movement now) was a Kabbalist in the eighteenth century. The interesting thing was that prime numbers are all different to each other, whereas non-prime numbers you can divide up and classify by. Prime numbers remind you of Paradise in Genesis, which Leibniz was obsessed by, in which everybody has a different name. Man is the naming animal; everybody is different. Then you get the Fall and you get these horrible regulations and classification. I wonder if you could elaborate on that a bit.

Marcus du Sautoy   Yes. I think a lot of numbers have their own different personalities and as you get to know them more and more you like certain numbers more than others because of that quality. For example, my favourite prime number is number seventeen.

RK   Mine too!

MdS   Excellent. There you go! There are several reasons why seventeen is my favourite prime number. Firstly, perhaps the greatest mathematician of all time was Gauss and one of the things which made him become a mathematician was his discovery as a child of a way to construct a seventeen-sided figure just using a straight line and a set of compasses. He started a mathematical diary with this discovery and that was what drew him into mathematics. He always wanted that construction to be put on his gravestone. I went to Göttingen just recently and it isn't on there, unfortunately. I felt like carving it in to satisfy his wishes.

Seventeen is also another wonderful prime where we seem to be surrounded by bugs at the moment. I think this is attracting all the bugs in London to the Serpentine Gallery. There is a fantastic little bug which lives in the forests in North America. I don't think it's quite come here yet. It has this very strange life-cycle: it hides underground for seventeen years doing absolutely nothing and then after seventeen years the cicadas emerge en masse into the forest and they sing away. The sound of the forest is so loud that residents have to move out. Then after six weeks the cicadas all die and the forest goes quiet again for another seventeen years. It's beautiful. Nature has chosen seventeen as its favourite prime number as well.

It's also the prime number that I play for in my football team out on the Hackney Marshes and I persuaded the whole of my football team to change into prime numbers and we got promoted after we did that. So primes are definitely my favourite numbers!

[Laughter]

RK   We had a discussion earlier about art as a form of knowledge and that seems to be a very important issue with artists for understandable reasons, maybe, although why should it be important? But anyway, do you have an opinion about it?

Pedro Ferreira   About art as a form of knowledge?

RK   Or in any way comparable to your form of knowledge.

PF   I think they are very different and I'm not going to go into the differences. I'm actually going to go into the similarities. One of the things that I've realised over the last ten or fifteen years of doing science is that a lot of the ways we pursue knowledge in science is guided by – I don't want to use this word, but I'm going to use it anyway – aesthetics. I work on the fabric of space-time. Another way of putting it, and people don't normally put it this way, is that I work on the notion of place and how dynamic place is and the life of place and how place is more than just somewhere where you put things in; it has a life of its own and you can describe its life and its evolution. The point when aesthetics, or this kind of creative line has come into play was when Einstein, for example, con structed his theory of space-time. He wrote down a set of equations which were – people like to use this word – elegant; they were very simple and elegant. And that has pervaded theoretical physics, that has pervaded fundamental physics, over the twentieth and twenty-first centuries.

RK   The elegance.

PF   The elegance. And we can discuss what this elegance means. It's probably a very classical notion of elegance, but it is this way of thinking that makes people make choices of what line of research to pursue in my field. So there is a kind of similarity. You do make a choice: you choose an elegant route, not an ugly route.

MdS   I think the quote of Leibniz you were referring to was actually one where he was comparing mathematics and music and he said music is the sensation of counting without realising you're counting, which I think is actually a very simplistic view of the similarities. I listen to a lot of music when I do my mathematics and I think that the sense of aesthetics is very similar between mathematics and music. Having an aesthetic sense is really important for me in finding a route through what can often be a complete mess.

PF   One of the things we do day-to-day is try and extend what Einstein has done, and obviously different people have different ideas. You pick a model, a theory, something to work on, which if you abstract, you step back, is probably as valid as any other theory, but you pick it for a reason which can be quite subjective. It should be based on how well it fits the natural world or some more basic objective principle, but it's not.

SL   Are you saying that God is throwing dice?

PF   No. This is different. This is the way we do science. I think the way we do science is much more subjective and driven by some personal direction and much less a methodical building of this edifice where we know what the next step is. It is what Marcus is saying: you cut a path, you find your own path and you go through it. It might be the wrong path but it's the path that you choose driven by your aesthetic judgement.

MdS   Yes. I think there are a lot more choices than people expect in a science, actually; you can choose many directions to go in. Mathematicians love to talk of themselves as artists rather than scientists. It's an art but an art under huge constraints, almost like building a building, I guess. You want to build something but it's got to stand up; what can you do within that?

HUO   We have talked about lots of different models of contact zones between disciplines, that idea of going beyond the fear of pooling knowledge, and Brian Eno who started the Marathon tonight talked about the very astonishing art school out of which he came, where for some years science and engineering and art came together. I was wondering how you feel in your own way you go beyond this fear of pooling knowledge within your dialogue. It's a question to the three of you.

MdS   Is the word 'pooling' knowledge?

HUO   Yes. Pooling knowledge and going beyond the fear of doing so.

MdS   I think one of the reasons why Richard and I met, actually, was a project where Richard kept a diary of what it was to be an artist for six months; two years later the Gulbenkian Foundation, which sponsored that, asked nine scientists to keep diaries. We did an event together, two artists and two scientists. It was really exciting for me to see the similarities and the big differences between what I do and what an artist does. The person I really felt that I had most in common with was a novelist, not actually the event we did at the Hay Festival but another event at the Royal Society.

RW   Was that Lawrence Norfolk?

MdS   Yes. Lawrence Norfolk wrote a fantastic novel and he talked about it in these six months. The way he was piecing together the narrative and the way things didn't work and then suddenly it all slotted into place, it felt like proving a theorem. My description in my diary was of what it was to prove a theorem. We suddenly said, 'My Gosh! We're doing the same thing, almost, here.'

RW   You both can say something about the relation of fear to desire, though. All your gestures just now were about the exhilaration of 'it fits' but there is also 'it doesn't fit' and the 'fuck it' factor.

MdS   In the diary I kept I was trying to prove this conjecture and it was all about beauty. All the examples I had had this beautiful palindromic symmetry and I thought, 'Wow! This has got to be true. Symmetry is always there'. I finished the diary and I was still working on it and a few month later one of my graduate students came into my office and showed me an example where the symmetry wasn't there. It was like, 'Oh my God! I've been trying to prove this thing for ten years. It's not as beautiful as I thought it was!' You have to take a lot of risks and be prepared to fail in order to have those few times where it does work out. But you have to be prepared for nature not always to be beautiful.

PF   I don't know if you find this but I find that some of the projects I've loved most are failed projects. Some of the projects which are the ones I really obsess about and I think I invested most of my intellectual and creative energy in are ones that didn't work. In retrospect it's obvious why they didn't work. Ones that have been incredibly successful and have had a lot of citations just happened, they just fell out.

MdS   Yes. There's a richness about things going wrong, actually, because suddenly you have a complexity there you didn't realise and then you can say something is beautiful and something is ugly. You have a notion of beauty there because these things are working and these aren't. That may be more interesting than everything working.

RW   But my whole work is beginning to look as if it might be about things going wrong! [Laughs] That's sort of disturbing, really, because you think this is a perpetual interest in the beauty of failure and I have a terrible eye for failure. I haven't found a good failure in here tonight, but the point is I don't look; they visit me. Actually the bugs are amusing – they are like a little 'whooooo'. They are almost intimate so they don't quite qualify. I'll always see the crack in the glass before I see the glass. Always.

HUO   Many thanks to all of you.

Applause, end of interview

Rem Koolhaas Our next guest is Ron Arad. Basically I've always felt an enormous sympathy for you, a huge respect, considerable admiration, but nevertheless never had the particular incentive to talk to you. Now I have to ask you questions. Do you recognise that kind of situation?
[Laughter]

Ron Arad Yes, I think I ran into you in the middle of the night in New York once. Maybe it's good the microphone was not on. Why do you think I need sympathy?

RK No, no, you don't need sympathy but these are the feelings I've always had for you without the need to communicate further.

RA I think it's right because I'm not a talker: I do things, I make things, I draw and what I do is things that didn't exist before I did them. Some people feel like talking about it, some people don't. You seem to belong to the second group.
[Laughter]

RK You belong to the second group?

RA You seem to belong to the second group. You do things, the phone rings and lots of people want to talk about it. Some people don't.

RK Yes. OK. Nevertheless there are a number of things we have in common, perhaps the influence of London, and I would like to ask you to talk about that. What has London done for you and what can you do in London which you could not have done anywhere else?

RA Well, I'm a foreigner in London; I'm not from here. That probably has a quality. I came to London from the beleaguered Middle East and I had a very exotic image of what London is, mainly thanks to New Realism films of the 1960s and 1970s and, of course, I didn't find what I anticipated. Every film that came from London was culture; everything that came from London was fresh. Of course it's not true. When I hear *Penny Lane* played on the radio it doesn't take me to Liverpool, it takes me to Tel Aviv where I grew up with it. So London gave me the chance to be an outsider, which I still am to a great degree. In the profession I found my self in, having defected slightly for a short time from architecture, design was a complete desert in London. There was nothing happening. If I went to Milan I would probably have had things to join. I am not very good at joining things so London gave me the chance not to join anything but to invent my own profession and to do what I do.

RK   To what extent is the shapelessness and roughness of London an important feature?

RA   I think it's great to work when there's great indifference around you; you are free to do what you want. I had it enhanced by the fact that when I first started, when I graduated from the Architectural Association, I started my own company, which I shouldn't have and I had a deportation order, which gives you even more freedom to do what you want because there is absolutely nothing to lose: you don't take notice of anything, you just do things.

Hans Ulrich Obrist   I wanted to ask you to talk a little about bridges between design and architecture and design and art. You've ventured into architecture on some occasions; at the same time you've had a close relationship to the visual art context, friendships and dialogues with artists like Cornelia Parker and Rachel Whiteread. I was wondering if you could talk about those two bridges.

RA   I think most professions want to be closed shops in some way. I think Frank Gehry once told me that when he was at the height of his career as a furniture designer he had to stop it to be taken seriously as an architect. People find it very difficult to perceive that you are very good at one thing and that you are brilliant at another thing at the same time – actually, I'm also a very good ping-pong player! I don't see any bridges between the two things; I just do things. Architecture, I think – was it you that said it's a tragic profession? Have you coined that sentence, Rem?

RK   Could have been. *[Laughs]*
[Laughter]

RA   Right. It is a tragic profession because it is a profession where you have to be asked to do things. You have to be commissioned, you have to behave yourself, you have to have Philistines commission you, basically. I just wasn't patient enough to do that so I did things that I could do without waiting for anyone to ask me to do or to like it or to finance it. I don't think I need any bridges. If you look at Italian masters of furniture, for example, they are all architects without any exception. There are no Italian masters any more since they started teaching design as a profession. You don't need to actually be busy defining the borders between things. I think it would be a lot easier if we divided things into charming and exciting things and boring and tedious things; it's a much more intelligent division than between what is art and what is design and what is architecture.

Scott Lash You talked about New Realist 1960s British cinema; there's a really strong ethos of the industrial worker coming through that kind of cinema as distinct from Hollywood. A lot of your work, maybe it's completely happenstance, works off notions of rapid prototyping, almost industrial-type principles.

RA I did serve my time welding and beating steel before we discovered computers. And I drive a car, I don't use a horse. Rapid prototyping is a very convenient tool for us to make things and we use it. It's very exciting in the first period, then it gets even more exciting for what you can use it for and after a while it becomes commonplace and you look for other drugs, other excitements. But I am sure it was very similar in the industrial era when they made exciting machines that could do things that couldn't be done before.

RK One of the reasons why I thought architecture was a tragic profession is that we only make prototypes.

RA It was you! You are admitting now! *[Laughter]*

RK Yes. That we make prototypes only and that we therefore can never really earn money. That is the great thing about furniture or making anything that is a mass product or potentially a mass product, that you potentially earn money with it.

RA This is the grass that is green on the other side. Most designers don't make money; most designers don't have mass-produced objects after their name.

RK I would like to ask you how your economy works.

RA In two words, very well. *[Laughter]*

I have three economies: I have an architectural office that struggles with pleasing clients and mayors and people like that – you know all about that – and a lot of idealistic work that is sometimes not rewarded as fantastically as you want it to be. Then there's the industrial design, that if you are lucky and you have the best-selling pieces to yourself – I am very happy that I have some – money comes in without you having to do anything. And then there are the studio pieces, that is playing the art market, which if you really want to know is the most financially rewarding activity.

RK   Of all.

RA   Of all three, yes. It finances the architecture sometimes, finances the industrial design at other times.

RK   And do you think that connection to the market could ever apply to architecture or do you think it would be a smart project for architects to establish that connection? Or what do you think is inherently the reason that we are stuck?

RA   We are stuck because we depend on clients. We have a very expensive, long education and our clients did not do any course in being a client for architects. Either they made some money somehow and they need a house or a building, or they were elected by someone for their views on something else and they find themselves in a position to commission us. But it's flawed; we know it's flawed. Once I entered a competition on architecture – I tend not to enter architectural competitions – and when I finished I thought, 'Am I mad working so hard for David Chipperfield to judge it?' That's how it works – or it doesn't. You don't want to be judged and selected and assessed; you want to do what you do, like you do when you do the studio pieces or when you are an artist. You do what you do. I always preferred customers to clients. Clients want you and they think they have a say. Customers, you don't have to know them. The best architectural client we had was Sheikh Saud of Qatar. In a discussion about his villa I said to him, 'When we do a scheme that you like…', and he stopped me. He said, 'I don't have to like the scheme. I choose the architect, the architect chooses the scheme. It's not for me anyway; it's for the nation because in my family we have a very short life expectancy'. Which, you know, is beginning to define a good client.
[Laughter]

It was not life expectancy that stopped the project. Unfortunately he was put under house arrest, which was something we couldn't predict.

HUO   You mentioned the three different layers of your activity, the three different economies, but also the three different contexts of production. It reminded me of a conversation I had with Ettore Sottsass some months ago. In a similar way he has different layers of activity. We are interested in models of older designers or architects of previous generations who have somehow been a toolbox for you or are a toolbox for you.

RA   Everything that's done before, until twelve o'clock, until they closed the Serpentine road, is part of a toolbox and Ettore Sottsass is a great example. There are lots of parallels: Memphis and his work, although I never liked it formally, gave us a lot of courage. We looked at it and said, 'OK there are other routes'. There are other ways of operating and you can create excitement around a chair, for example, without having to like that very chair. Ettore gave us a lot of courage and he writes beautifully.

HUO   Are you writing?

RA   Very little. I couldn't keep a diary to save my life.

HUO   I want to ask about your unrealised projects. Obviously in architecture there is usually a quite high percentage of unrealised projects and some of your architecture projects, like the house you wanted to build in Hampstead Lane, have remained unrealised. But I was wondering if in your practice at large, in design, in industrial design, there are any unrealised projects which are particularly important for you and which you could tell us about.

RA   Yes. All the projects that you invest time in are extremely important. Some of them exist. When I grew up and studied at the AA, no-one built anything. We drew bridges from London to New York and we did walking cities and we talked about Coney Island and whatever and no-one was building anything. If you did something that resembled something that was buildable, you had to apologise for it. It was in a period when architecture was very jealous of art; they talked about conceptual architecture, architectural murder in the park and all sorts of things like that. So I educated myself in a period when to build something was almost the most un-cool thing you could do. It changed, of course, and Peter Cook had his first building. He will tell you at six o'clock in the morning. Today, thanks to the digital technology, you have photographs and animations and films about things that are not built but for us are almost as real. But yet there is something very good about a product or a building or a physical thing that is better than the digital rendering of it. That is a real reason to actually realise it, because otherwise we wouldn't.

RK   Thank you.

HUO   Many thanks to Ron Arad.

Applause, end of interview

Hans Ulrich Obrist I would like to introduce Jane and Louise Wilson and say how happy we are to have you here with us.

We have talked about numerous notions of toolboxes tonight, things from the past being reactivated, and I have been very interested in the way your work in the last couple of years has somehow reactivated Brutalism, thinking about your piece *The New Brutalists*. You told me in previous conversations you have a big interest in re-visiting Peter and Alison Smithson, so I wanted to ask you how this started and which are the aspects in Brutalism you find relevant for our contemporary condition.

Jane Wilson I think we were very interested in Brutalism because of what the Smithsons had said about it, certainly in a post-war time when architecture was up for grabs. But there was this attempt to not just try and cosmetically conceal the post-war damage but to incorporate that into part of the design. To us that seemed like a really interesting concept. Also, following on from that we made the work *A Free and Anonymous Monument* filmed in the north-east of England. We took as our template for the installation the Apollo Pavilion designed by the artist Victor Pasmore. Who was a contemporary of the Smithsons.

HUO It's good to hear more.

Louise Wilson Pasmore described his pavilion as 'a free and anonymous monument, through which to walk, in which to linger and on which to play', and I think that's a really interesting starting point for an art work and also for the idea of a pavilion and the idea of a public structure. He didn't want to make a public building that had any real agenda behind it; it didn't need to be a social club or a church, it was a free and anonymous monument, which is a really interesting concept. It is a Brutalist structure that stems from a post-war period but also from his perspective as a painter and as an artist. He also designed the south part of the new town, Peterlee, an area called Sunny Blunts. I don't think there's any equivalence of that.

JW In this country.

LW In this country, yes. That an artist worked on a design of a new town.

Scott Lash	Another quick question on Brutalism: if you look at Le Corbusier, Brutalism, and then you compare it to what was going on in London and in England, it struck me that our good friend the Chinese architect Ma Qingyun, who had spent a lot of time in Paris and just came to London for the first time, thought Paris was beautiful but he loved London. He loved London because it was so ugly. Even the women, he said, and I don't agree with this, are ugly. Is there something wonderful about the ugliness of some of the Brutalism?
LW	Yes. I think it's function over form, in a way; its function dictates its form. It's out of that post-war period of building something that had a sense of utopia. For example a cantilevered roof that you could drive your car underneath, or something that made sense in terms of a space and use of space. Perhaps there wasn't that kind of impulse and understanding previously in British architecture.
JW	Peterlee was built on a landfill of an old mining town and subsidence was a big issue. The whole premise is not something particularly elegant and dynamic.
LW	Lubetkin was the first architect who was brought on board to design this new town and he proposed beautiful designs for tower blocks, but because of subsidence the project had to be shelved. I think he was sad he had to leave the project. Subsequently Easington District Council invited Pasmore to be involved in the design.
JW	It must have been a real challenge for Pasmore to design the housing and landscape the area.
Rem Koolhaas	There is currently a huge investment and optimism about what art and artists can contribute to cities and in general an incredible expectation of sparks in the encounter of architecture and art. Are you now optimistic about the same potential and would you be happy, for instance, if somebody asked you to work on a new city or to contribute to a new city? And what would you feel you would have to contribute as artists?
JW	That's an interesting question. I suppose we were looking at a certain precedent for that; Peterlee seemed unique in terms of Britain, for that to happen. Like Louise said, there doesn't seem to be any kind of equivalence here for that to have occurred. It would certainly be interesting. I know there are attempts to do things around the Hayward and the South Bank, asking artists to be in residence.

RK   But as a principle.

JW   Of course.

RK   In certain sections of the Continent it is now an obligation to involve artists and if you don't know about it, it's a huge growth market.

JW   It doesn't appear to be the case here in the UK.

RK   But what do you feel Pasmore contributed?

LW   Pasmore described his approach very much as a journey and I think that's interesting, the idea that space is about a journey and that you encounter different visual moments on a journey. That's quite a beautiful idea to describe space and to think about architecture; it becomes something filmic. The architectural journey has a sense of filmic duration.

JW   Yes. We often create video installations, which have that in mind so it's something about making a space that reflects that.

HUO   You have used a lot of those architectural spaces, actually not so much to document them, but thinking about your *Stasi City* it's almost that you make invisible cities visible. But the question leads also to your un-realised projects or your own utopias. I was wondering if you had a project which has not happened yet, which has been too big to be realised, too small to be realised, censored.

JW   Yes, we have had some projects that have been probably too ambitious to realise. For example *Suspended Island*, there were discussions to do something in Lincoln Plaza last year but it all became very difficult. So that is something that you often have to work with and yes, you do find that you can't realise certain projects.

SL   You did work in New Zealand last year.

JW   That's right, yes.

SL   If you go back twenty-five or thirty years, London was an imperial city. The Empire had broken up; London is a post-imperial city in a way. The work that you were doing in New Zealand had to do with Empire. Could you say something about that?

LW   They were abandoned.

JW   Yes, being in New Zealand, being in the South Island, it's very strange. It is very beautiful but you also feel it is very familiar, which is not what you're expecting, you know? You travel so far and then you arrive somewhere so familiar… Dunedin, a city in the South Island, is Gaelic for Edinburgh; it was modelled on the town plan of Edinburgh.

LW   All the buildings were south-facing.

JW   And unfortunately it was the wrong hemisphere, so they should have been north facing! But there was still that idea to carry a template forward to what were obviously the colonies, what was the Empire, as you said. It was very interesting to see this history still visible there; certainly one of the hospitals we filmed in had a panopticon design, which I don't think had really existed in this country for fifty-odd years. To see a portrait of the Queen in this panopticon hospital was like something lost in time. That was curious. And also just the number of sanatoriums in the South Island.

SL   Empty casinos to sanatoriums.

HUO   Can you tell us about one of your most well-known works? Certainly it would be interesting in this context, as we are talking so much in terms of the city, to hear a little bit more about *Stasi City* from 1997.

JW   *Stasi City* came out of our residency in Berlin; we lived there for a year as part of the DAAD [Deutscher Akademischer Austausch Dienst]. We had visited Berlin in 1989 so it was interesting to see it when the Wall was still there and then to come back in 1996 when it was in the process of reinvention. We travelled to Marzhan and visited Hohenschönhausen, a former Stasi prison, which was very curious because you realised it was situated at the end of a suburban street. It was the journalist who found it who nicknamed it Stasi City, because within the prison walls there was a Stasi motel, the phone-tapping service and a hospital, and there was the prison. So there were all these other elements but they were all cushioned at the end of this very benign suburban street, which seemed really quite sinister. So we were very interested to document it and to look particularly, not so much at the prison itself, but at the bureaucratic structures that supported it, so specifically the interview corridors, the rooms around it where the hospital was, basically where all the bureaucratic life was, not the actual prison cells.

RK   You must realise that you mentioned the word 'utopian' with a certain kind of longing. There is still some kind of utopia in the air, then, after the war but you realise that you are talking about utopias in every case and many of them are much more sinister. So what is your relationship with the dark?

JW   I'd probably like to ask you that question, having designed the Television Tower in China and seeing the level of censorship that still exists there. Perhaps there is real underlying darkness there as well.

We were talking about the Stasi and the level of control they exerted, but it could also be seen in some buildings that are happening right now.

RK   I don't know whether you were here but we were talking earlier about London having turned more into a completely observed, policed environment.

JW   You asked about darkness so I wondered what your feelings were about certain dystopias.

RK   I think it's too early to say that China is a dystopia.

JW   Right.

RK   I think we are working in a kind of situation that we know has a lot of problematic aspects, but we also believe that the building we are doing there has a certain potential in diminishing the negative and some potential also to actually focus their attention on media in a way which will make it unsustainable to continue the current practices.

JW   You mean there is more transparency to it?

RK   Not only more transparency. There is, for instance, a new twenty-four-hour English channel in China and I think that in itself is such an inevitable connection to the outside world that it has in itself introduced a series of modernisations that I think the building will encourage.

LW   So utopia. Good. *[Laughs]* Jane and I haven't actually named the last piece we did, the New Zealand project called *Erewhon*. It was based on a book written in 1879 by Samuel Butler and it was about this idea of utopia. It's a satirical novel and it ends up being about a dystopia. In fact it's about these people called Erewhonians. Illness is a big defeat in this new idea of a utopia.

JW   People get put in prison for being ill.

LW   Yes, they get put in prison for being poorly. So we were intrigued about this idea of a colonial arriving in New Zealand, which was, I guess, at that point an idea of an idyll and it's not as benign as you think it is.

HUO   Ken Loach spoke about the role of improvisation in his films earlier

	tonight. I was wondering what the role of improvisation in your films is.
LW	I'd say all. Yes, all improvisation.
JW	I think you have to respond to hidden things that you want to reveal, which is what we did in *Stasi City*.
LW	It's very hit and miss.
JW	And I think it's about an engagement that is developed over a period of time – improvisation comes from being comfortable with something that has become familiar.
LW	You immerse yourself, to get that familiarity.
JW	Yes and that's what makes for engagement and that's what makes for, hopefully, a level of improvisation.

RK	One more question, in a way a preparation for a question we will use later when we will be talking to Gilbert and George, two artists who work together. In addition to being two artists you are also two sisters.
LW	We're twins.

RK	What fascinates me is, does making as a team make your work more consistent, more intelligent, more coherent? It seems incredibly difficult to create an opening between the two of you or a wedge to create some kind of separation. I think working as a team must have enormous advantages in developing the narrative of your career. Does it work like that?
JW	Yes. We are seen as a unit, which may seem a bit of a tyranny, why would you want to live like this? Particularly in a society which ultimately acknowledges the individual. For us as sisters, twins, the individual is complex and tricky particularly if you live with an instant measure – how do you understand your place when perversely enough it's not through your individuality but through your similarity as well.

HUO	Many thanks.

Applause, end of interview

Hans Ulrich Obrist	Cerith Wyn Evans. Welcome. Michel Butor wrote this remarkable early text called *The City as a Text*; it is a text which, when it came out in the 1960s, immediately had a huge impact on the world of art; Dan Graham and other colleagues of his in America read it. I was wondering if you could talk about this idea of the city as a text.
Cerith Wyn Evans	It's a big one to start with and much has been written (and many foolish things have been written) about this easy analogy that can be made from the notion that cities somehow operate as a text. I would rather, probably, be more comfortable with interrogating the notion of text than the notion of city. Essentially it's a rather profoundly late romantic and rather banal idea of the city being some form of spectacle that presents itself as a kind of narrative textuality. I think my interest in this initial prescription is problematised by my, if I can use a word which is never used any more, 'haptic' experience of various cities and various different texts. I suppose on an autobiographical level I am interested in texts that I can't really quite fathom or understand or language that expands the possibilities of comprehension of where I might be. Another great writer about this has been Michel de Certeau in his *Practice of Everyday Life*. Yes, there's lots of work to do and I suspect the more interesting work will be done by women, actually, on this subject. *[Laughter]*
Rem Koolhaas	Why?
CWE	Because I think there are prejudicial gender conditions in relation to language. I am thinking of the way that Judith Butler talks about architecture, which she does rather rarely but very profoundly when she does. Or Beatriz Colomina. My heroes, actually. I like listening to women talking about things like this because it's such a cock-rock subject. *[Laughter]*
HUO	Beatriz Colomina will be here, actually, in the pavilion, on 18 August for a discussion with Thomas Demand. To follow up one of the things that have been recurrent over the last ten hours or so, there have been vari-

ous links to Situationism. Rem was wondering if what Guy Debord was to France, Cedric Price would be to England.

CWE   Much more. Cedric, yes. Guy Debord maybe.

HUO   We were wondering about your relation to Situationist ideas. Again it's a bit of a big question but it would be interesting to hear.

CWE   Yes, it's turning really nasty now. Can we be a little more optimistic? If we can speak a little bit about tying it back into this remit in relation to the city, I came to London in 1976 and I was exposed to the city as a kind of text which was in some cultural shift, some excitement, largely through popular culture and music and fashion, etc. Guy Debord was introduced to me by brainy art school teachers and they thought that it would correlate and chime with my interest by providing me with some form of art historical legitimacy. Subsequently I've learnt to loathe and love Guy Debord. I've learnt to identify partially with certain romantic impulses, namely in his confessional voice, which is one of a kind of ancient authority, and his notion of citation is, I think, profoundly well-versed. We had this conversation not long ago with my mentor John Stezaker. John still believes that Guy Debord has something to say. I think Debord has something to say – I mean I think he had something to say. So to that extent I think reading Flaubert is as interesting as reading Guy Debord and this revolt into style has become somehow predictable to say the least. In as much as I can appreciate in a melancholic, imaginary gene the *In Girum Imus Nocte Et Consumimur Igni* especially, the bleating of a sick old man, you know, there are interesting correlations. Artaud is much more interesting than Guy Debord. Guy Debord was a phoney and I think that's not such a bad thing to be, either. I have a complicated relation to that.

RK   I am stuck in a profession where being critical is almost impossible.
CWE   I wouldn't call this building stuck at all!

RK   OK. How do you think you can be critical in art and how do you think you can be critical in architecture?

CWE   Feeling the need that this critical capacity is de rigour is our problematic also. I'm with you and it's something that I've struggled with. At the same time I'm almost falling into the grumpy old man position of going, 'Why be critical?' The Arts Council are celebrating six hundred years of their patronage. They are doing this exhibition and they bought a piece of work by my good self which – it's a little bit complicated. There's this great big glass Venini chandelier made by the great Achille Castiglioni and first made for the first class Alitalia lounge in Milano Airport. So the likelihood – I always dream – of Sophia Loren drinking a Negroni under this is very high.

[Laughter]

They managed to obtain this marvellous relic and it somehow promotes and carries this text, which is a diary entry from the 1968–75 edited version of the great John Cage's diaries. The title is *How to Improve the World (You Will Only Make Matters Worse)*. Now the Arts Council decided to call this retrospective exhibition at the Hayward Gallery – all fine, and I'm sure there will be really seriously marvellous things there – well, they've robbed my title. They said, 'We are really happy with your piece' – they wouldn't lend it to our show in Paris, they wanted to keep it. I said, 'OK. Fine.' So they've called the show *[Laughs] How to Make the World a Better Place*, but they've left out *(You'll Only Make Matters Worse)*. *[Laughs]*

OK. I'm being a bit playful. Can I ask you a question?

RK   Yes.

CWE   What's this like? How did you decide how to do this? I haven't been here earlier. Maybe every other person has asked you about the interview Marathon. I am really honestly, genuinely proud to be part of all of this because I think it's a great event. But how did you decide who you should ask? Cathy and the gang have been super-sovereign because they've had to put up with people who have baby sitters or – I don't know – weird diets, to make it all possible.

RK   You mean how personal is this choice?

CWE   Yes.

RK   Partly. Only partly. Maybe a third. There is another third that I think is personal to Hans Ulrich and the rest some kind of statistical emergence that we were curious to encounter.

CWE   Do you know this marvellous poem by Robert Frost? It's totally anecdotal and I hope I am being a bit of light relief because I'm just not really interested in being very serious this evening. There is a poem called *Stopping by the Woods on a Snowy Evening*. I wish I could remember it. He could remember it because on the inauguration of J. F. K. (he was somehow the White House's poet laureate at the time) he had left his notes in the car or something like this and he couldn't remember the poem he had written at this great, important historical occasion. We look back to this moment in American democracy which was actually much more optimistic than what subsequently emerged. But Robert Frost could not remember the new poem. He had Parkinson's Disease or something like this; he was super-embarrassed and sweating and very nervous in front of the world's media at the time, which was tiny compared to now, and he said, 'But there's one thing I do remember and it's a poem that I wrote in 1942 called *Stopping by the Woods on a Snowy Evening*, which was the most extraordinary thing to send into this historical process of inauguration. I'm not going to be able to remember all of it. It's a very short poem; I only looked it up yesterday on the Internet. You just have to put in the title and it appears. I love archaic poetry on the Internet; John Donne on the Internet is specifically fine, Rilke also, fabulous and the typefaces they choose are really bizarre. Anyway, 'Whose woods these are I think I know', is the beginning. 'His house is in the village though. He will not see me stopping here, To see his woods fill up with snow'. And the most fucking fantastic line of a poem ever, 'My little horse will think it queer', *[Laughs]* 'To stop without a farmhouse near. He gives his harness bells a shake to see if there is some mistake. The only other sound's the sweep, Of easy wind and downy flake. I have promises to keep and miles to go before I sleep. And miles to go before I sleep'. *[Applause]*

HUO   Cerith, I have my only recurrent question but I am embarrassed because I have asked you this so many times before. I am asking you again tonight because I think it would be great to hear about your yet-unrealised projects. Maybe there is an unrealised London project.

CWE   Since you live in London now I thought it would be really good to raise money from the British Council and the Arts Council to maybe get – I'm a huge fan of Orlan so I think it would be really great if you had a sex change, Hans Ulrich.
[Laughter]

HUO   Many thanks to Cerith Wyn Evans. Thank you.

Applause, end of interview

Hans Ulrich Obrist   We are very happy to welcome our next guest, Squarepusher. We thought it would be interesting to start the conversation with some examples of your recent work.

Squarepusher   OK. If the chap with the CD player would like to oblige us, I'll explain briefly what we are about to hear. I am releasing a new record – this is not a deliberate plug, this is coincidental. I've a sixty-minute project consisting of twelve individual pieces which is going to be released later in the year. I was asked by one of the people organising the event to play a short piece of music and I thought it would be lovely to play something from this new album as opposed to exhuming something everyone's heard anyway (or maybe no-one's heard). So I've compressed my album into one and a half minutes; it will give you one per cent of the idea, the key of a few of the tracks. See what you make of it.

[Music]

OK. That was it.

[Applause]

I don't expect applause for that. Actually I think I prefer that version! '

HUO   Thank you very much. We spoke at the beginning of this Marathon with Brian Eno about the link between sound and the city. He thought it would be difficult to bring sound into the city because it's difficult to compete with the city and we spoke about the extent to which the city enters the production of sound. I was wondering if we could ask you the same question.

S   OK. Well, I could just start by attempting to articulate a particular sentiment I recall having around twelve years ago, which was associated with the *Ambient Works II* record by Aphex Twin. I remember distinctly thinking to myself how lovely it would be to hear some of this music in a tube station. I'm not sure. I have discussed that idea with people because a tube station has a particular kind of acoustic character and tube transport in general has a very particular social character, shall we say in that people are rammed together and yet they don't feel very comfortable, obviously, and they don't converse. This is something that I find intriguing. For example, I have this strange Superman instinct so if someone gets trapped in the doors I can't help myself, but jump up and try to help them. You look around and it's quite funny. Everyone knows that nothing bad is going to happen but you look around and it's as if everyone wants to forget it straight away.

So there is a social character, or a particular social demeanour, that everyone adopts. I think it would be interesting to try to interrogate that by introducing a sonic component to maybe just one tube station because if we did it to every tube station there may be civic unrest – or possibly not. Possibly, immediately it would have a positive effect but something tells me that these sorts of things would work most effectively if they were brought in bit by bit. And certain tube stations have certain acoustic characters which others don't have; for example, some are outdoors, in which case they don't have the strong reverberative character. That's the first thing that sprang to my mind when you talked about music in the city. Not being from London, these particular forms of transport and the associated atmospheres do stand out to me as quite bizarre, given that being a country lad I'll get on the bus and say, 'Alright' to someone, even though I've never met them before. You could assess that as having very little social value but that feels intuitively more pleasing.

Anyway, I'm diverting somewhat from the city. The city does have an extremely idiosyncratic acoustic or sonic character of its own. You might say that it would not necessarily require addition of music, bringing music into spaces, as much as trying to get people to reassess their actual perception of sound which is already existent. For example, referring back to my tube station idea, for anyone remotely sonically aware, these particular pieces of machinery create fascinating noises, sometimes very piercing ones, sometimes extremely physically reverberative. If you have the capacity to be able to screen out mid-range and high-range frequencies then you can sense some extremely disturbing sub-sonic effects going on in these environments. I would say it would be equally or possibly of more value to the individuals concerned to try to open people's minds a little bit to try to get people to look at sound not necessarily as their enemy, not something which is encroaching on their peace of mind, but something – maybe not necessarily enjoyable in the sense that a piece of classical music is, but at least as having character and being interesting. In general to be mindful of one's environment, I think, is a good starting point for a positive view of the city and life in general.

Rem Koolhaas	I think we can organise it for you.
S	Good. Thank you.

RK	The Director of London Transport was here and he talks on lines which are very similar. He would probably welcome it.
S	Who is that?
HUO	Tim O'Toole.
S	OK.
RK	Seriously.

HUO	One of the things we want to do with this Marathon is, obviously in a very incomplete polyphonic way, to map London and try to see if there is such a thing as a theory of this city. I was wondering why you moved to London. You said in a conversation that it had to do with the atmosphere but also with less distractions.
S	From London?
HUO	To London.
S	Just to clarify, I moved to London about twelve years ago, I moved from it about four years ago. I had a spell in London. What was the question?

HUO	What is your take on London now, how do you see the city?
S	I find it absolutely fascinating. I find it a sensory overload for maybe more than two or three days at a time, but I am not in any sense saying that marks it out as an unpleasant environment, just simply that my work necessitates an extremely open sensory system. To conduct my practice, if you like, I need to have my ears open, completely. I need to be able to fine tune very quickly to the sorts of sounds that I produce in my work. It's something of a knack and something which I haven't quite mastered, certainly over those eight years, as to how to be able to limit that sensitivity, if you like. I suppose it comes from the fact that London is not an environment in which I grew up so I always feel like a tourist. That's OK, there's a certain enjoyment in that, and I think there's a view which a visitor can have which a resident is almost certainly not going to have. Nonetheless, I think I am slightly embarrassed to say I am not the best person to tell you. I don't know.
	When you say 'theory of a city', do you mean a theory that you want to impose on what we see around us or you mean a theory on which it is to be based?

HUO Definitely not imposed.

S OK. This, for me, brings to mind the sorts of ideas that the Situationists had about the city, which has a certain resonance with my attitude to it. One of the ways in which I help myself feel comfortable when I move to a new area, is to undertake random journeys and random walks around the environment, and in particular I take the bike because there is a certain velocity and range that you can have on a bicycle and find some fascinating places. This resonates with something I discovered in Situationist theory which is to interrogate – in their terms – the capitalist and production-oriented town planning theory. If you were to leave the concept unquestioned, the typical ways which you would be directed around the city would be ways which were conducive to consumerist activity and to remaining in a state of semi-consciousness about this particular way in which you were being manipulated. That is something which I always take pleasure in trying to subvert by attempting to get away from where you are being shoe-horned and get away from where you are being pushed. There is endless fascination in that for me. If we are talking about theories, that would certainly be my input on what I consider to be a positive way of reassessing the theory, if that's what it is, of the city.

RK There is some overlap between architecture and music and it is acoustics. In my career I have encountered the phenomenon of anti-noise, i.e. a technology with which you cancel noise or cancel sound. I am always surprised that this is not something that plays a big role in music because I think the whole idea of cancelling or elimination is so unbelievably interesting.

S It's a fascinating idea. It does resonate very deeply with me, especially as our culture seems to be very intent on accumulating.

RK Exactly, and expanding.

S Yes, expanding. I am quite interested, at least as a way of trying to just bring that process into relief and contrast to say that's fine. What can we discard, because we are up to our necks in this shit? That links quite closely to the concept that you are talking about. I think it's a very, very difficult thing to employ, though. What I presume you are talking about is using phase cancellation, microphones and re-broadcasting the sound at certain positions such that it limits or effectively phase-cancels ambient noise. We are talking about environments we have around us which are pre-existent. Fascinating though this concept is, and as much as I would love to see it put into action, I cannot imagine that occurring because the sort of acoustic environment that you would require for that kind of level of control would have to be very, very carefully designed, as far as I understand it.

RK   Yes, but I am sure that with digital techniques we can really achieve it.

S   I think one thing that would be possible is to carry some sort of device around with you. It is not quite the same, actually, but there is hearing aid which is designed to help people with persistent ringing in their ears which generates a small amount of white noise, which according to psycho-acoustic theory is sufficient to effectively mask the sound. Something similar might be possible whereby microphones would pick up ambient noise but you would only receive the sound through positioned speakers or headphones, so thus you would have a mediated picture of the sound. Of course if we are talking wholeheartedly about modifying in the sense of removing sound. I think that would be quite easy to implement. It's not something I've tried.

RK   You are the first person this evening who has a pseudonym and it's very powerful because it combines the word 'square' with 'pushing'. Can you say why you chose it or what it means to you?

S   I could probably disappoint you with various sarcastic answers to that question but the truthful one, which is probably even more disappointing than those, is that I found it in a Thesaurus. It's not a currently used term, it's an arcane word for someone who operated a crossbow. I think it dates from the medieval era. The word appealed; as you say, it's powerful and it does have the fortunate aspect of being very evocative. Square-pushing in itself is perhaps not that exciting but it does, as people have said to me (and I nod like I knew but actually I didn't, I'd never thought of it), bring to mind operating machines, which is for better or worse something I'm heavily involved in and something I'm well known for.

HUO Many thanks, Squarepusher. Thanks very much.

Applause, end of interview

Hans Ulrich Obrist	It's a great pleasure now to introduce our next guest, Peter Saville. As this is the London Marathon we wanted to ask you about the city. In previous discussions we had in Manchester we talked a lot about the future of the city, so I was wondering if you could tell us about how you see…
Peter Saville	… the future of the city.
HUO	Yes.
PS	I find it difficult to imagine the future of London. I've been finding London very difficult these last few years. One of the things that helped me approach the Manchester Project was the fact that I feel London has almost reached a kind of optimum point and that the UK could really do with another city, not even a second city, just another city, a kind of comparable city, and that London is almost reaching a point where it is not rewarding to people now unless they earn a lot of money and have a lot of luxuries and privileges. It is strange that the UK doesn't have a really strong other city; there's such a gap between London and all of the other cities. So I have a certain amount of optimism for places which still have some development in them.
Rem Koolhaas	I have a totally different question.
PS	OK. Good.
RK	You are a graphic designer among other things. My theory is that graphic design is the most important and most powerful domain in the world right now. Would you agree?
PS	It is. I would agree with that. [Laughter]
RK	And since when do you think this has been the case and how much longer do you think it will last? And why do you think it is so particularly important right now?
PS	I feel kind of retired from it, partly for that reason. It's just that it happens to be what I learnt at college and the decision was made, I think, at the age of sixteen when an art teacher said to myself and my friend, Malcolm Garrett, 'You boys should consider doing graphic design', and

161

we said, 'What's that?' And he explained that there was a real job doing what we liked doing at school, so we decided we would do that. So I trained as a graphic designer. There have been many times when I thought I really should have done something else, but anyway that's where I started out. But I've always done it for myself; I've always tried to be in a position where I was expressing my own point of view and that is very uncharacteristic for the graphic designer. It's for others and to others. There is a great misapprehension about graphics at the moment that has something to do with self-expression and of course it isn't: you're a messenger for someone else. In a media-dominated society, in an information society, the messages that you are communicating are the things that people know. I have a vision of the world at the moment with a kind of net around it, a news net and it's your existence in that news net that gives you a presence in the world. Of course, because the communication arts broker the news net they are very powerful. The problem is that there are other people in charge of those messages; graphic designers articulate other people's messages. Graphic design is not your own message, it's somebody else's and communication design is about delivering somebody else's agenda – which doesn't interest me very often. Obviously if it's an agenda I am in agreement with and have some feeling for, then it's quite nice to be involved, but more often than not your client's agenda is not necessarily your own interest. That is why I've retired from doing it where possible.

HUO   What is interesting also in relation to that is that you have spoken recently about the fatigue of fashion and consumerism and I wondered if you could tell us a little bit about this. You have resisted this idea of a corporate office; many of your colleagues started to grow and grow and have big corporate design offices. You've kept the structure very small.

PS   OK. One bit at a time. A large design office, and Rem will know this, is the first step towards realising the level to which you are in business. Suddenly you find that you are doing work for the purposes of paying salaries and covering overheads, so you are not working on things that you care about, you are working on cash flow and that introduces you to the reality of what you're engaged in. My feeling about much of the popular arts is that the challenges to the issues that were there have, for the most part, been accomplished. So pop is the culture of the post-war period and whether it was in the form of music, design or fashion, it articulated the needs and desires of a new and democratised generation. The things that it had to challenge have now been challenged, so fashion is not really doing what it did twenty or thirty years ago, pop music isn't doing what it did thirty and forty years ago. It's pretty much run its course and become a commodity, an entirely commoditised activity, so it's almost like pop culture is in a condition of auto-repeat, like a tape going round. It's also a fairly limited palette within pop. Obviously there are more marginal issues, issues for more marginal areas of society, for people in other countries and other cultures, and there is something maybe vital that can inform a marginal area of pop, but in the kind of general it's pretty much run its course in my opinion.

RK The research for this event produced synopses based on CVs, etc. There is a sentence about what you're doing now which is really alarming and seemingly completely wrong and offensive if I hear what you're saying.

PS Yes.

RK It says, 'He now concentrates on his own creative projects, consulting for corporate clients, including CNN, Givenchy, Gucci and Selfridges on branding and identity issues and the development of fashion multi-media'.

[Laughter]

PS That's the Internet for you.

RK How does that reconcile with what you were saying?

PS A lot has changed.

RK Let's talk about what changed because you went from graphic design to branding.

PS Everything seems to be branding these days. Branding to me now is how you exist in that news net. A lot of people ask me about this topic. The work in Manchester started as a branding project.

RK And now what is it?

PS What do we mean by branding? Brand used to be like a logo; your mother would tell you to drink this or buy that, it's a good brand. Driving the car on the way back from Manchester to London I think about this kind of thing. My personal understanding of a brand now is that it lives in that news net, and obviously it has to be news and it has to be constantly

163

regenerating and entertaining. So a brand now is something that is in a process of constant regeneration, basically just continually looking for news. Unless you are continuously generating news you drop out of the news net. So I see a brand now as a virtual entity; it is not a logo and a brand is not necessarily a company or an activity, it's a sum of its parts, it's a sort of an entity. And it seems to me that these entities need to continuously regenerate, so I see a brand as a kind of news-generator. I get asked to give an opinion about these things. What I try to do, which is what I've always done, is give my own opinion about these things. That's my starting point.

RK   Can you give an example from this list?

PS   Yes. CNN is on that list; in 2000 or 2001, a client from the 1980s had moved to CNN and they had some problems at CNN Domestic in the US. David Newman invited me over to talk to his chief executives about design, about the image. CNN had been founded by some journalists who did their job fairly well but they were a group of guys who were not that sensitive to, or concerned about, the look of things. David asked me to go over for a couple of days and try to articulate why the look of things mattered these days. That's it. So I acted as a consultant on the look of things. We'll all have a bunch of different opinions about CNN. It's not an entirely bad thing.

RK   No.

PS   And it was very interesting; I went to Atlanta, I got to look inside a world news network.

RK   And did your work have effect? Did it change anything?

PS   I don't know. I think so. They then employed some designers to re-design the look of CNN.

RK   The studio?

PS   No, no, the on-screen. You will know this from your own work, Rem, the interesting thing is when there is a commission from clients we have to enter a little bit into their world: you're doing a building for somebody, whether it's a hospital or a hotel or a factory and you enter their world and you learn something. I find it interesting to learn things by these introductions. I learnt about fashion from the inside; as a young person I was kind of fascinated by fashion, I was fascinated by the music business. It was very interesting to see it from the inside. My experience in Manchester has taken me inside local government, inside politics; that's a very eye-opening experience.

HUO   I wanted to know more about this Manchester experience.

PS   They asked me to re-brand Manchester.

HUO   I am curious about how you responded to that.

RK   Let's establish first, what did they ask you? And what are you doing?

PS   Hans is right. It wasn't to re-brand Manchester, it was to guide the brand of Manchester: what do we do with it? Manchester has a certain kind of status; they wanted us to optimise the status. As I said, I have to go about these things in a tangible way that means something to me. Because I didn't build a big business, I didn't let a big studio develop around me. I'm not duty-bound to generate business. So I address these problems on a level that means something to me. Manchester is my home city so I felt a certain obligation, a certain responsibility, a certain pride to be asked, but also a certain duty. It was a bit like National Service. And I owed a lot to Manchester. All I did was say to myself, 'How can the future of Manchester be better?' That's how I went about the job. It's a fairly complex issue because cities are complex things. Two years ago that was the question I put in my own mind and that's the question I still have in my mind. How can Manchester evolve in a positive way in Europe in the twenty-first century from my own point of view?

The next step was to make some assumptions about what I felt would happen in Europe this century, obviously what would survive. Manchester is an example of a city which is now post-industrial and so much of what had been the *raison d'être* of European cities has now changed. The making of things has gone to the other side of the world. But the 'what to make' has not yet gone to the other side of the world. My understanding of things is that the financial management services are still here and to a certain extent the cultural and creative direction is still a remit of the West – I think. So I felt that a city such as Manchester had to have a place in that new industrial culture and to be pro-active in the creative cultural urban issues and that it could demonstrate some progressive ideas and thinking about the urban condition this century. One of the nice things about smaller cities is that they are quite empowering. Mega cities can be rather overwhelming to people; smaller cities do give you a feeling that something is possible, that you might tackle something in a new way. This was my recommendation to the city, to go about the future and to go about their contemporary problems in an innovative way and thereby hopefully set some kind of example to other places. I can go into it a bit more. Manchester was the first industrial city; that was the provenance of the place. I re-articulated that as the original modern city and sat with them and said, 'It's the first industrial city, as you know; it's a great provenance but it doesn't really give you a route forward, it's so historically facing. But we could look at the spirit of first industrial, and rephrase that as original modern. The values of originality and modernity could be synonymous with this place in the twenty-first century like they were in the nineteenth. You could attempt to take an original and contemporary approach to the issues of the city.

RK   The nightmare of branding for me is you always have the sense that in a hundred thousand cities similar to Manchester people are having equal ideas and working on the same programme.

PS   They have to.

RK   For instance, the city of Rotterdam is also totally interchangeable in terms of rhetoric and ambition.

PS   Yes it could be but, Rem, what you have to do is find something, whether it's a city or an organisation or an individual, which is to some extent true to them, and something which the people there can either do or aspire to being able to do. I would say that Rotterdam's position and approach to the world should be different to Manchester's position and if it isn't different then it isn't correct. In a situation like this I am attempting to give my point of view to some other people whose problem it is. The problem of cities is the problem of the city, it's the problem of the people there. You can give some advice, you can give an opinion; you can say, 'This is my take on it', and it's down to them how they respond to that and go about it.

RK   Isn't that both the strength and weakness of the consultant?

PS   Yes. Absolutely. But I am giving my opinion to people who ask; I am not going out in the world offering it. People have said, 'Would you like to do this for other places?' My answer has been, 'Not really, no'. Manchester's my home, they've asked me for my opinion, I've tried to give my opinion in a way that meant something to them. Hans knows that we do already have one positive outcome from this interaction, which is the festival that they're planning, but I do not wish to go around the world trying to be a sort of city…

RK   … Richard Florida.

PS   No, Richard Florida is Richard Florida!

HUO   You don't do most of the things on the old CV anymore.

PS   That's right.

HUO   What is interesting is what you do now and you have started to venture into exhibitions. At the same time you still sometimes have contact with corporate clients.

PS   Yes.

HUO   But then in a very different sort of negotiation. The other day you told me the very strange Adidas story. Could you tell us this story now, because I think it makes this negotiation clearer?

PS   Strangely, at the age of fifty I'm interested in doing things that I want to do. You know, the work I did at the beginning that people fondly remember me for was based on me doing what I wanted to do. I did record covers that I wanted and nobody stopped me so I just made the record covers that I would have wanted for myself. The real job of the graphic designer, this 'for others, to others', was something I spent all the 1990s struggling with and realised that I didn't really want. I learnt in the end how to do it but I didn't really want to do it. So these days I try to stick to doing things I want to do. I also do have to pay the rent, so occasionally I do something that I would rather not do, but I do have to exist. But increasingly the commissioned work is more on my terms so the one luxury that I have is that people do come to me as me, rather than just coming to me as a commercial artist. Adidas asked me if I would do a trainer project, an anniversary marketing campaign. I said, 'Thank you very much for asking'. It's very flattering when people ask you to do anything even if you don't want to do it; it's still nice that they ask. I said, 'Thank you for asking me but I don't want to do it'. They were surprised and said, 'Why?' I said, 'Because I don't believe in it. You don't really want me to do one and I don't want to do it. This is just another sort of gratuitous partnership liaison between somebody who has a kind of cult name and a corporation seeking credibility. These liaisons are meaningless to me. They're a press release. I don't believe in these things and I don't believe that kids out there believe in it either. So thank you, but no'. They were a bit surprised and said, 'But you can do what you want'. I said, 'I don't think you're listening. I don't want to do it'. They invited me to Germany to the Adidas factory. I said, 'There's only one interesting thing', and they sort of sat on the edge of their seats and said, 'What is that?', and I said, 'The brief basically exposes the gratuitous nature of the project. That's interesting. I wouldn't mind giving the brief to five thousand people'. They said, 'How do you mean?'and I said, 'Well, actually print the brief and share the brief. That I think is important, that's something worth doing; to bring some transparency to this process is a gesture worth making'. And to my great surprise they said, 'OK. We'll do it'. I said, 'You make me a pair of plain white shoes that I would wear and print the brief'. They said, 'We'll do it'. The scary thing is how awful the corporate monster is; you know *Forbidden Planet*? There's a monster in *Forbidden Planet* which is actually the angst of all the people and that's unfortunately how corporations are now. No matter if you even criticise them, they take that criticism into themselves and become almost bigger through it. I would like to hope that somebody got some kind of clarity from my version of the Adidas project.

HUO   Many thanks. Peter Saville. Thank you very much.

Applause, end of interview

Hans Ulrich Obrist	It's a great pleasure to welcome our next guest, Roger Hiorns.
Roger Hiorns	Hi!

HUO   Earlier this evening we had a conversation with Charles Jencks. I was very surprised when I met you the first time and you told me that it was actually not an art book but an architecture book by Charles Jencks which made you start your work.

RH   Yes.

HUO   So I was wondering if you could tell us this story.

RH   OK. Well, it was a long while back. I won an award at school and received a book voucher. The book that I bought in the mid-1980s was a really very grand, really very huge architecture book that was compiled by Charles Jencks. It went through all the different periods of architecture up to the present day. It drew attention to many subgroups and distinctions between architectural tribes. It was useful to see how these systems worked at such an early age. There are lots of flies in here!

HUO   More and more, unfortunately.

RH   [Laughs] Well, it was a pretty detailed book on the origins of postmodernism and also the later aspects of postmodernism; through that book you could explore the possible roots to its own exhaustion. Anyway, I used this book in a new piece of work which I was showing at the time. I was so enamoured by the fact that the James Stirling building of the Clore Gallery at the Tate was on the front cover. This was extra encouragement later as I did a project outside the Clore Gallery at the Tate, so there was a good long-term relationship which I was interested in exploring further at that time.

Rem Koolhaas   Hans, I am noticing a weird coincidence that almost every English story starts with school. Did you notice that, too?

HUO   It's fascinating.

RK   Is there a particular quality of the English educational system?

RH   Perhaps.

RK I would never have mentioned school in any interview, certainly not in a first reply.

RH It wasn't so long ago with me.

HUO It was from the first interview with Brian Eno on.

RK Everything starts with school in England.

RH When you come to this Marathon it's quite tricky. Quite uncertain, as you are not quite sure what to expect; so you want to start from the very beginning perhaps, a good place to start as any. Also there is the sub-text, the idea of talking about London, your relationship with it and how you came to London. I'm not originally from London. I arrived in London when I was seventeen and this was when I started working on 'things'. I am originally from Birmingham, which is another big city but big and complicated in a completely different way.

HUO Can you tell us more about London now?

RH Well, I've got a strange relationship to London at this point because I live above a public house on Fleet Street. The public house is very old; it was built by Christopher Wren to house his workers when they were building St Paul's and when they were building St Bride's Church, which is the church of newspaper journalists. When journalists have weddings or they die in combat and have their funerals, they are certainly at that church, so in every respect it's the faithful continuation of the Fleet Street journalist environment, the ailing tradition of free independent commentary and news gathering. There's nothing left of journalism in Fleet Street now; Reuters was the last group, and that's just recently gone. Historically I was very interested in the city of London when I first arrived as a teenager, so in a certain respect it's a continuation of that fascination for me. I remember my fascination originally being esoteric, magical and trying to get further into and under the typically darkened streets of the city, and now of course I don't believe in that at all, I passed those adolescent vapours. I didn't consider those same questions any longer. It's more of a passing space, a continuous walk-through for me. So this very old pub, which is from 1670, is an interesting place to live currently.

HUO There was obviously a very visible generation of artists here in the 1990s through the YBAs and you are clearly part of the new decade. (It's very strange that this decade still really doesn't have a name. Someone once called it the zero-zeros but that's a bit pejorative.) I was wondering if you feel there is a kind of a rupture with the 1990s, if you feel part of a new generation and how you would describe this new generation with links to other artists in London.

RH The relationship is quite problematic because we came from a generation that was viewing how things were panning out with the YBAs when I originally came to London. We went to shows, we saw what they were doing, we saw that they were becoming very famous, we were watching it play out its very early conclusions, priorities were set firmly, very early on, within a self allotted time-span, there were limitations within the DNA of many of those artists. We thought we should not follow these examples. Then there's a new relationship getting started with a number of galleries that were also showing work which was remarkably different from what the general YBAs were achieving at the same time in London. There was one gallery in particular called Robert Prime which I visited with my friends that I had at the time, so in a way you saw a different structure of intention, a different way of working, you saw this duality in attitudes.

RK In what way different?
RH In their way, they weren't celebrity-based like the YBA's self-referential and militantly authentic progress. There was certainly an aspirational aspect to the YBA generation, which wasn't really anything of interest to the way I always considered things to be done. Where did this spirit come from? It wasn't familiar to me. The closer and more intimate relationship built between the artist and the public was in no way practical, it shallowed the pools of the novel experience that contemporary art can create, it demands immediate interpretation and historicising. Ok, I think that there was an interesting development; the instantaneous biography, it's a-historical, it was interesting to bring that subject in because it was a remarkably relevant tool of the time, and still it becomes a more sophisticated device. You had artists making work which was self-revelatory and you also had a lot of similar journalism that provided a similar model, you had many publications that were also uniquely self-revelatory at the time of that work's genesis. So, it followed this pattern which was happening generally within the media and it made some sense that the YBA promoted itself from the media that fed its principles, as so suc-

cessfully a mirror of the aspirational. We were looking at these artists and they were making pieces of work, memorable things, seemingly iconic things, and they became a neat package, this strange view of individual artists wanting the same arena of narrow interpretation and nowness, media myth, very limiting in the future no doubt.

And then there were other artists showing in town, their first shows, some of them, the artists: Angela Bulloch, Liam Gillick, Kai Althoff, mainly European artists, and they were doing something that was remarkably different, providing completely disparate forms of activity. They were coming with completely different strategies and ideas about the way to action their subject. So yes, there was the real paradox of very different work happening in the same place at the same time. Historically it was an interesting event to watch, an otherwise static world gathering momentum. It was good that you had the alternative examples, if you didn't have such an attractive alternative, then who knows what else would have happened. I think it would of course have shaped things very differently.

[Silence]

HUO   Many more questions to come.

RH   OK.

HUO   In the 1990s there was a clear rupture with the 1980s and that was somehow manifested through a very different relationship to objects and maybe a doubt about objects or quasi-objects. I was wondering, less in terms of media or strategies but in terms of work, if you would see a clear difference.

RH   Now?

HUO   Yes.

RH   Tampering with the object, strict positivism. Re-tooling the workshop appears to offer a more rewarding future than the resultant object perhaps. Objects now require a specific breakage so that it can be re-analysed and re-positioned, looking at the objects' materiality much closer. We accept the objects' primary meaning on a conditioned impulse too easily, this narrow route to interpretation prevents any material progress into the next new forms. It's very general, but let's identify the objects and working methods for the next period, 'further' objects should identify themselves easily as adverse reactions to their present surroundings, it's a question of applying the right procedures to promising materials. So, it's important, a strategy to readjust material foundations. Is this pure strategy, a tricky one, there are all sorts of different strategies. You can come to having a strategy without having any strategy at all. The word exists but you don't necessarily have to use it, so people are actually aware now that there is a non-strategy situation, a naturalisation, and you can just do things and just be and do what you want, total formlessness, ze-ro structure, an ideology vacuum. Object-making can be tempered by strategies or tempered by the simple idea that you want to become a strict formalist. Your formalist attitudes towards things can be tempered even further by even more things, vacuum on much less, hence the esoteric nature of these shiftless works. It's a difficult question; there is either a lot of things that you can do, or not a lot of things you can't do. In real-ity I don't think there's anything you really cannot do. You can negate history with immediate biography, and you can think about things in terms of endlessly separating art from aesthetics, through a positivist cri-tique, etc. And you can just carry on. Let's leave it open. Does that make any sense at all? Probably not at this point in the night.

RK   I'm not talking as an expert on sculpture but when I look at your work I don't see somebody who's negating history. I see somebody who's play-ing with Brancusi, both in substantance and form; I see somebody who is playing with the colours of Yves Klein and Anish Kapoor; I see some-body who is playing with the aluminium of Frank Stella.

RH   OK. That's your opinion.

RK   It's not my opinion, it's my observation.

RH   OK. At the start, I think you can develop your process through an aes-thetic of proxy; you can develop yourself within a host aesthetic, your early aesthetic can grow mutagenic in a body of already set forms until it becomes eventually your own. It's not a critique, appropriation is an internalised transformation via already set forms. This bears an inter-esting complication for the ideologies and spirit that originally stimu-lated the tampered forms, a playful admixture of tested realities is a good position to encounter. You will transform your emotional and psychic self by learning another language, the profoundly unfamiliar eventually be-comes your primary interpreter. Simply, I think it's important if you're beginning your own language to find the fundamental building blocks within the other languages, ones you could never entirely grasp. Reference can be collided, you don't have to be precious to any single language, you don't need to care. I am interested in the gaps between pieces of work these problems create…

RK   I was intrigued that you combined the words intelligence and sacrifice.

RH   Yes.

RK   Can you clarify that? What does that formula mean?

RH   Perhaps disappointingly, the title is actually from an album by Alec Empire. He was a member of a band called Atari Teenage Riot; he brought out a solo album and I thought it was an interesting title, *Intelligence and Sacrifice*. I don't know what that alludes to with that piece of music at all. He's a fairly abstract artist himself. In a way there's no allusion; there's always a disconnection between the titles and the pieces. The titles always come after and they are unhelpful. They're a conditioning tool, a tradition we can allow to dissolve perhaps, they allow a direction to interpretation, a chaperone of reference – but is that necessary at all? I'm not a fan of titling and currently everything is untitled at this point; I'm going through an untitled period, then to move into the next phase after that.

HUO   You also have a writing practice and in the pavilion here we are planning an event with you which will be more the form of a reading, of a lecture. I was wondering if you could tell us a little about your practice of writing, if it's a daily practice and how it works.

RH   Sure. Writing is tricky. The history is that I was having to do talks to the general public and I was finding it a problem; I was finding that the connection I was having with the public was necessary but not directly from me personally. I was slipping into biography, into projecting personal subjectivity into the situation, and this was uncomfortable as it's not important to hear all this excess information, too many red herrings, so it's important to remain silent. I needed a barrier, perhaps an acted lecture, written by myself and delivered by an actor perhaps, and this grew into the monologues. In the work that I make there is a sub-text of detachment. I am interested in the encouragement of a detached way and nature. You can further isolate your present situations and circumstances through actions and activities. You can do this by using tools differently from their set intent: re-evaluating and disturbing their use can supply a new reasoning, insomuch a new logical detachment is a good result. So the plays or the writing came from a collaboration and collision of ideas I was currently thinking about.

So it goes, I wanted to have lectures prepared. I used to go into lectures and basically feel like this, just talk and see what happened, and there was no structure, so I wanted to write a play. My whole work became a lecture; it was scripted and I would become an actor talking within the role of talking about my own work. Then further... I was interested in an actor talking about my work so I wouldn't have to be there at all. It also negated the idea that there would have to be questions afterwards, which were always problematic. I worked on monologues and developed out of that. So yes, finally I write monologues which are about the action of detachment.

HUO   Many thanks to Roger Hiorns.

Applause, end of interview

Hans Ulrich Obrist   Welcome to Olivia Plender, our next speaker.
Olivia Plender   Thank you.

HUO   Olivia, I want to ask you the question we also asked Roger about the generation of the 1990s marked so much by the YBAs and this decade in which you started work. (Maybe we can come up with a name for this decade during the Marathon.) Do you feel that there was a rupture? How do the 1990s relate to this new decade and to what extent do you feel part of a new generation?

OP   I was hoping you weren't going to ask me that question when I heard you asking Roger but, trying to cast my mind back, I extremely disliked the YBA movement and I felt unhappy in London at the end of the 1990s when all that stuff was really coming to a head. It didn't feel like it was attached to anything that I was particularly interested in or creating a cultural landscape that I wanted to be part of. In that sense I think there has been some kind of rupture but I wouldn't like to name what that is. I don't think I'd like to give it any kind of name. Much as I find Roger's work interesting, I wouldn't particularly associate it with mine. London is such a huge art scene; there are a lot of different art scenes within it so you get – I wouldn't like to use the word 'movement' but for want of a better word – different movements happening within London that have absolutely nothing to do with each other. Some of the artists who are very active in London at the moment wouldn't necessarily participate in this kind of event. I think you can't put one title on whatever it is that's happened post-1990s.

HUO   When we spoke recently you mentioned your interest in counter-cultural, mainly esoteric, organisations. It's very interesting that many started very near the Serpentine Gallery in Kensington and in this neighbourhood. You also told me that the Science Museum and these esoteric organisations originated from the same kind of initiative. I am curious how this research stands right now because in terms of mapping London it is a very interesting project.

OP   I have been looking at Non-Conformist religious movements and how they overlap with social protest movements. Specifically, there are two religious movements I'm looking at, one of which is the Modern Spiritualist Movement, which started in New York State in 1848 and is a religion based on speaking to the dead. The medium replaces the role of the priest and mediates between the congregation and the spirit, which is the non-denominational equivalent to God or the non-gendered, non-specific equivalent to God. It became very big in the north of England amongst Non-Conformist religious communities like Methodists and Quakers. It started in Keighley in Yorkshire in about 1850, I think, and then spread south to London where, in a sense, it became more establishment. Kensington was very much the home of that sort of occult activity. For instance, there is the Spiritualist Association of Great Britain in a magnificent old mansion house in Belgrave Square, which I think was gifted to the movement at that time but is now decaying. There is also the Society for Psychical Research, which is a funny sort of organisation that I accidentally joined when I was using their library one time. Now because the membership basis is largely people over the age of seventy, they feel that it's very important to discover once and for all, empirically and scientifically, if there is life after death. But they have trouble getting younger members, so if you are under fifty and go in to use the library they will try and press you into becoming a member quite quickly. When that sort of activity was in the north it was very much about disenfranchised people, people without a public voice, using this very strange circumstance of claiming to speak to the dead as a way of making political statements in public. So, for instance, a woman at a séance in the north of England would give a political speech for three hours about why women should have the vote, but she would be channelling the ghost of Abraham Lincoln, so it's not her, it's the ghost of Abraham Lincoln saying that women should have the vote.

As I said, when Spiritualism got to London it became much more establishment. The Society for Psychical Research was set up in 1882 by Cambridge physicists and philosophers. Arthur Balfour, who became Prime Minister, was a member and one of its presidents. And then you have the Theosophical Society, also based near here, which represented a kind of elitist backlash. Occultism was a massive movement sweeping Europe and large parts of the world. The point of Spirituualism was that it was non-hierarchical and everybody could be on the platform. Even today when you go to a Spiritualist church mediums spend a lot of time telling the congregation, 'It's me up here but any of you could be up here. You just need to do a bit of work on your psychic skills and you could be up here in a couple of years'. But Theosophy was the reverse, it was about re-establishing the hierarchy and making all the sort of knowledge secret again and you could only attain occult knowledge through special initiations; Madame Blavatsky was at the top. Kensington was where Non-Conformism met the establishment, Non-Conformism as expressed through occult movements.

Rem Koolhaas What kind of shape do you give this research?

OP A bit of everything. At the moment I'm doing a book about it all, which is a graphic novel; I'm also currently making a radio programme. Sometimes I lecture, sometimes I make installations. The shape varies but I've been at it for a few years, so it does come out in different directions, in different shapes.

HUO And this idea of different directions, different shapes has also to do with this incredible variety of things you are doing at the same time. You are running and editing a magazine, *Untitled*; at the same time you are self-publishing, you have your practice as an artist and at the same time you are also venturing into more TV-related projects. That is something I am curious to ask you about because TV is something we have so far explored very little in these London Marathon conversations. Eric Hobsbawm said we should not neglect memory; the Marathon should be a protest against forgetting. A lot of moments have come up from the 1950s, 1960s and 1970s which are toolboxes for artists or architects or designers today. TV hasn't really come up even though there were very interesting TV things happening in England in the 1950s and 1960s. As far as I understand, you revisit certain of those 1950s and 1960s TV projects and I was curious to know if I'm right to assume that this is a toolbox for you and how you use those things now.

OP I think so. The work I've done about television is mostly about *Monitor*, which was the first magazine format arts programme on British TV. One of the reasons I'm revisiting that stuff, I suppose, is because arts programmes on TV have completely changed shape. The last decade of television is totally different from what it was when I was young. I think in the 1950s when television was a new thing and people were trying to work out the formats, they were related to older modes of expression, so a lot of arts programmes up until the 1980s, really, were based on the lecture format. For example *Ways of Seeing*, Kenneth Clark's *Civilisation* series and in a lot of the *Monitor* programmes there was Huw Wheldon speaking with a slightly paternalistic air to camera, delivering a lecture about the subject. But that kind of lecture format has completely disappeared from TV and it's a mixed blessing. I don't watch television – it might be a crass generalisation – but a lot of people in the art world and a lot of people I know don't watch television any more. I think television has ceased to provide much educational content, which maybe stopped with my generation of artists. When we were teenagers we watched TV. You might stumble across a Fellini film at two o'clock in the morning; you wouldn't know what it was but it was kind of incredible and it was part of a world you wanted to inhabit. You had no idea where that was but school seemed like the place to go to, in order to attach yourself to that.

HUO So you revisit these moments. How does this work? Can you tell us more about this TV project?

OP There's a couple of things I've done. One was an interview that I did with Ken Russell, the British film maker, who worked for the *Monitor* programme for about a decade. He made documentaries about artists, everyone from Romantic poets like Shelley, Keats, Coleridge, Wordsworth, those sorts of people, to a very well-known documentary called 'Pop Goes the Easel', which was about the Royal College of Art and young pop artists. I spent about a year trying to track down Ken and then met him in a village hall in the Lake District in front of an audience which was the local cinema club. He used to live in the Lake District as it's the home of British Romanticism. A lot of the people in the audience had either been extras in his films or had some contact with him, seen him in the supermarket in 1982 or something, so that felt like an appropriate audience to invite. I built a set that looked like a television studio and interviewed him in the style of a c. 1972 television interview, so very much in the old format. Now on TV you don't get so much of that; a TV interview would not be an hour long. It would probably be more like this in fact, where each of us gets about twenty-five minutes.

This leads on to something I would quite like to do, which is to ask you two a couple of questions about the situation we're in now. I'm quite curious about how you arrived at this format and the idea of the twenty-four hour interview and what the purpose is. It's an interesting project to embark on but do you see this as research or is it a performance? How do you see this process yourselves?

RK   It's not really a performance, at least not for me. It's an articulation of our curiosity about London and about the simultaneous existence of so many ways of thinking in one particular city at the moment that it is really confronted with many of its own contradictions, seemingly on its way to becoming radically different to what it used to be. So it's really an inventory.

HUO   And it's also a continuation of many interviews Rem and I have recorded together.

RK   Some of them very long.

HUO   Yes. It's a kind of a continuation of a marathon we did in Tokyo where we tried to map a movement. The idea was to look for a 1960s movement with a manifesto. We found after research that the Metabolist movement could be a really interesting project because all the protagonists were still active. At the same time there is a big interest in Metabolism right now among younger artists and architects. Obviously we interviewed everybody, not just architects but all the other participants, the critics, the engineers...

RK   ... the politicians...

HUO   ... very important – and that took three days. When we started to think about the programme in London the idea was to do this. We started, actually, with the idea that the interviews would be forty-five minutes to one hour, but the process developed dynamically and there were many different practitioners from different fields we wanted to talk to. Little by little that's how it evolved. It didn't really have a master plan at the beginning!

Thank you very much, Olivia, thank you.

Applause, end of interview

Sophie Fiennes
Russell Haswell
Anat Ben-David
Damien Hirst
Ant Genn
Shumon Basar
Markus Miessen
Åbäke

Hans Ulrich Obrist We are very happy to continue the Marathon and to welcome Sophie Fiennes. Earlier tonight I asked Zaha Hadid about London and her still unrealised projects related to the city. She said for her London was still an unrealised project. You're working on London right now and we could say it's also an unrealised project; it's on its way. I am curious to know more.

Sophie Fiennes It's actually a fictional project whereas all of the work that I've done so far has been documentary. I really enjoy a certain chaotic way of working that documentary brings. You never know what you're going to get and you have to be very responsive to the subject. But I've been developing something fictional based on some areas of London that intrigue me, near where I live. One of them is this waste disposal site on the river where there are big barges that take the waste out of London; six hundred tons every day. I am interested in this work, this mechanism of emptying the city of its waste, and in the very old-English, Victorian feeling of this location; it seems almost nineteenth-century. And then there's another area very nearby, with modern, light industrial depots that also features in the project. It's a ghost story that I'm setting in these two locations, one of which is this waste-disposal area and the other a postal sorting office.

Rem Koolhaas And is it a feature film, a full-length film?
SF I intend it to be that, yes.

RK It's really interesting because you are not here the whole time but we hear certain things and certain words repeated. You are the fifth person who has used the word 'ghost'.
SF Really!

RK Yes. What made you do a ghost story?
SF Actually it's a ghost story set amongst two different times. It's a kind of a ghost story but it's a pre-life story. It's the haunting of something that hasn't come into being, not of the dead that have passed. It's a kind of haunting from the future rather than the past.

HUO It's not the first time you have worked on London. I am very interested in the impossibility of making a portrait of a city. The idea of making a synthetic image of a city is a priori impossible, as cities like London are so complex. Could you talk a little bit about this idea of a portrait of a city and how you work?

SF I made a choral portrait of the city [*Because I Sing*, 2001], which was an Artangel project in collaboration with Alain Platal, a Belgian choreographer and theatre-maker. It was something that they invited me to do because they had got together choirs for a live performance and they wanted to make a film of it. It was a way to make a portrait through one thematic basis. Sometimes it's best to make a very tight frame in order to go further into ideas and this choral portrait was, in a sense, very contained.

HUO Can you tell us more about it?

SF There were many different choirs; there was a gay men's choir, there was a Women's Institute choir, and they all seemed to represent different communities that made up the city. But of course when you make observational documentary it becomes quite paralysing because there's such a contingent, ongoing expansiveness of people and moments; it's very touching when you really go close into very intimate situations. So instead of being about scale it becomes about trying to find individuality in documentary moments within the vastness of a city like London.

HUO How do you feel London has changed in the time you have lived and worked here?

SF It's changed in its texture in a big way. When I was about twenty-one I worked on the film called *The Cook, The Thief, His Wife and Her Lover* with Peter Greenaway. I was the Art Department Production Manager and it was in the late 1980s. I had to go around and salvage lots of objects from various places like old factories. Mrs Thatcher was closing down all the hospitals so we went to the Moorfields Eye Hospital and extracted all these old cookers and took light fittings. We salvaged things from The Isle of Dogs which was then this red brick, heavy Gothic spectral landscape. It had this ghostly quality of Victorian London which you see disappearing and replaced by this light industrial, neon-strip lit, disposable architecture that you feel is there for a very brief time, it's not there to last. So in that sense I feel Victorian London is disappearing really, even if warehouses get turned into loft apartments, the sense of it has changed.

HUO I mentioned earlier that one of the triggers for doing this interview project was the very long conversations David Sylvester had with Francis Bacon. Obviously doing documentaries on one person means having very long conversations and I was wondering if you could talk a little about those sorts of conversations. I think you are doing a film right now on Grace Jones.

SF It is interesting to be here on the receiving end of a conversation or interview, because I very rarely embark on interviews in my work. I kind of enjoy myself as a presence behind a camera; I think I even hide behind a camera, really. I have conversations with my subjects to balance the observational nature of what I am doing, but I very rarely do interviews as such. I think they are very hard to do. I also just feel more excited by being a free-floating eye that sees in a certain way, and framing things in one way or another changes them emphatically.

HUO Can you tell us a little bit about previous documentaries you have made on specific people?

SF Following on talking about portraits of cities, I made a film called *Hoover Street Revival* [2003], which was a portrait of Los Angeles through this Pentecostal church community. It was a portrait of that community, but it was through the relationship of the sermons that were preached and the response of the parishioners and the tension between this very idealistic, ecstatic Holy Ghost-filled life in church and then this incredibly flat life outside. It was very anchored around this fixed point of the church. It was little moments with the people in the community who were affected by the sermons of their bishop. I am interested in places where there is an attempt for some kind of ecstatic experience. That was interesting to me. The singing portrait was the same thing.

RK I want to ask you about the classical division between documentary and feature film. One is supposed to be authentic and the other one is supposed to be artificial and manipulated. I also see that you have worked with Lars von Trier and Dogme, and Dogme seems to be taking an interesting in-between position of wanting to be authentic fiction, so that's almost a triangle. How do you see that?

SF   This is a question that I always enjoy because actually I don't consider myself a 'proper' documentary film maker anyway, because I'm *not a* journalist. I'm much more interested in the kind of material that you create by observational shooting and then creating juxtapositions. In fact, fictionalising reality, playing with the grammar of the cinema that constructs a three-dimensional space in the mind of the viewer. Imposing that kind of grammar onto reality was the premise of *Hoover Street Revival*. It was a way to try to see the fiction in reality itself, or the sense that a cinematic feeling was as close to reality as an interview is supposed to be.

RK   I completely understand. In that context, how do you see what Dogme was doing, or is doing? And how do you interpret their following?

SF   I think Dogme was really about recognising that when you make any piece of work you have a set of rules. Lars von Trier made them explicit and then he broke them a lot of times; it was about pushing himself out of the unspoken rules that he had already. It was a way of pushing himself beyond a certain aesthetic that he didn't want to repeat. That was how I saw it.

RK   Do you still follow him?

SF   Yes, I thought his film *Dogville* was fantastic. I loved the fact that it was just on a black stage; all reality had been stripped away and yet when you watched it you had a very strong sense of the community that it was portraying.

RK   In architecture there is a certain kind of analogous movement. What would be the analogous movement in art, Hans?

HUO   To Dogme?

RK   Yes.

HUO   What is it in architecture?

RK   I think maybe some of its representatives will be here later. Caruso St John has talked about it.

HUO   No, I don't see it as a movement in contemporary art. In poetry Oulipo comes to my mind.

SF   You mean creating rules?

RK   No, I mean when the issue of rules becomes so explicit and becomes almost a movement in itself at some point.

HUO   I think with exhibitions it's always about rules of the game in some way and I think something we'll hear from Richard Hamilton, hopefully, later tomorrow. It is this whole idea that if an exhibition doesn't invent a new rule of the game, which very often is a display feature, it's already doomed to oblivion anyhow.

RK   OK. I have a different question. Almost all the people we talked to were adamant that in London there are no boundaries between professions and that therefore there is an unusual cross-contamination between them. Is that true for film as well in London?

SF   No, I think the film world, unlike the art world, is very enclosed here. It always wants to be closer to commerce than art and there's a lack of confidence to do anything that is perceived as a risk. Every time I make a film I take the attitude that I don't care if they don't commission another film from me again because it's the only way I can then work to my own rules. I don't know whether I'm really answering your question, but from my experience of looking at British film it's not that alive. I look for inspiration from other fields, looking at how other people work. I enjoy that connection with other people, like Michael Clark, who was here before, whom I worked with. I enjoyed sensing how he thought being a choreographer, being a dancer. It seemed to generate a very different way of thinking.

HUO   You mentioned inspiration and I am curious to know more about what inspires you, particularly in terms of the past. Are there any filmmakers or other practitioners from the past who are a toolbox for your present activity?

SF   The people whom I have enjoyed in the past and have been very formative for me are European filmmakers, basically from the 1960s and 1970s.

HUO   So would Jean Rouch be someone who matters for you?

SP   My background isn't in documentary; it's much more fiction. I found myself making documentary because of these small cameras that enable you to make films. The mechanics of trying to get funding – a year spent having lunches with people! This is what I mean about the anxiety for me of trying to make fiction. I'm scared that I'm going to lose the creative freedom that I have in shooting digital video and making films, forming them, editing them myself on Apple Macs. For the last project that I did on cinema with Slavoj Žižek I cut it myself at home in my one-bedroom flat.

HUO Can you tell us about this Žižek film?

SF Yes. It's called *The Pervert's Guide to Cinema* [2006] and it was originally commissioned as a forty-eight minute film for Channel 4 but when I got the material and looked at it I realised it had to be bigger in length, so I finished up making a three-part film, three fifty-minute pieces. I found it fascinating to look at fiction from his perspective because it was this imaginative way of responding to images, and about form really, ultimately beyond narrative. In fiction, particularly in funding bodies, there is an obsession about script, an obsession about plot, and when you see cinema through Slavoj's method of looking at it, it's in fact what he calls 'the libidinal density of forms' in cinema, this is where the real enjoyment is. That was the kind of, as he would say, the transcendental agenda of the project.

HUO Many thanks, Sophie Fiennes. Thank you very much.

SF OK.

Applause, end of interview

Hans Ulrich Obrist	It's a great pleasure to introduce our next speaker, Russell Haswell. We will start with an audio clip of your work. *[Audio]* *[Applause]*
Rem Koolhaas	It was completely contrary to what I expected! It's not about the sound but about the image. I see centrality in everything, symmetry, rotation, but always counter-clockwise. Can you explain? Each of those movements would normally be associated with classicism.
Russell Haswell	Yes. But these things weren't created with that in mind.
RK	But nevertheless it's quite surprising to see such a dedication to symmetry and centrality.
RH	Yes.
RK	Can you say something about it?
RH	In this instance these recordings were generated using a computer system with a graphic input, so the audio which you heard at sub-standard level was derived from drawings and these drawings had symmetrical and rotational features and these different methods of composition were applied to this process. But I'm quite interested in the synesthetic experience from making drawings, turning them into sound, being a non-musician. They exist but they're not the core of my interest.
HUO	How, as a non-musician, did you come to work with sound? I am very interested in finding out the extent to which software generated your kind of sound. You use a lot of generative audio software and I remember your concert in Yokohama had to do with a laptop and conversion. I was wondering if you could describe how this started.
RH	I guess my interest in these areas came when I was at art school and trying to draw but also trying to make sound. Being a non-musician I was quite excited by the fact that you could actually draw a wave form and start to play on this microtonal level, this microscopic level. I guess about 1990, or probably just prior to that in 1989, I had my first experiences of using computer software where you could physically draw the wave form. From then on it became a preoccupation of mine to try to

189

find ways to draw sound. I guess between then and now I have been spending most of my time trying to find these possibilities and trying to utilise any software that had been made in this fashion. If it hadn't been made already then I've been starting to work with people who could realise those things for me.

HUO   Were there any toolboxes or composers from the past who were helpful in developing this trajectory?

RH   Xenakis is the only one, primarily in the sense that he developed this computer music system where you do draw the sound. I worked on the possibility of using that system and managed to do that.

HUO   You re-visited Xenakis, together with Florian Hecker. Can you tell us about this?

RH   We didn't visit him, we worked in his studio and with his devices. He was no longer with us at that time, unfortunately.

HUO   And what did you do with his work? You just used the studio?

RH   We used his graphic input music system, which is called UPIC.

RK   Is that used in the recording we heard?

RH   Yes.

RK   You know he did a pavilion once?

RH   Yes, of course.

RK   There is a degree of similarity; I recognise the shapes.

RH   Yes.

RK   People have talked about ghosts today.

RH   I don't believe in ghosts.

RK   OK.

RH   I only believe in the physical and real.

RK   So there are no ghosts.

RH   There are no ghosts. There is no God.

[Laughter]

HUO	I have an image here in front of me called *The Brutal Truth* from 2002, which sort of fits the context of tonight perfectly because it's all about insects. Can you tell us a bit about this?
RH	It was a piece I made when I was on an artist's residency programme in Stockholm called IASPIS. I spent nine months there, which was longer than I should have been there because somebody was kicked off the programme for being a necrophiliac and it fucked up the programme. Consequently I stayed there longer and I made this piece called *The Brutal Truth*, which was a video of cockroaches I'd managed to acquire in Stockholm from a reptile shop (people feed them to their lizards and snakes and so on). I decided that it was quite interesting to slaughter these cockroaches with Chanel nail varnish, which I proceeded to do and document. It also became for me a process to create automatic drawings because when you apply Chanel nail varnish to a cockroach its legs and its underbelly start to draw trails until the nail varnish sticks to the body and it can no longer move. Then it stops and becomes encased in a hard nail varnish shell, encapsulated, which produces quite a nice physical drawing that includes this insect. For me at the time art was a little bit more popularist than my attitude as an individual. That piece was really an attack of what I saw was considered to be popularist at the time. I'm a bit more objectionable than that, really!
HUO	On the numerous occasions we discussed sound tonight we tried to establish the link to the city. Brian Eno, with whom we started the Marathon, said carrying sound into the city is really difficult; it is difficult to compete with the city. There is the other question of to which extent the sound of the city would enter the work of a sound practitioner. I was wondering how you would answer these two points. Squarepusher was talking about bringing Aphex Twin, I think, into the London Underground.
RH	I guess there are a lot of possibilities in this city. I don't know.
HUO	To pin it down to your work, do you intervene in the city with sound?
RH	I used to but currently what I'm attempting to do is try and remove myself from those scenarios, so hopefully there will be appropriate concert houses and venues to present things. But at the moment there aren't any appropriate venues of the appropriate size with the appropriate sound

system to really work in this city compared to the other metropolises in the world.

HUO That's interesting because we have also been discussing models of cultural institutions; Joan Littlewood and Cedric Price's Fun Palace was mentioned. So you think there is a kind of missing institution in London in relation to that.

RH Yes, sure.

HUO Can you describe how this institution would work? What is missing?

RH A good music venue, really, something that's in between music and the exhibition of contemporary art, I guess. I don't know. I remember experiencing in Europe, particularly in places like Vienna and in Switzerland, in the early 1990s you could go and do a concert in a museum. When that kind of things happened at that time I remember coming back to England and thinking, 'Why don't they do that in London? Why don't they have concerts at the Tate?' Actually now they are beginning to do that. I guess programming becomes an issue then, as well as who is chosen to play or present their work. I think there's a lot missing from this city.

RK That's really interesting to hear because you are the first one to make negative comments. The whole evening has so far been almost an unadulterated declaration of satisfaction with the city.

RH I left. I'm out of here!

RK So it's very refreshing to hear something is missing.

RH I think there's a lot missing, really.

HUO What else is missing?

RH Oh shit! Jesus! Where do we start? It's endless, the list. I don't know. Give me a clue. A good cinema.
[Laughter]
A good nightclub. A museum that we're really happy with.

RK Oh my God!

RH Exactly. Not here, not yet.

RK I think this is a perfect moment to end.

HUO	I do have a last question. I want to ask if you have unrealised projects, projects too big to have been realised or censored; the unbuilt roads of Russell.
RH	Yes. I'm trying to make a film at the moment, a 35 mm film which has no image.
RK	No image. Sound.
RH	*[Nods]*
HUO	Many thanks to Russell Haswell.

Applause, end of interview

| Hans Ulrich Obrist | It's a great pleasure to introduce our next speaker, Anat Ben-David. |
| Anat Ben-David | Hello! |

HUO Can you tell us about your collaboration with Douglas Gordon?

ABD I wish I'd brought a video or something because usually I perform, you know, and I thought since people are probably quite tired maybe I should do a spontaneous performance.

HUO That would be great.

ABD I'll just do a text.
[Stands; removes microphone from stand]
OK. This is one of my texts. Whooo. *[Shakes upper body]* OK.
[With energetic body movement, rhythmic delivery of text]
Journalists over celebrity scandal. You're too much to handle. You're too much to handle. Clicking in chat rooms, faking male stars. Getting no too much, so get in touch. Why are you holding from saying your piece? It's not insane, it's you or them. Call of the century, on your guard. The poor are fat, the rich are sad. Hey rock and roll. Your blood is clean. You eat organic and go to the gym. You're suing the kids from snapping you tunes off the Internet. They make you yet. They distract you from deciding which car to get for your lawful wife. Get a life! Call of the century. On your guard. The poor are fat, the rich are sad. Heeeey! What' it about? Trend is filling application forms, posing around in community fairs searching for action. It's just not there. Hey greed! You have too much. You can't spend enough you want to get more. Hey! Hey Knock on the door. The rich are sad, the fat are poor. Call of the century. On your guard. The poor are fat, the rich are sad.
Thank you.
[Applause]

Rem Koolhaas There are probably very few rich people here.

ABD I'm certainly not rich. I don't think it's so good to be rich because you get really comfortable, right, and then there's no point in it. So it's quite good to be poor, I guess, sometimes.

HUO   Thank you very much for your performance. Could you tell us more about your collaboration with Douglas Gordon?

ABD   Oh, Douglas is great. He's really fun. We watched football together. He's really into football. Did France win in the end? No, no. That thing happened with Zidane, which was a shame. Douglas did a film with Zidane and he was really into that so while we were recording in the hotel room we muted the TV because we couldn't, of course, record with the TV on loud. We were watching the football and recording a song together called *Art Rules*. The T-shirts that I gave you say 'Art Rules'. We wrote and performed the song together with Douglas and it's going to come out on a single, hopefully, somewhere. We need a place to launch it, so if anyone has an idea that would be really fun. We did this really great performance in MoMA around the big sculpture of Balzac. He was standing in the middle and we were jumping around doing our performance around it. They put a fence around it. This is a huge sculpture of Balzac made out of bronze or something and even if there was a bomb coming right down nothing would have happened to it. But still they were really afraid we would touch it and we were trying to poke it a bit with some fabric we had and the guards from MoMA were jumping around trying to stop the show because we were touching the Balzac sculpture. So anyway, that was fun. What was your question?

HUO   You have answered it.

ABD   *[Laughs]* OK.

RK   I would like to know more about your contribution to *Wonder Years*.

ABD   Oh, *Wonder Years*! Yes. [Wonder Years *was curated by Avi Pitchon, Adi Nachman and Hila Peleg*]

RK   The way it is described is a new Israeli generation that is taking liberties with the Holocaust and introducing humour and frivolity about that issue. I would like to know more about it and whether you think that is a promising direction, for instance to address the current moment.

ABD   Holocaust. Yes. We grew up in Israel with a notion that everyday life is all about the Holocaust and what happened to the Jews before the Second World War. Blah, blah. In school every Holocaust Day we had to stand and when the sirens were sounding we were trying not to laugh because everyone was doing funny faces and stuff like that. You have to find a way to deal with it, to exercise your humour about it in a way. We know what happened and it's terrible and all those things but these are historical facts and when you go into the human side of it then you deal with it in a very personal way and the personal way that we as contemporary people deal with it, our generation, or this specific group of artists, is with humour and with a more popular approach because these are our tools. Some people thought it was quite provocative but actually the stuff that I did or Tamy Ben-Tor, my best friend, was not.

RK   What did you do?

ABD   I translated songs from that period into pop songs. I made videos of myself performing songs which I really love by Marlene Dietrich and executed them as video clips and projected them in that way. I didn't think it was non-respectful or anything. It was very personal and emotional for me but it was not the usual way people like to perceive those kinds of things. A lot of artists did the same kind of personal thing and it doesn't really fit always to what it's supposed to be like, very heavy and depressing.

RK   That was only in Berlin or did it travel?

ABD   It was only in Berlin. It didn't really succeed. I don't think it went anywhere else, but it was a good experience. And then since I knew that Hugo Boss were involved in art and since Hugo Boss himself was actually a Nazi, I thought maybe I should ask them to be my sponsors. I just wanted some suits to present in my art work. They freaked out and didn't want to give me anything. Then after a month I was performing in one of their parties and in the middle of the show I said, 'Oh that's so great. Look at it. I love Hugo Boss; they are giving us all these things, suits and shoes and stuff, but the thing is you know, you know where they started?' And I began talking about the Second World War and stuff and people didn't really appreciate it. Later on I heard that they were really freaked out by it. I thought it was very appropriate.

HUO   I was wondering if you could tell us a little bit about your performance activity and your band. It says in a text here that in your performances you want to create and generate a total vision using your body and appearance and at the same time you write songs and text and perform as a member of a band.

ABD I wasn't a musician originally. I'm an artist. I did painting and all that stuff. When I did my MA at Goldsmiths my dissertation was about the relationship between the fascist leader and the pop star. Since I could not become a fascist leader, unfortunately, I decided to become a pop star. So I wrote some songs and recorded them really, really fast. Then I toured with a band, with Chicks on Speed and with Peaches, and extended my experience and I got more and more into it. I believe that everything I do is generated from performance because I think that the live interaction or whatever happens in my performances is the most important, relevant thing and all the rest of the stuff, installation, video or whatever, is generated from that experience. But this is the route and the most essential thing for me as an artist.

HUO Do you have unrealised projects?
ABD Ooh! So many!

HUO Can you tell us about some of them?
ABD I have a lot of stuff. I want to do a solo show. I haven't done a solo show yet. I am very realistic, you know. If there is something that I know the limitation of, I will just take the limitation and work with it as something that I can build on. I work all the time; I don't have time to think about projects that I want to make happen. I just work and work and collaborate and do stuff and if I have an objective then I address it. I can't dream all the time; I have to work and do stuff all the time.

RK You talked about your show in Berlin, you talked about MoMA in New York and playing with their values, you talked about your life in Israel. London is a highly un-charged place compared to all these examples that you mention. Why are you here in a city where it is so hard to locate a place that you could insult or an issue that could be provocative or a value that could be compromised?
ABD Actually I think London is a really great place. At the moment I think it's a centre for a lot of things that happen. Just living where I do in Shoreditch it's close to the White Cube but then you've got all the Vietnamese restaurants and you have Caribbean and Hasidic Jews and Turkish places. Then you also have the suits that work in the City. The big capital is right there, and simple people. Everything is just there as a palette; you can see the whole reflection of humanity if you want in that

instant. At this point of my life I think I need to be right in the middle of things and I believe London is a great place to be. I walk out of my house and just see the truth in front of me, so it's very inspiring.

HUO   Many, many thanks.
ABD   Thank you. Bye!

Applause, end of interview

Hans Ulrich Obrist	I am very pleased to introduce our next speakers, Damien Hirst with Ant Genn. Welcome.
Damien Hirst	Hello Hans. That fruit doesn't look very good. That fruit's been there since the 1960s.
HUO	Maybe we could start with London, as this is the London interview Marathon. Damien, in an interview we did you were talking of London as a good soup. I was wondering if you could tell us a little about this idea of the city as a good soup.
DH	Jesus! I can't remember 'a good soup'. Do you mean with loads of layers with art and music? How long have you been doing this? Since 5 o'-clock? What's the next question?
Rem Koolhaas	My next question is, why did you want to be interviewed at this time? Is your mind working best at this moment?
DH	Hans asked me five or six times to do it and I didn't really want to do it. *[Laughter]* But in the end, he is so persistent that I said, 'Give me the worst time'. I thought four o'clock may be the worst time.
Ant Genn	It is pretty bad.
DH	I went to bed for about two hours and then got up again, which was stupid, and my neighbour was just going to bed as I got up. When I said I was going for an interview at the Serpentine, my neighbour thought I was going to be interviewed for a job. *[Laughter]* She said, 'Good luck with the interview'. I said, 'I hope I get it'. Brilliant.
HUO	The idea was also to do an interview with you and with Ant. Maybe you can tell us why we are doing this with you two together, how it came about.
DH	You said you were doing people from all walks of life and Ant's in a band called 'The Hours' that he's been doing for a while. I have been helping with it, doing a lot of the artwork and things like that, so he came along.
HUO	Have you been working together?
DH	Yes, I do all the singing.
AG	Yes, he does the singing and I do the art. *[Laughter]*

HUO	He's got a record coming out – when? Next year?
AG	Yes, and a single in October. Damien and I have known each other for a long time and worked on various collaborations over the years.
DH	So that might fit your multi-faceted London idea.
AG	It's all merging together like one beautiful thing!

HUO	Can you tell us about the projects you've been doing together?
AG	What was the first thing we did?
DH	I wrote poems called *The Cancer Chronicles*, which were about cancer. John Malkovich read them and Ant did the music for them. We have not quite finished it yet.
AG	No.
DH	It's pretty dark.
AG	It's fucking dark, mate.
DH	It's not very cheery.
AG	It's not what you'd put on at a kid's party or anything like that.

DH	Did you ever see that Tommy Cooper sketch where Tommy Cooper comes in and says his father had died and he'd been left a Rembrandt and a Stradivarius? He has a painting and a violin in his hand and he goes 'But Stradivarius couldn't paint and Rembrandt couldn't really make violins'. And he smashes them. *[Laughter]* You should do the artwork and I will do the singing. It would be much better.
AG	And remember the first thing we ever did, years ago, the TV sculpture thing that you did on Channel 4.
DH	Oh yes, that was good, wasn't it?
AG	Yes. With the TV with flies in it being zapped and killed and it was like you were looking on the inside of a TV.

HUO	Was it a nuit blanche thing like tonight, all night long on TV?
DH	No. They gave artists half an hour to do something on TV and it was called *TV Sculpture*. I forget what other artists did it. I emptied the TV out and filled it with flies and tried to make it look like the TV was actually filled with flies but it looked shit and it didn't work. *[Laughter]* Then Ant saw it and said, 'It would be great if you put music on it'. So we put music on it.
AG	We put *Flight of the Bumblebee* on it and it was all 'diddlediddlediddle diddle' and they were all getting zapped, bzz, bzz, bzz.

DH	It was brilliant.
AG	And then we put in loads of soundbites and it went into loads of channel-hopping, so it was like, 'bzoobzoo', 'how many points do you want to try for?', 'no', 'zing', 'ooo', 'incorrect'. That kind of thing.
DH	And they put it on at midnight so nobody saw it.
AG	Yes. It was just left for us to talk about it.
DH	Can we go to bed now?

HUO	I want to know more about this new album. Damien, I think you were co-producing the new album.
DH	Yes, we helped make it but now it's been taken over by the record company.

HUO	Ant, can you tell us about this album?
AG	I've been involved in music for a long time and I have always been in bands with people and been in other people's bands. My friend Martin Slattery and I both used to play with Joe Strummer together and we used to be in a band called Black Grape and years before I was in a band called Pulp. A couple of years ago we went to see a Radio Head gig and we were totally blown away that they were just completely existing on their own terms. It was entertaining but it wasn't entertainment; it was really exciting. We came away from it and turned to each other and said, 'Fuck, what are we doing with our lives? We've got to make something that's our own. We've got to sing our own song, quite literally'. So we decided that we were going to try and do that. I said to Damien, 'I want to do that' and Damien said, 'I'll finance that!' And gave us loads of money to go and make a record and indulge all our musical fantasies, so we went away and did that and we've worked on that for a couple of years. We have just signed the record to A & M Records, who have re-launched in this country. Damien has been doing all our artwork and all that kind of shit. It's an amazing thing for us to be able to do what the fuck we want and not be tied down by a record label. They push you and pull you and all that kind of stuff. Damien said, 'Do what the fuck you want'. Which we did.

DH	And now you've got a deal, which is great.
AG	We signed a record deal and it all fit together. I think when we first did it, people said to him, 'What are you doing that for? You're mad!'

DH   It was after Joe Strummer died, really, because Anthony and Martir Slattery were in The Mescaleros as well, which was Joe Strummer's band

HUO   And you also knew Joe Strummer well, didn't you?

DH   Yes, pretty well. In the glory years. *[Laughter]* When men were men.

AG   Joe was an amazing human being.

RK   In October we want to do a second Marathon.

DH   Jesus Christ.

RK   When we will talk only about three things: money, art and globalisa tion. I think that we are living for the first time in the moment wher the relationship between money and art is not only through collector and artists, but artists themselves have become serious owners of rea estate, money and riches. You are, in a way, perhaps the best exampl here. Does that feel a burden or a beautiful condition or a pleasure o all three?

DH   I think money is a very dangerous thing, a very complicated thing. It' a key, isn't it and there is always a big conflict with money and art. have a great business manager who is very good, who has helped me a we've gone along. He says that you have to be very careful, and I agre with him, that you don't chase money with art, you've got to chase ar with money. It has always got to be that way around. The moment yo do it the other way around you are fucked, basically. Money has alway got to be secondary.

RK   So you are using it to give other people finance?

DH   Have I got dollars in my eyes? *[Laughs]* No, I'm only kidding you. I d it for the money. *[Laughter]*

RK   Is there a connection between your religious paintings and money?

DH   Religion is big money, isn't it? There aren't any answers to all thos things. I think money is a lot more powerful than I thought it was orig inally, but I come from a background where I didn't have much mor ey. You just kind of hope for it. I used to think having too much mone was the same problem as not having enough money but I don't think is anymore; I think that's stupid. *[Laughter]*

HUO   Maybe to come back to the city, one of the things this interview Marathon tries to do is make an incomplete mapping of certain aspects of London. Damien, you have been telling me about an incredibly encyclopaedic drive to map all the pharmacies of London.

DH   Oh yes, that's a kind of map project.

HUO   It is an unfinished project, an incredibly thick book which involves conversations with every single pharmacist. I was wondering if you could tell me a little bit about how this book is coming along and about how the archive works.

DH   Yes, it's a great map of London really. We've been doing it as we've been going along; we've been trying to get permission to photograph every pharmacist inside the pharmacy and every pharmacy from outside. It depends how you define London as well, as Greater or Inner London. I think we've got three or four thousand altogether and we've got permissions for most of them. It's an amazing thing because they are all different. There are a lot of Boots pharmacies and it's all changed in London. It is really multi-racial as well. It's just going to be a very thick book which just has them all in, and not many words, called *Pharmacy*. How about that? It took me ages to think of that. *[Laughter]*

AG   That's why you get paid the big money.

DH   *[Laughs]*

HUO   One thing which would be interesting to discuss, which has come up in previous interviews, is the idea of a lack of boundaries, a very porous situation in terms of different roles. More and more practitioners, whether artists or architects or designers, are assuming several roles at a time.

DH   Cheese rolls.

HUO   *[Laughs]* You also have your publishing house right now; at the same time we are going to show you as a collector at the Serpentine in November. I was wondering if you could talk about these different roles. I am very interested in knowing more about your new publishing initiative in relation, also, to discussion of this book, *Pharmacy*.

DH   I've always done lots and lots of things, really. Whenever I do anything I always try to go in a different direction. As we've gone along I've always done my own books or got very involved in books. I think books are great because when you do an exhibition it's the only thing left after the exhibition, so it's great if you've got a big trail of books behind you as an artist. So then we just decided to have our own publishing company. We took on a designer who had worked with us before, Jason Beard; we employed him and he works with us now. It is great. We have started doing lots of other books. We did a book with Thomas Scheibitz and we've got the publishing running at its own speed now, doing other people's books. It's great. Do you want to do a book?

HUO *[Laughs]*

DH I want to interview you. Aren't you tired?

HUO No, it's only just begun.

DH Which was the worst bit?

RK I think it's very interesting that we have had many artists this evening before you; for almost all of them you are a serious form of oppression.

DH Oppression?

RK Oppression. You are such a strong presence that somehow they have to define themselves and inadvertently you probably contribute to a huge sense of oppression.

DH Oppression. O-P-P?

RK Yes.

DH I thought I was like a shining light!
[Laughter]
Why did you get these flies on me? What are these little flies? It's the fruit. *[Points to fruit on the table]*

RK I don't know whether you remember, but we spent the night together in Venice.

DH Oh yes. You were great! I was amazing!
[Laughter]

RK *[Laughs]* I was totally impressed by your lack of pompousness and yet through your reputation and status there is a weight of heaviness that accrues to you. How do you outwit that? Or is it an issue to outwit it?

DH I don't know. Maybe when I walk in it walks out. I do get aware that have a reputation. Cab drivers always say, 'You're OK, really'. I think 'What made you think I wasn't?' *[Laughter]*

RK That's my point.

HUO Maybe some questions to Ant. We are asking most of the participants in the Marathon tonight about London and about how London changes. What is your view on that? How do you feel London has changed?

AG How has London changed? I have lived here eleven years. I came here in the mid-1990s and from a musical point of view it was an explosive time. I came from Sheffield. I was on sickness benefit in Sheffield one minute and the next minute Brit Pop exploded and I'm having a piss next to Elton John at the Brit Awards. *[Laughter]* Literally that is what it was like. I remember me and Jarvis going to the Brit Awards. I believe at the time we were intoxicated on the sometime-marvellous drug, Ecstasy, and we were like, 'Fucking hell. That's Tom Jones!' We were just walking around. We were just kids off council estates and it was all mental to us. So there was a massive explosion in the 1990s of that. It was a kind of period in the music business when we went to the Brit Awards and it was still Wet, Wet, Wet and Simply Red and that kind of scene and then there were these thugs from Manchester, Blur and Oasis and Pulp and Black Grape and we were all fucking out of our minds on drugs. You could see them all going, 'Oh no! Who are these people?' But it had its own energy; it exploded and took over the music industry and what was known then as Indy music became totally mainstream. The whole 1990s was then this massive hedonistic period and very creative for a time and then I think a lot of it got washed down with drugs because a lot of people took a lot of drugs and had a great time for a long time. That took its toll and it seems that after the 1990s it simmered down a little bit and went back into a pop music thing and it all went a bit safer. You get a lot of bands now, no disrespect to them, bands that are good bands, like Coldplay or whatever. I don't really go to award things any more but I went with Jarv to the Q Awards when he was presenting an award to Scott Walkerand. I looked round the room. We had been in that room a few years earlier with all those people I talked about and I think there was Coldplay and Feeder and they all looked like they were going to have a cup of tea and a bit of celery. I thought, 'Fucking hell! This has all changed a bit!' It had all got a bit safer. Things do ebb and flow and things do change. Personally, I'm ready for a change again. I'm ready for a bit more fucking madness, you know. I'm not talking about drugs, I'm just talking about big characters. The drug does not make the man, it was just more the big characters: there was Sean Rider, Jarvis, Liam and Noel, all that kind of crew.

HUO	Something is missing?
AG	I don't know if something is missing.
DH	More celery.
AG	I suppose it's better to be macro about it than smackro about it. *[Laughter]* In the long run, for your kids and that. But we are here for a good time not for a long time. I don't know. *[Sings]* 'Life is a roller-coaster. You've just got to ride it', as Ronan Keating said. *[Laughter and some applause]* It goes up and down, doesn't it? Things change.
HUO	Damien, can you comment on the change in London?
DH	I haven't really noticed a lot of it. I remember I wrote a letter to Alex James from Blur and called the time we had in London 'the glory years'. We took a lot of drugs and drank a lot but I had three or four brilliant years.
AG	Yes, absolutely.
DH	He wrote back and said, 'What glory years?' I thought, 'Shit. He must have seen it completely different to me.'
AG	There's a lot of debris from that time but a lot of excitement as well. A lot of the young bands that came out of that after the 1990s, came out of that possibility. I think what happened in the 1990s was it kind of smashed down a lot of barriers. People thought there was massive possibility; you could come from nowhere and be massive, you know.
DH	Yes.
AG	Not that being massive is the point but just that it is a possibility and if you shoot for the stars you might hit a lamppost – or if you shoot for the lamppost you might hit the fucking kerb!
HUO	The first person we spoke to about this Marathon was Eric Hobsbawm and he thought it could be really essential and urgent to protest against forgetting. One of the things we have done throughout the night is that we have asked the participants if there are ideas from the past which are somehow relevant for their work, not so much in a nostalgic way, but as a toolbox for now.
DH	Toolboxes.
HUO	Yes.
DH	I did a quote in an interview some time back. I don't know what the hell I meant but I like the sound of it. Somebody was asking me what it was about. I said there has only ever been one idea in art, which is

what you are wearing tomorrow. I don't know what the fucking hell it means but it sounds great.

AG   I don't really understand the question. Are you asking what is inspirational about that?

DH   About London.

AG   About London or about music or about life or about art or what?

HUO   It's a very open question. It has to do with things from the past. There has been a lot of interesting discussion tonight about Brutalism or the Smithsons being an inspiration box for artists and architects now.

DH   Where do you get your ideas from?

AG   I had an interesting conversation at your opening in New York with Jim Jarmusch, and it was about what was important in our art was following your heart and keeping your eye on the prize. It's about making the shit; forget about what's happening outside of it, forget about money and all the rest. We said that a lot of our heroes never made any money – people like Erik Satie, whose music is very famous and is on commercials and all the rest of it. He is a guy who wore the same suit every day and played in small cafés in Paris to make money and did a few collaborations with people but never made loads of money. I said, 'Yes, and Mozart was buried in an unmarked pauper's grave at thirty-four'. He said to me, 'And do you know who the richest guy in Vienna was when Mozart was alive?' I said, 'No'. He said, 'Exactly!' Who gives a fuck? There are no monuments to that guy. I think that's an important thing for me. In a time of such affluence and focus on wealth and making money, ultimately when you are dead all that is left is what you did.

[Applause]

RK   There is an interesting phenomenon: before midnight, every speaker spoke about politics; after midnight not a single speaker spoke about politics.

[Laughter]

DH   It's not allowed. You turn into a pumpkin.

RK   What do you think is the connection? Can you say something about politics?

DH   Not after midnight! Jesus Christ, are you mad? I prefer what Ant was saying and I agree with that. There's that great quote: 'There are no pockets in a shroud'. I really like that as well. It's like we will all be remembered for the size and ornateness of our gravestones. I think it's death after midnight, isn't it, politics before?

RK   OK. Death.

DH   We love Tony Blair.

AG   Politics. I don't know.

RK   Religion?

DH   No, I don't think I'd like to talk about that either.

HUO   Politics: we are going to have Chantal Mouffe later on tomorrow morning. She wrote the book, *The Return of the Political*, where she says, 'Because it is indeed the political which is at stake here and the possibility of its elimination'. So the return of the political.

DH   I remember there's a great piece by Sylvia Plath called *Context* where she wrote about atom bombs and nuclear explosions going off in her time and she was saying that she can't feel anything from that. She wanted to make something that was political, to write a piece about living in a time when we can destroy ourselves, and she was saying that she couldn't. In the end the most political thing she could think of was the thoughts of a tired night surgeon or a baby forming itself finger by finger in the dark. I think that's the sort of angle I'd come from. Picasso did *Guernica* but I think it's got to be in a much worse crisis than we are at the moment to get artists to operate on a political level. I'm more interested in it on a much smaller level.

RK   Shall we end there?

HUO   I have a last question, which is the recurrent question about the unrealised projects. I ask you both if there are any yet-unrealised projects which have been too big to be realised or censored: your unbuilt roads.

DH   I once tried to do a sculpture, which was of two dead cows fucking, with hydraulics, called *Couple Fucking Dead Twice* but I never managed to do it because they were decaying in a box. Because of all the methane that gets produced when they are decaying, you can't have electronics to make the movement inside because it might explode. At the moment it's on hold. I'd still like to do it.

RK   Maybe because cows don't fuck.

DH   That's why I like it. It's just so stupid on every level. The idea of trying to move forward impossibly. There's no evolution there.

HUO   Ant, any unrealised projects?

AG   Since I did *The Cancer Chronicles* with Damien, I have got into writing orchestral music and I suppose modern, contemporary classical music, which is something I have no training in and I do it by trial and error. Because I have no training in it I go to a lot of classical concerts, the Proms and stuff like that, because I like to learn how the sounds are made. I haven't got time to go and learn it at school. One thing that struck me in my discovery of classical music is how kind of outdated it seems and how classist it is; there are no black people there, there are no people in trainers, and how there is this exciting music but it's all about Richard Strauss's *Alpine Symphony* or things like that. So I decided that I wanted to write a symphony called *Symphony for the Twenty-first Century Drug Addict* and write a piece of music that was actually about homeless people scoring crack and shooting into their groin and express that in a musical form. That is something that I want to do.

DH   That would be great.

HUO   Many thanks to Damien Hirst and Ant Genn. Thank you very much.

Applause, end of interview

5.15 am   **SHUMON BASAR** with **MARKUS MIESSEN**
and **ÅBÄKE** (Maki Suzuki and Kajsa Stahl)

Rem Koolhaas   We would like to introduce our next speakers, Shumon Basar and Markus Miessen. They have brought Kajsa Stahl and Maki Suzuki, of Åbäke, a collective of four graphic designers which includes Patrick Laceyand and Benjamin Reichen. They have just produced a book together, *Did Someone Say Participate?* For anyone knowing the writing of Shumon Basar, *Did Someone Say Participate?* is rife with ironies. Can you say something about that title?

Shumon Basar   There's been a lot of appropriation, I think, this evening and our title was a straight-out appropriation from an essay Slavoj Žižek wrote called, 'Did Someone Say Totalitarianism?' We simply replaced the word 'totalitarianism' with 'participate'. The sub-title of the book is just as important: *An Atlas of Spatial Practice*. That notion of spatial practice is really what the book is concerned with.

RK   Can you say how?

Markus Miessen   There's also an issue in terms of the participation because we don't necessarily mean participation in the sense of community-building, but rather our participation in alien fields of knowledge. So in a way from our background, which is architecture, the idea is that you venture out into different areas of knowledge.

Hans Ulrich Obrist   Is it about re-invention? The notion of participation was very authentic at the beginning with people like Yona Friedman or Giancarlo de Carlo and then became instrumentalised and, I would say also, very degraded. When I visited Giancarlo de Carlo four or five years ago in Milan and asked him about this kind of problem, he said, 'I agree with you. If you consider the era of the 1960s there were at the same time two things which were very important. One was the rebellion of the students and the other one was a new consciousness in the trade unions. During that time I had made two projects, one was for the housing complex in Terni and the other was the urban plan for the new centre of Rimini, both based on the idea of participation. After that moment a more bureaucratic period began when participation became something very

210

formalistic and stupid. The problem to me had changed. The question was how to make an architecture that could be intrinsically participative; and this becomes a question of language'. So, 'intrinsic participation': I was wondering, in view of this degraded aspect of participation, whether your book is about the reinvention of participation.

SB   If an authentic version of participation exists, ours is possibly a very inauthentic version. As Markus mentioned, there's suddenly a lot of participatory projects happening today, whether in art practice or architecture or political work. We're not really dealing with that. For us the notion of participation refers less to the idea of a public 'participating'. We are much more into the proposition that practitioners of different disciplinary backgrounds participate in alien fields of knowledge production. Something that might help in understanding this is a term that I have tried to coin, which is the 'Professional Amateur'. He or she ventures out and deals with the things he or she is not officially trained to do. That's something that all of us here find incredibly fundamental to our practices: it is somehow not entirely based on professional expertise. We are constantly putting ourselves in situations where we are quite ignorant.

MM   That's also one of the issues we try to address with the spatial practitioner because we are trying to get away from the idea of the architect being the one in charge of space. I think that would also be something interesting to ask you; for example, what do you think in terms of your role in a project like Dubai, how do you think you can intervene in a place like that as an architect?

RK   Maybe I should explain that after a total focus on China we have recently begun to work in the Middle East and, in order to increase our knowledge, engaged in it in a massive way so that we are now working in Kuwait, Bahrain, Doha, Dubai and Abu Dhabi, so that we really covered all things. As with the beginning of any architecture enterprise, it's partly based on interest and ignorance, and so what we are trying to do is to reverse this ignorance in a very quick and efficient way. I was talking, too, with Zaha Hadid; her whole explanation was very precise, that the Middle East, instead of perhaps being a zone of inevitable absurdity, could also be a zone where some serious work can be supported or imagined.

SB   Perhaps the reason that Markus asked the question is that when I was in Dubai in December 2005, there was a sense in which if you pointed at most buildings and asked people, 'Who designed that?' the name of the architect was not only absolutely irrelevant, it was usually unknown. What mattered was the name of the developer, of the construction company, and possibly the engineer. The architect's status ranked pretty low down. One of the construction companies told us that they only work with four architectural firms in the world, all of which are the anonymous acronyms few of us have heard of. Right now is very interesting. Dubai is inviting people like you Rem and Zaha Hadid. One wonders whether your position as signature architects will fit within that specific kind of hierarchy or whether you'll be able to transcend it.

RK   Well, I think there are a number of firms there that rule, not only Dubai, but in fact the whole world. Actually there was an interesting discussion with Peter Saville where he was asserting that the West is still leading in creativity. I think that is a really sad illusion or lack of awareness. If you are in Dubai what you really see is that we completely lost the initiative or authority or maybe abandoned it or deserved to lose it. So there is an enormous amount of new firms like Atkins, Halcro, that no-one, frankly, has heard of before, that are doing work that is eighty per cent identical to the work of star architects. So I think that the beauty of that situation is it will probably kill the whole notion of this kind of architecture. As far as I am concerned personally it has forced me into a serious investigation of our own work and tactical adjustment of our own work towards a more generic, boring style.

SB   It produces a kind of generic signature architecture. The architect is brought in as the set designer, as the one who adds ornament or dressing to the economically derived product. There is something quite liberating about the honesty of that.
     If one observes these mutations in terms of the power of the architect or indeed the impotence of the architect in the global context, I think what we have been trying to do with our book is look at the flip side. This is the empowerment of those controlling space who happen to not be architects. In a sense, we have been looking at the kind of increased capital value of constructive space, be it in notions of geography, politics, philosophy, or graphic design, etc. Whilst there's been a lot said about the growing impotence of the architect over the last ten years, one can at the same time see an empowering of architecture, but par-

adoxically not through architects – through everyone else. That's one of the things that the book tries to explore.

Perhaps I could hand over to Maki here because Åbäke could nominally be described as a group of graphic designers and yet there's a poverty of description at play – in the same way as describing Peter Saville as a graphic designer is inadequate terminology. The way the book is put together is an absolutely instrumental collaboration with Åbäke. The way in which as 'graphic designers' their emphasis is on content and the form of content has been quite fundamental to how the book reads. Maki, perhaps you'd like to say something about the nature of the practice of Åbäke.

Maki Suzuki   It's less, maybe, about us but just before we go too deeply into the book itself…

Kajsa Stahl   … we made a PDF of the book and what's just passing by on the screens around the pavilion are the end-papers. It's kind of a reaction to the book itself and what's inside it. We took all the different shapes of all the flags in the world and separated them, so you will find all the stars and all the eagles separated. We also made it into a little font dedicated to the book so you can, in a way, construct your own flag by typing different things.

MS   Maybe it's better if you have a look at the book itself. I'm not suggesting that you should buy it now…

MM   Why not?

[Laughter]

MS   I wanted to explain why we are dressed up. It's not necessarily for this occasion; tomorrow we are going to the wedding of a friend, who is an architect, and we were thinking of a present for him. Obviously the book was the cheapest option and we were also thinking how to make it a bit more interesting for him. I would really love it if everybody could sign it. Not everybody knows him, but you probably know someone who got happily married, so if you could think of that and add to this particular book – I'll put a pen with it – please do so.

HUO   Of course. As Robert Filliou said, 'Vive la mariage'!

A question to Markus and Shumon because there is clearly a change of format here: the interview has turned into a book launch. You proposed including Åbäke and that has a lot to do with the incredible promiscuity of collaborations in which you operate; there are other collaborations with your magazine. I was wondering if you could talk a little bit about how this collaborative practice works.

SB   What can we say about our open relationships with each other? I don't know. There's a commitment to promiscuity, I think, if I'm going to be coarse about it. Several of us graduated in the year 2000, which makes it very easy to mythologise, and Markus graduated a few years after that. Towards the late 1990s I suddenly became very aware of collectives, particularly in graphic design, funnily enough… Suddenly there was a resuscitation of 1960s collectives and groups, the Archizooms, Archigrams, Superstudios and so forth.

In the 1990s I worked for Zaha Hadid and Markus worked for Daniel Libeskind. If the 1990s were an attempt to emulate our masters and mistresses, by the time we got to the 2000s we completely changed our minds. There was a 'fuck it' attitude. Again, new efforts were made to come up with something alternative to the notion of an individual star character and that somehow has ended up with us being in a series of incredibly free-form, promiscuous relationships. Promiscuous but probably within quite tight circles. We [pointing to Maki and Kajsa] are three of seven who produce a magazine called *Sexymachinery*, which is a kind of art publication collective, and we [pointing to Markus] are also part of a new PhD programme that Eyal Weizman is directing. If I could swerve the topic back to London – because I am anticipating your London question, Hans Ulrich…– I'm quite openly sentimental about attributing part of this authorship to London in the sense in which we are all self-exiles here and that state of self-exile means that you often get lonely. This loneliness can be satiated by meeting each other in productive ways.

MM   I also think that there is an issue in London about optimism. There are a lot of other places where that optimism is not quite so radical and I think that really helps for this kind of collaboration.

HUO   Maybe it's interesting to hear from Åbäke about London because in an interview you gave you said you chose London by default.

MS   We met at the Royal College of Art; the course was an MA and most of the people came from somewhere else; we already decided at college to work together. Kajsa is from Sweden, Patrick is from Wales and Benjamin is French; so am I. It is by default because we didn't know where to go back to and it would have been completely undemocratic to choose one of our home countries, so we just stayed and we are very happy to have done so. But then as a consequence, since we were working from here, we had to be democratic again. That's why our name is Swedish and our email address is French.

MM   Where does the Welsh come in?

MS   He's over there.

SB   Patrick is Welsh and needs to be represented somehow.

MS   But he doesn't speak Welsh.

SB   That's true.

MS   The thing is that the nature of graphic design is also something we've been very anxious about and we had the preconception that maybe we would be at the end of this shitty stick where we get given a content which we can like or not, but then we have to design it. Obviously it's very difficult for us to polish a turd.

So one way to make sure that this doesn't happen, or help this to not happen, is to be a bit more pro-active in terms of content. So that's why co-editing this magazine with architects or textile designers is vital, but also we started a record label because we were very anxious to design a record of musicians that we wouldn't really like so much.

RK   For one moment I want to abandon all pretension that you are a collective and really focus on you, Shumon, as a writer of amazing fluidity and versatility, as much at home in irony, gossip, seriousness and earnestness, with a very wide repertoire. How did that happen?
[Laughter]

SB   Thank you. I'm going to be speechless now! If it 'happened' I am just finding out now, Rem…

RK   I think that part of the incentive is what used to inspire writing in general, the obligation to produce to earn money.

SB   *[Laughs]* Probably, as with everyone, it goes back to one's parents, but in an inverted way. Being second-generation Bangladeshi with a doctor father, I knew that there were three legitimate professions that you were entitled to grow into: medicine, law and accountancy. When I mooted to my mother that I might do English Literature, she said, 'Well, I don't think so. What sort of job are you going to get with that?' I tried again with Fine Art. She said, 'What? You're going to be an artist?' and laughed me down. Then I said, sheepishly, 'Architecture?' The reply was: 'OK. Architecture's fine'. I think architecture is fine because you can be mediocre in architecture and still make a living, whereas if you're mediocre as an artist or writer, there is a system breakdown. Writing became an unrequited, secret love, done in the spaces where it was permitted, or in invented occasions. My time at Cambridge – with my mentor of sorts, Peter Carl – was very bookish. I just read and read and had the opportunity to discuss everything I was reading. This was phenomenally exciting. It formed a kind of intellectual foundation for everything subsequently. By the late 1990s, writing in the so-called progressive architecture world had got incredibly onanistic and completely devoid of any sort of relation to the world we lived in. Everyone was reciting the same two pages from Gilles Deleuze, never having read all the other 328 pages or whatever. I contributed to this turgid morass myself – but then discovered thinkers such as Slavoj Žižek and Dave Hickey who were able to deal with heavy theoretical issues but through the textures of pop culture. Writing for magazines taught me how to be terse – I respect economy of expression greatly. When we began *Sexymachinery* our mission statement was that there is Mies van der Rohe in David Hasselhof – and vice versa. These are no longer 'low' and 'high' registers in the Adorno sense. We should be well beyond that. The morality has to take place elsewhere, not at the scene of the references, but in the seriousness of the question asked. But being serious doesn't mean being dull. I insist on entertaining, somehow. Jokes are subversive for a reason. They do it by being funny. And this is what I try to approach in my writing.

HUO   That may be a nice conclusion.

SB   Could we ask you a question?

RK   Yes.

MM   Hans Ulrich, you said the Marathon is going to be fantastic. It's going to be like Woodstock. Another day it was going to be like Deleuze's *Mille plateaux*, which is very interesting. Somewhere between 1968, 1972, happenings and Woodstock. What is the nature of this revisionism? In terms of your reinvention is this romantic nostalgia? What is the nature of it because it is too obvious, it's too in our face to be discarded as anything other than that. Could you please say something about that?

HUO   We have tried to address in numerous of the conversations the idea of a toolbox rather than nostalgia. I think it's always about repetition and difference, so I don't think it is nostalgia. I don't think I can answer the first question about the pavilion because I actually don't think that the pavilion would have been built this way in 1968. Rem, what do you think?

RK   *[Shrugs]*

MM   Maybe in terms of the content there is also an issue because you are talking about taking a slice of London at a particular time and Damien, for example, was really nostalgic about the 1990s. How do you think that fits into the content of this Marathon?

RK   I think that as a slice it is working very well. I believe that is also totally different to Woodstock. I think Woodstock was not a surgical effort but more a kind of gloating or inarticulate celebration and if anything, this is an evening that is drowning in articulation. *[Laughs]* So that's a big difference.

HUO   It's just thinking about how one can invent different rules of the game. My main activity is organising exhibitions and the medium of exhibition throughout the twentieth century has been subject to all kinds of different rules of the game. Many, many things have been tried out in terms of gallery gestures, in terms of display features. We are going to have Richard Hamilton later, one of the great pioneers of invention of new display features, But new ways have not really been tried to the same extent in discursive events like symposiums or conferences. They still usually follow the same round table format, they usually happen in the evening from seven till nine or six to eight or whatever. Maybe there is a question and answer session afterwards followed by a dinner. That's true all over the world. Very simply, we think this is an extraordinary opportunity to think about different formats. I realised this for the first time when I started to do conferences; we cancelled a conference but maintained it anyhow, so everything took place except the conference and it became a kind of extended coffee break. All the speakers were there, slightly confused because the conference was not happening, but a lot of things were actually started. Ever since I have actually thought we should experiment more and more with this format, and in this sense it has only just begun.

MM   I really didn't mean it in any way disparagingly.

HUO   No, it's a very good question. I have a question for you. We cannot leave for the break before asking you the only recurring question in this Marathon, which is about your unrealised projects. What are the unrealised projects of Shumon, Markus and Åbäke?

MM   You should ask that question in thirty years but maybe we could turn it around. What is your unrealised project, Rem?

RK   No comment.

[Laughter] Too numerous to mention.

SB   Perhaps I could answer in a very glib way: to have *many* unrealised projects. Visiting the *Future City* show [at the Barbican] makes you understand the profound importance of projects that are put forward that never happen. In a sense they are more often the ones that actually really count in the long run. Many more unrealised projects!

HUO   Thank you very much.

Applause, end of interview

Iain Sinclair
Paul Elliman
Gilbert & George
Adam Caruso
Ryan Gander

| Hans Ulrich Obrist
Iain Sinclair | Good morning, everybody! We are very happy to welcome Iain Sinclair. Thank you. |

Hans Ulrich Obrist
Iain Sinclair

Good morning, everybody! We are very happy to welcome Iain Sinclair. Thank you.

Rem Koolhaas

Hi! Basically you are both lucky and unlucky in the sense that you are beginning the second half of this Marathon and that means that we have been able to discover certain patterns. I would say one pattern is that from 6.00 to 12.00 we talked about politics, from 12.00 to 6.00 we talked about death; inadvertently it was a thread that went through all the presentations. And so you can set the tone and decide what we talk about between 6.00 and noon.

IS

OK. Well, I think the thing about London is it has always been a Manichean city; it's a city of contraries, darkness and light, from its founding. Therefore, if you are going to talk about politics and death, you are talking about the same thing. I think we talk about politics and poetry – and those are the two contraries that fight for the soul of this city. This space, this kind of strange high junk space – because I think both of you move across the global landscape so fast you probably feel that everywhere is like an airport or a hotel room – this in a sense is a combination of that and of the Giant's Causeway. So it's a very interesting place to find yourself early on a Saturday morning in the city.

RK

A second pattern that we have discovered is that at least one out of four people talked about the relationship between their work and Situationist theory. You yourself have indicated that, perhaps inadvertently, you are responsible for a neo-Situationism or a Situationist brand, so there is clearly an awareness of that. I said earlier the great virtue of Situationism has been for me that it was really a movement that was the direct result of, and strong contrast to, the incredible formality of Paris. In a certain way, as someone who has lived here for a very long time, I have never been able to discover what the formality of London is and therefore I am really questioning the effect of a *dérive* on a city as chaotic and shapeless as London. Can you talk about these two issues?

221

IS   Yes. I grew up in the 1960s, coming to London first in the 1960s, and I was aware of Situationism as something intriguing but alien and very pertinent to Paris, as you say, and this idea that you could maybe superimpose a map of Paris over Venice, whatever. This is the kind of thing that is now happening to London. With the Olympic schemes, these grand schemes that are being imposed on the Lower Lea Valley in East London, it is a form of junk Situationism. I think what I have done with Situationism is to cannibalise it, and to incorporate what you speak of as the chaos of London, so that more poetic and mystic ideas about key lines and lines of energy and force can be adapted to the French concept to create something else which has had a vogue as psycho-geography, although I think this is the wrong term. It's more like *psychotic* geography; it's a new sense of engagement with London and with the city. I think that's been an exciting thing to be a part of.

RK   Any book that mentions both Mussolini and Andrew Parker-Bowles in one arc is obviously a very impressive combination of different registers. We have also heard a certain repetition about what the qualities of London were; we have heard the word village many times; we have heard shapelessness, we have heard the amazing ability of many cultures to live together in London many times. One of the great virtues of Situationism was to really make us see things in a new way or to create a vast difference in terms of how we understood something. I think *London Orbital* [2002] is a wonderful book but what would you say it identifies as new, or is it a further inventory of what is wonderful, chaotic and typical about London?

IS   I think what it does is try and make an elegy out of entropy; it's a sense of a city at the centre losing its dignity and losing its human strengths in the Thatcherite period, to bring in politics. There was this critical moment in 1986 when the GLC, which was the civic identity of London, was abolished at the same time as the markets were de-regulated, at the same time as this posthumous motorway, the M25, which if it had been built in 1949 or something may have been visionary and pertinent and instead of this is a kind of weird leftover of nineteenth-century science fiction. So setting out on this road is actually a way of journeying into the past rather than into the future. The relevant aspects of the road lead you into Bram Stoker's London at the east side in Purfleet, where he set Dracula's Abbey, and sets up metaphors of vampirism, distribution, storage, all of these great themes – and H. G. Wells' *War of the Worlds* in the Surrey commuter belt, sets up all the metaphors of invasion and destruction and technology. I think that's the interesting thing about exploring the edges of cities. We have a great writer who has spent most of his career doing that in J. G. Ballard, who sat outside the centre of London at Shepperton and has always said to me that the historic London is boring; he is only interested in the London of retail parks and marinas and, indeed, this very kind of excitingly disposable architecture.

HUO   In an interview he told us that his favourite building in London is the Hilton at Heathrow.

IS   *[Laughs]* For him the Hilton at Heathrow is the Hilton anywhere; it's a kind of nowhere. He says that the road into a city from the airport is the same in every single country.

HUO   Tim Newburn talked a lot about surveillance earlier tonight. That is something J. G. Ballard also told us; he talked about the spy camera as an Orwellian nightmare disguised as a public service. I was wondering if you could comment on that.

IS   Yes. As anybody who spends a huge amount of time walking and navigating the city must realise: what you are doing is signing on to be in the movie; you are constantly filmed. On the other hand, you are not allowed to record the cameras recording you. I have been in endless stand-offs where I have simply been photographing camera poles and security people emerge. The question they always ask is, 'Don't you know there's a war on?' This might be out in Tilbury in a wasteland of nothingness, which I actually walked through with a Dutch artist who makes all her work about recording security personnel. You think this is the commonplace army of Europe because the people who have to guard the gates of these things are now the bottom of the food chain. They are often illegal immigrants or people who have to take on this kind of job and they are policing industrial spaces and yet I am being filmed looking at these same industrial spaces, so there must be, somewhere, a huge image bank of anonymous figures gawping at razor fences and perimeter fences.

RK   Are you writing about that?

IS   I have written about that a little bit in various of my books. Currently I'm writing about Hackney because Hackney has all the things that I think are likely to be lost in terms of a proper human city. I think its geography has been totally remade, in that the Docklands zone is creeping along the canals, the old industrial water systems, and turning the warehouses into apartment blocks for city workers, and is meeting the city itself, the old City of London, coming north into Hackney, to create a new area of anonymity; people who sleep there do not necessarily live there. There is a new category of person who has a house but doesn't live in that house, they don't inhabit the geography. Once we lose our grip on the old geography of the city, the city loses its identity and I think is swallowed up in grand schemes and future projects. The era of the Millennium Dome.

HUO   That also leads us to a recurrent question: Eric Hobsbawm said that it is important that we somehow protest against the idea of forgetting, so I was wondering what role memory plays for you in the research about the city.

IS   Memory is the most important thing for me. I think we are living in a city of memory and the privilege of navigating this city at 4.30 this morning, to come across here, meant moving through a whole genealogy of memories. I passed through Farringdon Road; this morning it was full of clubbers coming out and there was a marvellous vignette of two people dancing, learning a South American dance on the pavement, very dignified. This was the spot where I remembered there had once been the book stalls. Farringdon Road was once a book market, which was itself the greatest reservoir of memory in London because it swallowed up all the great libraries and disgorged them onto the street. In fact Saturday morning is the time you would have fallen on these books and discovered the memory of a lost city Everywhere you move in London is a chapter of memory, is a narrative of memory; it's all the other times we've been here and I think we are dealing with these huge layers and accretions and it's quite difficult to insert objects or buildings into this without respecting these memories.

RK   Without destroying them.

IS   Or destroying them, yes.

HUO In relation to your walks I have a quote from *Lights Out for the Territory* [1997] where you said, 'Walking is the best way to explore and exploit the city; the changes, shifts, breaks in the cloud helmet, movements of light on water. Drifting purposefully is the recommended mode, tramping asphalted earth in alert reverie allowing the fiction of an underlying pattern to reveal itself.' I wanted you to talk a little bit more about walking, because we haven't really talked a lot about *flânerie* in the Marathon so far. I was wondering if there can be a non-nostalgic approach to walking.

IS Yes.

HUO The Swiss scholar Lucius Burckhardt founded a quite eccentric science in Germany called strollology; it was the science of having a walk. I was wondering what your strollology would be.

IS I think walking and the city are totally dependent on each other and walking is the only mode to really operate within the city. I think the notion of the Situationist walk is too conceptual for me and too conceptual for London. I thought what we needed to do was more a kind of stalking than walking; you set off with a notion that you want to explore but you are open to all the changes and references of the city. I think that the great writers of London have been walkers; I think of De Quincey setting up a form of early psycho-geography or Situationism, partly because of his obsessive need to find sources of drugs. Everybody has a different methodology of exploring the city according to their own obsessions. Some people would only see this junk connection, some people would see relationships that they want to pursue; whatever it is, there is a motive that draws them across the city and writing becomes a form of reading the city. I think with architects and planners, what I'm disturbed at now is that instead of using a walk which gives you this panoramic, cinemascope version of everything, it's the helicopter view that's becoming dominant. You see endless images of people in yellow hard hats and pin-stripped suits being helicoptered over a piece of landscape and if they find something that's blank like Thames Gateway, which is on the flood plain, they will say, 'This is what we must exploit'. If there's anything left. While I think if you walk it, if you set out to walk from Aldgate in the city down to Southend through the A13, you discover all the unknowns of the city and you discover where the city gives up its identity. So walking is really the only way to do it.

RK   I want to quote Baudelaire to you, who perhaps was the most programmatic modernist. He famously said that it was necessary to be resolutely modern and was completely willing to face the beast of modernity as an inevitable part of urbanisation. This has always been, I think, a paradoxical situation of the English mentality to be in a way so nostalgic that they have never been able to genuinely embrace the city. So if you don't really embrace the city, what are you nostalgic about?

IS   I think you do have to embrace the city; whatever the unpleasant elements that come into the city as part of modernity, they have to be embraced as well as embracing the past. I don't think you can respect what emerges unless you live in that past and understand it. For example, there are buildings I might not like, as the famous Gherkin, because of its hubris, because it inserts itself everywhere; everywhere you look, this dildo-like object is confronting you. Though I don't like it, I do feel that London will swallow up and absorb whatever is put into it. Equally, as a writer or thinker about the city, you have got to be prepared to absorb whatever manifestations of modernism appear, whether you like them or don't like them. London will take it on. In the same way through this event, all the multiple voices that are here actually in the end break down into a single voice. It just becomes an organic thing of bits and pieces layered on top of each other and doubt is cleared away. A particular spot in the park now has a small crystal of memory and argument and discussion and debate and slightly misunderstood questions moving backwards and forwards, and slightly weary answers, but it makes a nice junk-filled pot that cooks up and gives you something that is equivalent to the city of London.

HUO   That makes me think of Peter Ackroyd and his biography of London. In the preface to this book he writes about the city as a body, quoting Daniel Defoe, for whom London was 'a great body which circulates all, exports all, and at last pays for all'. But Ackroyd shows that this idea of a portrait or even a biography of a city is obviously an infinite kind of project, an ongoing wandering and wondering. In terms of this infinite process of mapping such a complex body as London, what are the yet unrealised parts of your mapping?

IS   I think Peter Ackroyd's sense of London, rich as it is, is based around the conservative notion that there are eternal qualities that cyclically appear, time after time. Essentially it never changes; there is no way of evolving into any other form. My own sense is to try and go backwards and forwards. As I said, I have lived in the same part of Hackney, by accident really, since 1968, and just being on the same patch of ground has provided me with a lot of things I want to go back to, so my current project is to try and recover elements of my own memory and to challenge them, but also to layer on top of this all the forces I see aggressively coming in. For example, yesterday I was taken round this amazing area called Hackney Wick, which is a sort of island abandoned between motorway systems and canals which will be largely wiped out by the Olympic Zone when it comes. The guy taking me around was a Sicilian photographer and he is determined that whatever city he goes to, and he has spent time in Rio and various African cities, the first thing he wants to do is to define where the edge is and to be in that edge as a point of access and to listen to whatever is going on there. What he showed me out of his window was that down beneath him were groups of Russians who had dug in, there were white street gangs, there was a Jamaican club, there were all kinds of weird multi-cultural things that the grand project wants to support in theory but is actually going to destroy. There was also a garden allotment of eighty people of all nationalities digging and planting and producing extraordinary things, exactly the kind of ecological benefits that the city says it wants to create but which are already there and which will be destroyed. So I think you are living in two places: a virtual city, which is the computer-generated city the planners and politicians want to impose, and this dirty, grungy, chaotic mess which is actually there. I think I would like to move into an argument between the two things.

HUO   Many thanks Iain Sinclair.

Applause, end of interview

Rem Koolhaas	Our next speaker is Paul Elliman. This evening or this morning – I've lost the sense of time a little bit – I suggested to your colleague, Peter Saville, that graphic design is the most important profession in the world today and I would like to suggest the same to you. While he totally agreed with me and didn't seem too unhappy about it, I noticed when I first met you that you emanate an anxiety about the issue.
Paul Elliman	*[Laughs]* An anxiety about everything! Getting up on time for this event. I gather he has his own fairly fraught relationship with the profession of graphic design anyway, for various reasons, and I have similarly fraught relations with aspects of the same industry, but for different reasons. As a graphic designer Peter Saville lacks nothing in professionalism, let's be clear on that. I, on the other hand, probably lack quite a few things. In the past I said something about whatever it was that I lacked in professionalism I tried to make up for in ambivalence to being a professional. But I also agree with what you are saying. One of my interests as an artist is in graphic design's power as a cultural form, perhaps, as you put it, the most powerful. Money is often described as the bloodstream of the world but this could just as easily be said of graphic design. The entire spectacle as a product of all the techniques of graphic design. I think that's what you're touching on in terms of its power or importance. That's what interests me. Though it shouldn't require having to have a career as a graphic designer to come to that understanding. Or to that anxiety.
RK	I love the word ambivalence because it's a luxury that very few in this decade – which Hans doesn't stop repeating still doesn't have a name – can afford. How can you afford it and what is your economy that allow you to afford it?
PE	I'd like to say that I've perfected a technique for counterfeiting money but unfortunately that isn't the case! I don't know. You find your way to afford it. Or include it. I've already more or less said I don't have faith in any particular professional pursuit. I think it's a case of diversifying your practice in ways that allow you to survive, allow your ideas to survive, exploring those things you are interested in through other forms

I make a living from my writing as much as from anything else. But then the world that I'm writing about tends to be the same world that I'm making design about – for want of a better way of putting it, or since I'm usually defined as a designer. Anyway, just as design feeds into so many things, these things feed back and disrupt our lives as people, why shouldn't they disrupt our practice as designers? Sometimes even to the point of ambivalence. But I would add that I'm not at all ambivalent about the power of the profession of graphic design. I think it's obvious.

Hans Ulrich Obrist I was also curious to find out about your form of resisting the virtual because your work very often uses test patterns or typefaces or the human voice, all kinds of moments of resistance to the purely virtual. I think that, in an interesting way, relates to our attempt here to map the city. Scott Lash talked earlier about the different senses of mapping the city – taste, hearing, balance, smell, seeing, touching. One of the most interesting things we found here in our research for the London Marathon was your interview with the voice of the London Underground. To make a long question short, I wanted to ask you to tell us the story about this London Underground voice and then in more general terms about these different senses and eventual resistance to the virtual.

PE I have room for the virtual in terms of perceiving life in any dialectical sense. I have room for the virtual in my awareness of how things are manifest through a materialism, through the body, through people or through things. You find your own balance for that I suppose. I'm interested in the ways that our language is produced and one of the forms in which it is produced and through which it produces us is typography. Typography plays out across every aspect of modernity: mass production and standardisation are things that can even be shown to have begun with the production of typography for example. But another way in which language is produced is of course through the voice. Produced and reproduced. I'm interested in the use of voices in public space. Voices transmitted or implemented as signs I mean. Just like typography. Derrida discussed in great length a category of language that connects writing and speaking. The recorded voices that we hear on public transport or in public spaces are just one of the many common examples of that everywhere around us today. Voices having all the inscriptive fixity of text becoming something we take for granted. Never mind the gap. The voice of the London Underground, or the voice used on at least three of the lines anyway, belongs to Emma Clarke. I thought it would be interesting to have a conversation with her. These voices are always a kind of monologue that you're not supposed to have dialogue with but of course it's always an actual person who has provided that voice. I've been trying to communicate back to these voices. Trying to apprehend them in terms of what they are as a cultural or social form, a professional discipline, a sonic and material thing in the world, and to apprehend them simply in terms of the person who is providing the voice in the first place. Of course I am interested in the idea of synthesising a voice or in language-modelling a fully electronic voice. In fact there exists a software that can enable a voice to be reconstructed from the voice patterns of almost any existing recording of someone speaking. Anyone's voice could be recreated to speak again. But I'm particularly interested in the announcements that are human voices. And for use in public space, most voices are recorded and probably will be for a long time to come. I've got a recording here in fact. It is very short. Could I play it?

HUO   It will be great if we can hear it.

PE   This is a recording I've just made in Madrid. I'm doing a piece of work for a show in a gallery in Madrid in January, at the time of ARCO, and I was quite curious about the two voices of the Madrid subway, which are male and female. New York also has male and female voices on the newer trains. You're probably familiar with the guy who says, 'Stand clear of the *ker-losing* doors, please!'. A dramatic male voice providing those paternal words of advice, along with a female voice offering the more functional directions or the locational information: 'The next stop is Spring Street' or 'Change here for the A and the E', etc. But these two voices are more separate in fact. The way that it works in Madrid is through a much more tightly choreographed vocal syntax in which the female completes the male voice's sentences. The man's voice will begin, 'The approaching station is...', and the woman's voice completes the sentence by naming the station. Retiro. Or Colombia. Then he will say, 'Change here for...' and she will add, 'Linea una'. I managed to get hold of the two voices, a man called Javier Dotu and a woman named Maria Jesus Alvarez. Real people, you can touch them (sometimes!), you can make them laugh, they're ticklish. It turns out that Maria Jesus is a voice from Spanish radio and Javier is a voice from Spanish cinema.

230

He's what I think they call a *doblero* – it turns out he's the voice, for Spanish cinema-goers, of Al Pacino, which I thought was a bit of a bonus. So I have them here describing how to get from the gallery in the middle of downtown Madrid, via all the various modes of public transport, to my office – which isn't so far from where Iain lives in Hackney – in Bethnal Green. It starts off with the actual audio jingle and then goes into those fabulous voices.

[Audio clip]

So this is the point where they are actually leaving Madrid... Now we are at the airport. And now arriving in London. (Which of course they're not supposed to be able to do.)

[After reference to Liverpool Street] This is where it gets a little bit frightening for me because they are getting closer and closer.

That's my street. And number 84.

Very scary!

Where were we? *[Laughs]*

RK   Scary, even for us.

PE   The virtual.

RK   One observation. We all benefit and suffer from globalisation; in many of our cases it has extended the territories where we can work and even though I think graphic design is the most important and most powerful force right now in the world, there is one almost comical limitation which is that you are limited to Western script and an enormous part of the world does not use it. Western script is probably shrinking in terms of its overall coverage.

PE   How do you mean?

RK   There is more and more Chinese script, presumably more and more Japanese, Korean, Indian, Arabic, Russian, etc. There is a very classical limitation to the Western.

PE   Except in something like coding languages, for example, which are pretty much Western.

RK   Are you interested in, or do you work in, other scripts?

PE   I haven't. Maybe through not having enough experience of them. I've worked briefly in Seoul and Tokyo, I've written about Maori oral culture, but I haven't worked directly with non-Western scripts. Though I have, because I've ended up with this vast archive of found typograph-ical letters, been thinking about it for some time. How to find similar or equivalent characters in a Chinese script, for example. At one point I was making a font by loading the found characters into a programme that allows several versions of each letter. You could have five different e's, for example, and never have to repeat any one of them in a single word. And in fact this is a programme that was developed for Arabic writing, where some of the characters acquire a different shape when they sit alongside certain other letters. The font programme (Open Type) was developed so that the electronic writing format could accommodate those kinds of changes or culturally specific conditions. It could be as easy to implement via the keyboard as it is when writing with a pen or by hand. But no, working directly with non-Western characters isn't something that I've done. I'm not sure how or even if I would deal with that without working closely with somebody who was of that language or knew it intimately. Western typography is the Roman alphabet, im-perial by name and by nature.

HUO   I have a very last question I wanted to ask you about the unbuilt roads of Paul Elliman. Could you tell us about some or one of your unrealised projects, utopias, or projects which have been too big or too small to be realised or forgotten projects?

PE   This is a famous question of yours. One of them is still an answer I gave you the first time you asked me this, which was that I had written to the BBC about fifteen years ago to ask them if I could select my own readers for the Shipping Forecast, the famous UK sea-areas weather re-port produced by the Meteorological Office and broadcast four times a day on Radio 4. There is something contentious in the proposal when you think about the kinds of voices other than trained BBC voices that could instead be allowed to read that forecast. But I was really just think-ing of using seven of my friends whose voices I was very familiar with, not special voices in any kind of professional way but for me just ordi-nary voices, special only in the most personal sense. This was a project that was probably completely ignored by anyone at the BBC. I mean I'm unknown anyway. And as it happens, the Met Office is an executive agency of the Ministry of Defence. Though of course I like that aspect of it. But I realise it also means that they are never going to allow just anybody to become involved with it at this level. The other thing though is that it wasn't something that I wanted to realise as an art work so much, but as something produced in real time and space through those very real cultural and institutional forms: radio, weather tracking technology, environment, language and the human voice.

HUO   Many thanks Paul Elliman.

Applause, end of interview

Hans Ulrich Obrist	It is a great pleasure to welcome our next guests, Gilbert and George. Welcome Gilbert and George.

[Applause]

Preparing the interview for this morning I have been re-reading this publication about your work which came out in France, which has all to do with the city. It puts E1 in twenty words: 'From art for all to Brick Lane to city to Cockney to dirty to docks to fiction to history to Gothic to Green to immigration to Jack the Ripper to maps to marginality to neighbourhood to religion to street writing to strikes to textile to violence'. So I wanted to start with asking you about the city and the role the city plays within your work.

Gilbert　I would that say we really are city boys. We only like big cities. If we are half an hour outside a city we are lost; we don't like it, especially because George always believes that once you are in the greens you become a different kind of person, you don't understand people any more.

George　We always believe that an excessive love of nature leads to totalitarianism.

[Laughter]

And we can prove the dangers of nature because we once went to visit our late friend Daniel Farson in a very beautiful village in north Devon and we stayed in a neighbouring hotel. We got up early in the morning because we wanted to see the estuary with the beautiful river birds and the whole village was very quiet and the sun was just coming out. We came up the village high street and there was the lovely parish church with the bees buzzing around the graves. Outside of the churchyard was a very beautiful young couple with a small baby in a pram. And it looked so sweet, so perfect, such a wonderful part of the world, completely ideal and exquisite. We turned and said, 'Good morning', and the young man turned and said, 'Fuck off you weird-looking twats'.

[Laughter]

Rem Koolhaas　Nevertheless, I can remember as one of your most beautiful works a kind of hand-drawn series of yourselves in the middle of nature with extremely lyrical proclamations. Was that an earlier life?

Gil	Ah! That was before we discovered alcohol! Can you imagine?
	[Laughter]
Geo	Probably as baby artists we had a problem to face the city and other people and we used nature – which wasn't really nature, it was always London parks or Kew Gardens was the farthest. And then I think in the mid-1970s we suddenly realised that the chaos of that nature was much better than what was reality around us, the streets, the people.
Gil	That's why to understand London we always take a – what do you call? – a bus to the end of the line and walk back towards Fournier Street, and that is extraordinary.
Geo	The 133 is one of our favourites. That goes all the way to... we get off at Streatham but it goes even further – and we have lovely coffees in Arab cafés there, where they are extremely friendly.
Gil	And sometimes we used to make a – what do you call? – a list of streets from, let's say, Liverpool to Crystal Palace. It was an extraordinary walk.
Geo	Just on one postcard that tells you when to turn left; just like those machines they now have in cabs. It was exactly like that, just on one postcard. So we walked from Fournier Street to Annerly to have lunch with someone. It took all morning and we just had this one small postcard.
Gil	The city is just extraordinary, especially in the east of London; walking up Kingsland Road or Commercial Street, the urban streets of London are just incredible.
RK	And they are still incredible because we have heard a lot of nostalgic descriptions of this disappearing from London.
Gil	We don't care about that. Last night we took a bus back at ten o'clock; in front of us it was like Falaraki. Have you heard of Falaraki? Unbelievable! Misbehaviour in a big way. Just thousands of people outside in the open at ten o'clock. Extraordinary!
Geo	There are dozens and dozens of people literally sitting in the gutter in our street. They are all very middle-class people. They are not Cockneys, they are not rough, they are not aggressive, they are all people who are training to be doctors – or architects!
	[Laughter]
	And one of the clubs at the end of the street is exclusively for drugs and it's totally accepted; no police interfere. People just go there for drugs;

it is extraordinarily modern in that way. We used to describe London in the 1970s as the city that was the most stressful and we rather liked that because we were very stressed. We said you just have to look at the thousands of people emerging from Liverpool Street Underground in the morning: they are all frowning and worrying and they are all desperate that they have to go and do this terrible office job. This is no longer true. They are all coming out of the Underground now with their friends, full of music. You can't tell the difference between the builder and the young city man going off to the gym before work. It is all much more democratic and much more friendly and very safe.

Gil   But the rucksacks. We are quite against the rucksacks because in cafés, wherever you go in, they have these enormous rucksacks and when they turn they smack you in the face.

[Laughter]

RK   I agree. Rucksacks kind of make mankind twice as voluminous.

Geo   It's dangerous on the escalators as well. You get on just behind someone and one third of the way up the escalator they push you over backwards.

HUO   There has been a series of protests throughout this long night. We started with a protest against forgetting from Eric Hobsbawm, now we have the protest against the rucksack. There has been a lot of discussion about the impossibility of making a synthetic image of something as complex as London is. One of the things I wanted to ask you was in terms of your mapping of the city: it has very much to do with Fournier Street and the streets around. You very early found the whole world within these streets.

Gil   We always said that Liverpool Street is Jerusalem for us. The best way to see the City of London is to go up to Crouch End and look down; it is a golden city, it is just extraordinary. Don't you think George?

Geo   You can see all the way through to Docklands and everything. Every major building stands out from there. Extraordinary.

Gil   Like Alice in Wonderland. It's just fantastic. We do believe that at the moment the East End of London is the centre, in some way, of the world. If you understand the East End you understand the world. I really believe that because everybody is there. Everybody. There are thousands of different languages being spoken and a thousand different people. George is the only English person there.

[Laughter]

RK   It is a really very striking difference; the two of you are optimistic in a very robust way. Has your single, combined identity affected this, making it easier to be optimistic or to resist anxiety?

Geo   I'm sure that's true, yes. To be two removes self-doubt. Normally the artist has to look at the empty canvas and think, 'What am I going to do? What am I going to do next? Should I put another cow in the field? Should I lower the sunset?' And no answer comes back. When there are two of you there is always someone to say, 'Oh, put another cow in, go on'.

[Laughter]

We used to describe London to people who had never believed it in the 1970s or the 1980s. We used to say if a spaceship was coming down on Planet Earth and telephoned and said, 'We've just got five minutes to film Planet Earth to take a report back to our people. Where should we do it?' we would say, 'Brick Lane, Liverpool Street'. That's typical Planet Earth. If you go to most places in the world they won't be typical Planet Earth, they will be typical 1930s, typical 1940s, but London is much more actual. Even the look, the gaze of people, the eye contact, is totally different from other parts of the world, we believe.

RK   Is the fact that you are working together, and have been working together for such a long time, also the secret of the consistency of your work? And also the secret of its longevity and its freshness?

Gil   I think it's driven in madness. It has to be combined: totally organised and totally disorganised, that's it. But in the end we don't care. We have to liberate ourselves totally. George?

Geo   Normally it's mixed gender couples who say, 'What is your secret?' And we say, 'It's a secret'.

[Laughter]

We always think when we are being asked about London that the important thing about London is that it's always London in the world. If you ask about most cities it's about that city there. And that's not true of London. We always remember the first visit by an Italian art dealer to us in Fournier Street and he came on an aeroplane and then went into the Underground, so he emerged for the first time in London at Liverpool Street; we were there to greet him. He looked around himself; it was his first visit to London and was obviously familiar with the clichés from the movies and he looked around very mystified and said, 'Where is the famous London fog?' *[Laughs]*

RK   Obviously you have a very particular economy of your overall effort and I think part of your secret, although I don't want to understand your secrets necessarily or expose your secrets, is repetition. A large part of your life, I can testify as a witness, is spent in very repetitive, almost ritualistic, moments that seem to be identical every day.

Geo More evolution than repetition, I would say, wouldn't you Gilbert?

Gil Yes, we are like monks, yes. Every day George gets up at five thirty, five o'clock to read dirty books and we always have breakfast at half past six. We start working at half past seven. We stop at exactly five o'clock and we start walking at seven o'clock to our restaurant. Eight o'clock we arrive at the restaurant, even when George sometimes takes a different route. At ten o'clock we leave and take the bus number 67 and at ten thirty we are at Fournier Street. And that's it. Every single day the same, except when we have to go out and entertain people.

Geo Or like this morning.

HUO Obviously the morning hour has to do with breakfast but it also has to do with newspapers. One of the things we discussed a lot in our previous conversations about London was your amazing archive of different newspapers.

Geo Our favourite recent story is about our favourite newspaper seller at Liverpool Street, whom we've known for forty years. The only thing we've ever said to him is, 'Good Morning', bought a newspaper, and he says, 'Good morning Guv'. And that was it for forty years until one morning recently when he said, 'Here Guv, have you heard this one?' And he said, 'My sister Lily is a whore down Piccadilly. My mother is another down the Strand. My father sells his asshole down the Elephant and Castle. We're the finest fucking family in the land'. We think that's an amazing thing to hear from someone you've only ever been polite to. [Laughter]
I said, 'Would you write it down for me?' He said, 'It's only a bit of fun, you know, Guv'. [Laughter]

RK   Last year in Venice I was completely amazed by the impact of Arabic script in your work and the force that had and sense of really doing something completely new. Can you say something about that?

Geo Because we are surrounded by foreign language newspapers. There are dozens and dozens of Arabic and Hindu and Bengali scripts all around us which we don't understand, but I think it's very important to use it because somebody can understand it. It doesn't matter to us that we can't understand it. It's all a big confusion. For instance, we did a picture called *Mullah*, which means a Muslim priest, in 1980, and from that day on everyone used to say to us, 'Why mullah? What does mullah mean?' And then those two aeroplanes went into the buildings in New York and nobody has asked us what a mullah is ever since because from that moment, everyone knows what a mullah is. The world is changing in that way and we want to show that we can be with it.

Gil   Every time we see these mullahs I always see this finger coming at you. I always would like to cut off this finger because they are always pointing to you.

Geo   Yes.

Gil   The mullahs on television. It is an extraordinary idea. Just preaching. And that is why I'll never like a priest any more. I was brought up a Catholic and they all did the same, all this pointing the finger at you. I will try to cut off that finger one day. But I think our biggest revolution is because we have turned ourselves to do it all on computer.

Geo   It's extraordinary.

Gil   That is the new brain for us. We transport our ideas direct into a screen.

RK   Since when and how?

HUO   I think there was a transition period.

Geo   I think probably we took a year to change over in 2001–02.

Gil   We stopped working for one year because we had to research what we actually could do. It was very difficult because computers were not powerful enough. We were not able to make big pictures. But now it's unbelievable.

Geo   In fact we started with the *London East One* pictures that you have in the little catalogue; those were the first pictures created with the computer. A lot of people say, 'Don't you miss the old dark room?' We say, 'Not at all. We are very happy. We don't have to get up early in the morning to switch on all the water and all the horrible smell of chemicals. And we were working for twelve hours completely in the dark'. We were very happy to leave that behind. The only thing we miss is the rubber gloves.

[Laughter]

HUO	And what changed in the way you work? It is very autonomous. What I think is also very interesting is that you don't have lots of assistants but you now actually do even the biggest catalogues yourselves. You do all the pictures yourselves. It gives you a high degree of freedom.
Geo	It gives enormous freedoms.
Gil	In some way, we are the total artwork from the beginning to the end; we design the installation, we design the catalogue, we design the artwork. When we go to the museum to put up the art we have total artwork. Nobody is involved except ourselves.
Geo	Even our assistant, who has the little room next to our studio, we send away when we are designing the new pictures because we want to be totally alone at that time.
Gil	Except recently we had two or three helpers. They were all architects. It's very funny because we prefer architects to artists. Artists are more dangerous. So they did all the scanning for this big book that we are doing with one thousand two hundred pages, maybe two thousand images. And we did all the proofs ready in Fournier Street. It was an extraordinary job.
Geo	But that was only possible because we weren't creating pictures at that time. If we were we wouldn't be able to have people like that around.

HUO	What are the unbuilt roads of Gilbert and George?
Geo	We do what we want.
	[Laughter]
	There are lots of projects waiting one day.
Gil	We are doing it. We are doing every day what we want. That's it. I think that Aleister Crowley said that once.
Geo	'Do what thou wilt shall be the whole of the law', I think.
Gil	'Do what you want is the whole of the law', yes.

HUO	Aleister Crowley is interesting. I heard about German novelist Christian Kraft the other day, who was trying to find the house of Aleister Crowley. That reminded me that you had told me a lot, years ago, about Aleister Crowley. Can you maybe tell us a little bit?
Geo	We were fans, briefly of him. Didn't he live in Hastings? The house was in Hastings, I thought. The wife of the person who ran the market café, Clyde at the market café where we had lunch and breakfast for thirty years, his wife, Naomi, was an occultist. She was a great follower of Crow-

ley and of Austin Osman Spare, who did the automatic drawings. She was able to leave her body and float to the top of the staircase and look down on herself, which was rather surprising as she was a very big lady.
[Laughter]

Gil   But he has an amazing head; the photograph.

Geo   Aleister Crowley, yes, extraordinary.

Gil   666 but an amazing head; it is monstrous.

Geo   We do have a copy of his rather rare book, *The Book of Lies*, signed by him, '666'.

HUO   What about the future? How do you see the future?

Gil   We told you many, many times. We want to be there in the future. Every single day. There is nothing more exciting than that.

Geo   We are all doomed.
[Laughter]

HUO   Many, many thanks to Gilbert and George. Thank you.

Applause, end of interview

Rem Koolhaas	We now talk to Adam Caruso. It's actually the first time we have talked or even met.
Adam Caruso	Yes.

RK So for that reason I am very happy. I have always felt that there was a curious discrepancy between your writing and your building. Do you feel that is true, or not? Do you think one reinforces the other?

AC It's nice to meet. I think there is inevitably a difference. Writing is a different thing from designing; it's a different way of engaging with the world and with different situations and maybe you could say it's less intuitive. So it's inevitably going to be different and I think what you can make your buildings about is not always what you can write about. Maybe when you write – and I find writing a lot more difficult – it is still as an architect, but maybe a little bit less so. It's maybe more as a human so that you try to engage with things that you aren't able to engage with in architecture.

RK But I think the interesting thing about your architecture is that it's very adventurous and your writing can be very moralistic.

AC *[Laughs]*

RK That is, for me, surprising because usually writing is a sort of escape from the ardures of architecture; here it seems that architecture is an escape from the ardure of writing or the moralism.

AC I would prefer to think of the writing as trying to have an ethic rather than it being moralistic. I think morality is a difficult concept and I do try to avoid being moralistic. But maybe you're right. It's the inversion of what you're saying; I find designing really difficult, too, but I think when one makes architecture you are trying to do something constructive and I try to be positive all the time. I don't think it's worth making architecture against things; it's just not worth the effort. It's constructive, whereas especially if one isn't writing a novel, but even if one is writing fiction, one can look at ugly things as well and try to engage with them and unpick them and understand them. So maybe the breadth of emotions one is dealing with is broader. I tend to write more about what I am against and maybe the architecture is more what I'm for.

RK   That is a beautiful explanation.

Hans Ulrich Obrist   I found a quote from you in a catalogue where you said if you do something that makes everything around feel poor, actually then you have done the place a bad service. Not being from the world of architecture and having an outside view on this field, I've recently observed that there is something one could refer to as a new normalcy. I've discussed this with Rem and we've had discussions with Nikolaus Hirsch about this topic and he referred to you and also to Peter Märkli, the Swiss architect whose studio I recently visited.

AC   Good, because I won't remember it! Is the first question about whether one can ameliorate situations with one's architecture or if that may be an important role for architecture? I don't think it always had to be a role of architecture. I think there used to be so many levels of consensus amongst people who had power in society that architects, and artists I think, didn't have to think so much about acting in a constructive way in their projects. I think it was very difficult to be transgressive until recently, actually.

RK   Until when? The 1980s?

AC   Yes, with the ascendancy of neo-right liberalism.

RK   When you began?

AC   Yes. I guess I was really lucky or unlucky because even the 1950s was a time when there was a heavy consensus and one could really believe that one was creating a new world in one's discipline. I think now there isn't this consensus any more, so when you act today, it comes with a responsibility.

RK   Isn't it simply that the initiative has shifted from the public to the private sector? Isn't that the dominant given or is that not true for you?

AC   I don't think that's the case because the nineteenth-century English city, for instance, was largely driven by the private sector and yet there were shared ideas which produced an incredible urban artefact. With lots of buildings today, I think their only *raison d'être* is to put everything around them in the shade. However, I think there was only a very short moment when this was possible because there quickly emerged a new kind of normalcy in this hyper-market context, where it's impossible to put anything in the shade because everything is as big and empty as its neighbour, and size no longer equates with impact or with presence. I think there are so many projects today that make you wonder where the support for this gigantism comes from, its emptiness is so starkly obvious. This is the new kind of normalcy which is not the normalcy of Märkli. Maybe we're interested in the normalcy which can span between quite modest things but also grand things. It's about choosing the pitch at which you're going to work in each situation. I think if you look at the City of London now there's a gigantism where it's as if normal-sized ideas get pumped up bigger and bigger and they become stretched in their volume and attenuated in their content.

RK Can you give an example?

AC [Laughs] There's a kind of new orthodoxy about a completely reduced glass skin which is stretched like Clingfilm over an enormous volume of building. The volumes of office buildings have been allowed to get bigger because there has been a political decision within the City that they have to build these enormous volumes in order to compete with other markets. I guess an example would be it doesn't really matter who designs these buildings; they are all the same because the territory of the architecture has been so reduced. The floor plates are very, very deep with the peculiar logic that goes along with such plans. There is a weak, vaguely abstract formalism which is prevalent at the moment and then the whole thing is wrapped in a skin, usually made by the same manufacturer because there has been a dramatic consolidation in the cladding industry, as there has been in the financial services industries that will occupy these buildings.

RK So what would you do if you were invited to participate in that? Not participate?

AC I don't know. We never have to confront it because we're never asked. [Laughs]

RK When I first saw images of your art gallery building in Walsall I was really excited that there was finally a kind of irony in England that was vigorous and not introverted and I was also really happy that there was an influence of Venturi. Is that a true influence?

AC Absolutely, yes.

RK   So what has happened to that influence? Recently your work has become more expressionistic, or is that a misreading?

AC   Our work is very eclectic. I think there's a big potential in eclecticism. When we started practicing, the number of architects in this country who would admit to being interested in Venturi could be counted on one hand and I always found this strange because Venturi is such an Anglophile and his work has so much to do with English culture and English architectural eclecticism. So yes, since we started Peter and I have shared a real interest in Venturi. But I don't think it's disappeared from our work. We're finishing a building now for the Museum of Childhood in London that is the most Venturian project, I think, that we've done, so it's still an interest but perhaps it's more latent.

HUO   We have a sound document here of an interview with Denise Scott Brown which can be listened to at any time. It's very much about Venturi's book, *Learning from Las Vegas*, having a lot to do with England in the 1950s and Denise Scott Brown's contact zone with the Smithsons. She also mentioned the importance of Henderson's photography which was a crucial influence. We have been speaking a lot about positions from the past which can be toolboxes for now and talking about this new normalcy. Would the idea of 'as found' of Alison and Peter Smithson have been an influence for you?

AC   We looked a lot at the Smithsons' work when we started our practice. Some of their buildings were very interesting but it was even more about them as people; they were quite unusual amongst English architects in that they actually articulated why they were working, what their role as architects could be in wider cultural issues. They wrote, they produced books, they did all sorts of things that we were interested in. Their broad engagement with culture was very unusual at the time and it's even more unusual now. It's funny that English architects have a phobia about engaging with a wider culture and it seems that the less articulate you are the more successful you can be. One of the reasons for the lack of professional success on the part of the Smithsons could be that people were suspicious of them; they talked too much, their opinions were too strongly held. I think that now a lot of people in other countries have rediscovered the Smithsons' work and we always get phoned up to write a little piece or whatever for upcoming issues of magazines – maybe one gets a little bit bored but it's still important.

HUO   Your practice has done a lot of collaborations with artists and we are sitting here in the pavilion of Rem Koolhaas and Cecil Balmond underneath the freeze by Thomas Demand. It is the first time the Serpentine pavilion has connected to what was inside the gallery. It was one of the first things Rem wanted to do so he visited Thomas Demand's studio and this is the outcome of the dialogue. I saw an exhibition in Paris where you developed a display feature for Thomas Demand so I thought as we are sitting here for twenty-four hours underneath his art work it would be really interesting to hear about your dialogue with Thomas Demand and maybe the specific collaboration for the Fondation Cartier.

AC   We have done three exhibitions for Thomas and he's now a friend of ours. Just to go one step back, we have collaborated with artists, but the more general influence of contemporary art has been even more important to us. At the same time as looking at Venturi and the Smithsons we have looked very carefully at contemporary art production, it has been a very good source of ideas, of things that we can steal. Contemporary art shows how wit and irony can be a part of very substantial work, that being witty is not the same as being frivolous. I think this is lost with most architects and I think that a lot of good art and architecture is witty. Working with Thomas has been a big influence on us. I don't think it's been such a significant influence the other way. He has enormous interest and knowledge about architecture and when he comes to the studio we always show him what we're doing and he always has lots of things to say, which we take notice of.

I think there is a message in the way he works, the way he makes images and intensifies the kind of feelings of these carefully selected, but found images. These places, which are architectural, are full of pathos. They are often a bit sinister. I'm not that interested in our work being sinister, but in the idea that work can have pathos and a bit of failure and that it doesn't only have to be triumphalist, that is of interest. But then the act of materialising a project gives it a kind of wholeness, maybe, that makes it convincing as work so it doesn't fall apart. I guess that's a strange combination of things. Fischli and Weiss are artists whose work Peter and I greatly admire. Their work has that combination of failure and accomplishment; it has this incredible pathos and even kitsch, and yet it never feels like they are taking the piss out of their subject matter or out of the audience. It always seems to be done with respects and in good faith. Maybe that sounds earnest but that's where I think the great potential is, in making things: you can put all those things together, you can have something that has an incredible presence, and yet the message or aura it's giving off is one of pathos and incompleteness. There is something very, very powerful about that.

RK   Thank you very much.
HUO   Many thanks.

Applause, end of interview

Hans Ulrich Obrist	It's a great pleasure to welcome Ryan Gander now and actually we'll start with a two minute film.
Ryan Gander	I thought I'd give you all a rest for two minutes by showing something, and I have the idea that not a lot of people will know what I make and it will give you a bit of an idea.

[Film clip: young girl's voice]:

'… definite and there's quite a lot of questions about this one. That's why I think it would be good to introduce something else. I think it looks a bit like a music video because the music videos, they try and set them in the most desolate places you are never expecting about the voice. I think they try and make them questioning or just like a short film. I think it could have been that but I think it's a name for a computer game but I think it would be difficult because it's very quiet, sort of, even though it couldn't be noisy because there's no sound to it. It's very quiet. It's a soft image and in computer games there is always a challenge you have to overcome but you have to look at it and there's nothing more to sort of achieve. I think probably music video. That's difficult. It's difficult. *[Pause].* It's difficult to say if it is real or if it's made by a computer because it's very close to reality but you can actually have something that was real and sort of that exact vision, that exact view with the car so I think it would probably, if you think of it, it was made by a computer. Not really, not until you get very close to the car. It's probably because of the shadow. I do think the colour of the shadow is quite good because you don't usually get that. I think that sometimes you do get sort of blue…' *[End of clip]*

HUO	Many thanks. To begin with the beginning would be great. Could you talk about the film we have just seen?
RG	The film lasts eighteen minutes and the actual visual part is a one-minute loop that you just saw twice. It fades from black up to white and the white merges into a ten-second snippet of computer generated animation of a car in a field of snow. I sent that DVD to a seven-year old child, three days before interviewing her in a sound studio, for her to watch and to think about. Then I put her in a sound booth and put me

in a sound booth opposite her. We talked to each other with a glass screen between us so that we could record our voices on different tracks and then edit it from about three hours of recording to eighteen minutes. Then I took my voice out so it's as if she's talking to herself.

Rem Koolhaas Why did you remove the traces of your questions? Why did you turn it into a monologue?

RG I don't like the sound of my voice. I wouldn't have been able to watch it afterwards if my voice was there; I would find it irritating. There's a thing at the Basel Art Fair called the Statement Section, which is a solo stand in the Art Fair for a younger artist, and it was made specifically for that. It works in other places but it works best there because a lot of what I asked her was about the nature of art fairs and the nature of walking around them, so she makes a lot of anecdotal comments. She is the child of someone who works in the art world so she has been to art fairs and she knows about art. At one point I asked her what an art fair is like and she said, 'You know when people call the art world the art world, well the art fair is the art world because there are streets and there are people and there are small houses'. And that's the way the art world is in her imagination.

RK It is a world.

HUO I was wondering if you can you tell us a little about your Bologna project, which is a topic relating to many of the previous discussions about London, about notions of mapping of the city. I was just reading your small booklet which is nine projects for the Pavilion de l'Esprit Nouveau, a project which happened this spring.

RG Yes.

HUO I was wondering how you revisited this pavilion and if you could tell us about the project.

RG Like you say, there were nine projects, but the most significant project there for me was to produce a time capsule which will be opened in fifty years, with the idea that I won't be alive in fifty years. I don't know, maybe I will; maybe I'll be lucky. Fingers crossed! But I like the idea that a work would be produced after the last work that I had made, in a way. It was logistically very difficult to organize; it involved passing a small by-law in Italy and opening an arts trust which would ensure someone would have the work produced in fifty years. The work is new curtains for Le Corbusier's pavilion in Bologna, which was a gift to the city of Bologna from the city of Paris in the 1930s. The city of Bologna didn't decide to build that particular pavilion for fifty years after it was given as a present to them; they didn't have faith in Le Corbusier or something. So I thought it was nice to take that fifty-year time span and move it forwards beyond this moment into the future. In fifty years, if the Trust works the way that it should, a child descendant of Le Corbusier will be traced and be given a set of instructions and using the original interior colours Le Corbusier chose for the pavilion, asked to make a painting. The painting will be sliced into sixteen sections, revolved, and screen printed onto curtains. The curtains in the pavilion will then be replaced. That's the idea. Whether it actually works out or not is a different thing, I think.

RK   Can I come back to the movie? I think that you are the first of our speakers to introduce the issue of innocence and so far children stand for innocence. But your questioning and her obvious sophistication make it a lot more complex than that. What are you trying to do with the thing in terms of reality? What is your comment?

RG   I don't think it's to do with innocence. I think it's just to do with children not having all the stigmas of knowledge attached. I wouldn't say that was the same thing. I'd say they have a lot more courage to believe in what they think without listening to what everyone else says and mixing that with what they think.

RK   But yet everything she says, and that's why I am asking why you removed your questions, is uncannily precise and accurate.

RG   Why did I remove the questions?

RK   Everything she says is so sophisticated, so accurate.

RG   It seems sophisticated but that's eighteen minutes from three hours. If you listen to the entire recording it wouldn't seem that sophisticated. It's just that I took the most interesting bits, probably.

RK   OK.

HUO   How do you see the current moment?

RG   It's funny you should ask that. *[Laughs]* I've got a new project. Next year I am taking the year off because I feel a bit tired and I feel that timespan between production and exhibition of the works that I've made has just decreased and decreased and decreased. I remember about two years ago I had five works in front of me which gave me time to digest them before I spat them out and I have lost that and am chasing my tail a bit. I find that a bit frustrating, so I am taking a year off next year. The other thing is I found myself with some money and there is something I always moan about in London, which is that there are too many bad artists that have exhibitions. I moan about it a lot, so as a sort of self-help therapy I started a gallery which opens in September.

HUO   What will it be called?

RG   It's called Associates. You can write that down. It's at 92 Hoxton Street and it's a small shop. I don't imagine myself as a gallerist, it's not one of my ambitions or anything, but there will be twelve solo shows over twelve months. After the twelve months is finished we will end the project. It will just be for one year. The artists that are being shown have not had solo shows in London before and they are all not yet represented by galleries. It is different to an artist-run space because it is not run by artists; it's managed as a professional venture and we will sell work but one hundred per cent of the money from the work that we sell will go to the artist, rather than us taking a commission to fund the gallery. We just worked out what it would cost in a year and I paid half and then asked people to give money, so there are fifteen people who have given money towards it. So how I see my future is a bit strange; I'm not used to it at all. It's like becoming a chef, or something, completely different.

HUO   It is fascinating that you would say that you planned a year off. About a week ago Dominique Gonzales-Foerster was here and was telling us that a year and a half ago she had made exactly the same plan as you. She said it more or less in the same words: too many exhibitions, she needed a year off, would go on a world tour. But in a post-planning condition, after only two or three weeks, plans drastically changed and she bought a house in Rio and opened a scientific research lab in this house. The world tour had ended and work started in a different way. So I was fascinated by this idea of planning a whole year.

RG   Yes, but the nature of the job is that if you aren't strong enough to say no, things always come along and you end up saying 'yes'. It's really difficult to say 'no', so it was important to define a real period of time. I shouldn't call it a year off because it makes me sound lazy. I should call it a research sabbatical or something.

HUO	To liberate time, maybe.
RG	Yes, exactly.

HUO	We were wondering about London. You live in London, you work in London; the city enters your work and your work enters the city. How do you see London now?
RG	I see it as very expensive and very unfriendly to people. It can be a depressing place to live. I look forward to going out of London and I get terribly depressed when I drive back in. This is the first time I have been this far west in about three months. I just stay in the east and I only move east or north; I never go west or south. That's my strange compass. To be honest, I would hate to be an art student in London. I think it would be a terrible place to study. I studied in Holland, so I am kind of lucky because I had the best that you can get, really. I went to the Jan van Eyck Academy in Maastricht and then the Rijksakademie in Amsterdam and they are two really nice places, friendly places to study, with enough money and a nice place to live. I couldn't imagine studying in London at all. I wanted to. I am from Chester, which is in the north of England, and when I left Chester I applied to go to Goldsmiths, because all my friends were applying to Goldsmiths and it seemed to be the right thing to do; I didn't get an interview. That happened with a few London colleges. Actually I feel like it was a bit of a blessing in disguise now, because the amount of time it takes to actually live here just doesn't leave you with enough time to think or make work, and I don't think that would have been very good for me. But it's alright if you've got somewhere nice to live and you've got a job that pays money and if you've got a chauffeur and a helipad. *[Laughter]*

HUO	It is interesting because Rem, you were mentioning that we had relatively few more pessimistic impressions of London, but there was change with the passage of time. Before midnight it was all more pessimistic and then it changed.
RK	Almost nobody has been even remotely critical of this city.
RG	Really? No-one has?
RK	It's been euphoric.
RG	I'm sorry. Terrible start to the day! *[Laughter]*
HUO	One of the things I was curious to ask you, the only recurrent question in this interview Marathon, is about your yet-unrealised projects, your

unbuilt roads. I was wondering if you had any projects which were too big to be realised, too small to be realised, forgotten projects or censored projects.

RG   I have a list of projects and most of them are too big to do. It's an A4 list with little boxes that you tick. I'm about three down out of about thirty. The third one was this gallery. I would quite like to design my own house, with me in mind, my own coffin (I'm not sure about that), I'd like to make some jewellery, I'd like to make a pop video. There are loads of things I'd like to do. The list is endless. Actually it seems like half of them you could never achieve.

RK   Just out of curiosity, what would your house do or look like?

RG   I'd stay in one place and the house would move around me. It would make it easier. Pneumatic pistons behind all the walls that would move the space. I don't know anything about architecture, so I don't know if it would work... *[Laughter]* Maybe it would be blue.

HUO   Many thanks Ryan Gander.

Applause, end of interview

Julia Peyton-Jones
Doreen Massey
Mary Midgley
Mark Cousins
Patrick Keiller
Jonathan Glancey

Rem Koolhaas   The Serpentine Gallery is, perhaps, in terms of the relationship between aura and footprint, the most efficient artistic institution in the world. I don't know a single institution that per square metre achieves as much and creates such an incredible reputation. That in itself is an enormous achievement, particularly in an environment and at a moment when all museums have been expanding. I think your strategy with the Pavilion, which is to expand but also to destroy and take back the expansion every year, is incredibly smart. Yet you have expansionist plans and I'd like you to talk about that.

Julia Peyton-Jones   Rem, thank you for being so generous. Can I also salute you and Cecil Balmond at this point of the Marathon and say what an incredible achievement this wonderful structure is, and how special it is to be seated in it? [Applause]

I think the thing that's interesting about the Serpentine is the way in which we can be like a lung: we can inhale and we can exhale, so that we can do events like this, which is part of an expanded programme. But I suppose the thing about an institution of this scale, which is so modest – the size of a house – is that any territory that's gained is already a huge advantage. The expectations are low because a small scale usually equals a rather modest ambition, so with that in mind, it's interesting to see where the gains can be made: gains of territory, gains of practice, gains of skill, gains of experience, gains of audience and so on. I talk quite a lot about hand-to-hand combat, because it feels like we're at the very sharp end of the development of artistic and architectural practice, and also the forging of the public programmes, of which this Marathon is part. Bearing this in mind, we're now embracing, relishing and enjoying the fact that we're small. In the past, if somebody said we were small, I used to shudder and feel embarrassed about it because, compared to larger institutions like Tate and the Museum of Modern Art in New York, it felt slightly humiliating. Now, I think it's the most glorious thing, because it gives us freedom. The freedom is to take the backbone of the Serpentine Gallery – the building, the exhibition programme, which has been going since 1970 – and then to expand it in the way that we want. So we can have your Pavilion here for three months, and when it goes, we have a piece of lawn that's so small, you can't imagine that anything could possibly have been there in the first place. Then, in case people forget, the Pavilion comes back next year, designed by another architect.

But in terms of a global ambition, it's also interesting not to think in a small way, but in a large way, which is why Hans Ulrich was invited to work at the Serpentine Gallery. The fact that the Smithson interview was played just before this session is fortuitous in terms of my memory, because the plans that Hans Ulrich and I hatched were the result of a very chance remark that we shared in a taxi back from seeing that interview at the Courtauld. It was a joke about doing something in London that we both agreed would be professional suicide. And from that throwaway comment, a whole discussion between us unfolded about what a public institution could really contribute in a meaningful way at this point in time. What could it contribute to the situation in the UK, but also globally? So we worked on a matrix of ideas, a layering of ideas that embraced the global in a most ambitious way while also addressing the local. It's like a column, and from the column tentacles expand outwards. So it's a very long answer – and clearly the length of my answer shows the degree to which the question still intrigues me. And of course, it's very nice to have Hans Ulrich at the Serpentine Gallery.

RK   Can you be a little more specific? I think I can say without revealing any secrets that even the Serpentine has mentioned the word 'brand' in relation to itself. What would you say are the potential consequences of that?

JPJ   The first time I seriously considered the idea of the Serpentine as a brand was when you used the term when we started working together. A brand assumes, for me at least, influence and a certain degree of power outside the specialism that the organisation may be known for – as part of a much wider context. And we're now exploring what would happen if the Serpentine branched out, not only in Western culture, but also in Eastern culture, outside our terrain both digitally and in reality. This isn't in terms of setting up institutions that we'd be running elsewhere, but, as one of our distinguished Chinese colleagues said recently, the concept of 'one gallery, one world'. For example, the Agency of Unrealised Projects was launched very soon after Hans Ulrich arrived here. This is a programme presenting the visions of architects, artists and designers that we may realise in the future – a document of these incredible endeavours. So we're expanding our programmes into areas that we haven't explored before.

Hans Ulrich Obrist Eric Hobsbawm recommended, as part of a protest against forgetting, that we address memory in this Marathon. Museum pioneers – people who've invented curatorial models – perhaps represent the field where there's the greatest amnesia. In America there's Walter Hopps and Pontus Hulten. In terms of your permanent reinvention of the Serpentine, which started a long time ago, who were the British museum-pioneers who were your models when you began to think about art institutions? Who, for you, would be analogous to Peter Smithson or Cedric Price in architecture, in terms of the museum?

JPJ When I started here in 1991, the landscape was hugely different from now. There was a sort of cultural poverty. You were saying earlier that now everybody's talking about London in a quite romantic way. But thinking back to that time, it's astounding that London in 2006 can be a world player in the arts. It's the only thing that I feel really patriotic about – not about British art, necessarily, but about the arts in general terms having a really strong, important place within this culture and that this is being recognised abroad. So this really seismic shift is almost incomprehensible. When I first came here as director, the director whom I most admired was Nick Serota, when he was at the Whitechapel Gallery, and the reason for that was because he did the most extraordinary range of shows by artists who hadn't previously been shown here. There was a corner of the art world, particularly in London, that was doing remarkable work on the same level as our institutional counterparts elsewhere. But that was very unusual, because the culture – not only the public at large but also the art world – was relatively closed. The extraordinary flowering that has happened since has been well documented, and is a reflection of the city – and the city is a reflection of it.

HUO You mentioned another pioneer who's been forgotten in the UK: Joanna Drew. Could you talk about her?

JPJ In a quite romantic way I have two art-world 'parents': David Sylvester and Joanna Drew. They were both my mentors when I came into the museum profession after being an artist for many years. Joanna was head of visual arts at the Arts Council at the time. She was a remarkable woman. She started as a dancer, and she ran this extraordinary empire, which included the Hayward Gallery, the Serpentine Gallery and the Arts Council Collection. It was a huge empire. And also she was responsible for bringing into the profession Nick Serota, for example, David Elliott, and many others. She brought in Catherine Lampert, who ran the Whitechapel Gallery, Susan Brades, who ran the Hayward Gallery – these children of hers, so to speak, who then went on to play such an important part in institutional life here.

David Sylvester was at that time an advisor to the Hayward Gallery and I worked with him. He was a very significant figure. And as you know from one of the earlier speakers, Ken Adam, David worked on his last show here at my invitation. David was so ill, and as we'd worked together for such a long time, I wanted to work with him again – it was very important for him to continue practising as a critic, as a writer, as a curator. So I asked him, if he had the opportunity, what show could he imagine might take place at the Serpentine. Those of you who knew him will remember he was very lugubrious; there were very long silences in his telephone calls, so you thought you'd been cut off. So there was a very long silence and he said he wanted to think about it. He rang me back the next day and said, 'I want to do a show of Ken Adam'. I thought, 'Who is he? This is absolutely awful. I don't know who he is. I can't show my ignorance.' So I played for time and asked my friends and nobody could help me, and then the epiphany came. The Ken Adam show was born and it was a great pleasure to work with both of them and, as Ken told you, David died shortly after his last interview with him.

RK   You call the Serpentine a public institution. How does that work, and how public is it? I don't have the feeling that a lavish subsidy guarantees your survival ad infinitum. How does that fact of being public position you in terms of the private enterprises of a comparable, if not larger, scale that are proliferating, such as White Cube, and how embattled do you feel vis-à-vis the explosion of the private?

JPJ   I think people are broadly divided into two categories, although I think possibly I span the two, and indeed the Serpentine may also to a certain degree. If you're in the public sector, not for profit, the audience is a key part of what you do; it's important. Personally, it matters to me how many people come to see Serpentine shows or visit the Pavilion or participate in our public programmes and everything else we do. In that sense, size absolutely matters to me because it's an incredible effort to do what we do – not only for me, but for the whole team. If you make a big effort and have one and a half people to see exhibitions, which used to be the case – there was something rather noble, even, about only one and a half people coming to see exhibitions because it was generally considered that those one and a half people were of such supreme intellect and understanding that only they could really understand what they were seeing – but I'd rather have 150 thousand people, working on the assumption that not one and a half but maybe fifty and a half will have a life-changing experience.

Running hand in hand with that, there's also this strange business of being very poorly subsidised – all our dear colleagues from the Arts Council, and elsewhere, please note! – and then what do you do with the fact that you don't have enough money to do anything? That in itself becomes a rather interesting question: what can you do if you have nothing? There are many reasons, not financial or indeed to do with generating visitors, why the Pavilion programme was born and has become so interesting. How can you commission really great architects to design something if you have no budget at all? Of course, we have a huge amount of good will, but the principle is, if you have no money, you can't do things. So seeing what you can do becomes interesting as an idea. We need to be very creative about how we get it all to work; that's part of the interest and also sometimes part of the frustration.

The private sector goes back to the size thing: institutionally, we'll soon be smaller – I'm being extreme – than all our colleagues in the commercial sector, who are building bigger and bigger edifices, producing bigger and bigger power structures. So that then gets back to the question, which is what Hans Ulrich and I are working on together with the team here, how can you be relevant when the power has shifted so radically? This is a very considerable question and one that's the most pressing of the day for the not-for-profit sector.

HUO   What would be your dream institution for the twenty-first century? Do you have any vision of how the public institution would work?

JPJ   It's very interesting, because it's no accident that the exhibition *Freeze*, which launched Damien Hirst and colleagues in the late 1980s, was a result of the most extraordinary rebellion against a situation that did not support that generation of artists coming out of art school. The most important lesson of my professional career was that if the situation does not work for you, you have to invent your own. It was the circumstances at that particular time in this country that resulted in this incredible creativity, invention and real flowering of contemporary British art. So there is, I think, a great deal to be said for that creative tension. But there's also a point beyond which it becomes reductive and unhelpful. So that balance is a very fine one.

HUO   Thank you very much.

Applause, end of interview

Rem Koolhaas

Of the people who've spoken about London so far, there have been almost forty extremely positive reports, including from Gilbert & George, for whom the East End is a kind of Jerusalem, and is still a Jerusalem after twenty years. But I think your critical interpretation of London is extremely necessary, particularly of the myth that London is a great and voluntary assembly of many races. Your *London Inside Out* is one of the rare texts that actually question that mythology. Can you talk about that issue?

Doreen Massey

Yes. Do you remember the day after the July bombings in London, when Ken Livingstone was still out in Singapore and we'd just won the Olympics? Livingstone spoke about London in a really moving way and called it 'the future of the world'. He spoke about the collection of cultures and ethnicities that are gathered here in London, and there's no doubt if you look at it statistically and qualitatively, in loads and loads of ways, that that's the case. And there's no doubt also that there's both, I think, a political level and a street level commitment to anti-racism in this place. That doesn't mean there isn't racism; it's horrendous. It doesn't mean that there aren't daily monstrosities going on in the streets, but I think it's nonetheless in a very general sense an amazingly 'tolerant' place. Ken celebrated that, and in celebrating, he said that this was London's character as a world city, as a global city. I don't in any way want to go against that. What I would like to do is turn that question around and ask about London as a global city in terms of its effects on the rest of the world. There are lots of ways in which that works. First of all, it's quite interesting to look at multi-culturalism outwards. Yes, there are loads of different groups, loads of different ethnicities gathered here in London, but Ken said they've come here to be free, to be able to be themselves and things like that. In some senses that is true, but people have also come here because of poverty in the rest of the world, or because globalisation has made it impossible for them to keep living on the land on which they've historically lived. They've come here too because of wars. One of the questions I want us as Londoners – as far as we are Londoners – to ask is, is what goes on in London in part responsible for poverty in the rest of the world? That's

263

one thing. To question that other side of London global city, which is London as a propagator of de-regulation, privatisation, neo-liberalisation. It started here. London isn't a global city just because it's open to the wider world. It reinvented itself in the 1980s (and if you want to come back to this, I think the 1980s was absolutely crucial). It reinvented itself in the 1980s on the back of privatisation, neo-liberalisation, the commercialisation of everything. I think we as Londoners need to question that.

But there are also more ordinary ways in which London affects the rest of the world. London couldn't go on without the immigration that comes to this city. One example I give in the article you mention, Rem, is nurses. We absolutely depend for the running of this city, the daily, social, ordinary reproduction of this city, in a whole host of ways on people who've come from the global South, and also increasingly now, from the East of Europe. The example I give is nurses from Ghana. What we're doing is taking skilled labour from those countries. I read a statistic the other day that between a third and a half of all professionally trained people in Ghana are not in Ghana; they're in First World countries, servicing our needs. That's a hugely difficult problem because I don't want to say people shouldn't come. Those of us on the Left are caught in a vice here: on the one hand, we want to say 'Of course there should be free immigration'; on the other hand we want to stop the brain drain from the Third World, from the global South. It's those kinds of issues that I'd like to put on the agenda, not to *not* celebrate London – there's a load of stuff to celebrate here, but to also ask some of the difficult questions about what that celebration depends on, and its effects in the wider world.

Hans Ulrich Obrist   I'm very interested in the local and the global in relation to this argument; you mentioned that it's necessary to look beyond the local place to trace its implications around the world.

DM   Yes.

HUO   *London Inside Out* was a key text for Rem and me when preparing this Marathon. There was one thing I wanted to ask you to explain: you talk about the global production of the local and the fact that very often the local is seen as a kind of victim of globalisation.

DM   Yes.

HUO   You say we shouldn't only look at that, but also at the local production of the global.

DM   I think very often in political campaigning around globalisation we see the local as the product of the global and thus the local as the victim of the global – global forces coming into your region and smashing it up in various ways, causing the destruction of local communities, causing the closure of factories and all those kinds of things. In many places that is absolutely true. In industrial towns in the North of England, that's the dominant thing that's going on. In many places in the global South, that's the dominant thing that's going on. But it seems to me if we generalise that story we end up letting 'the local' off the hook; we're exonerating the local. Because the global isn't produced 'up there'; it's not always somewhere else; it's not some kind of ethereal sphere that exists nowhere. Globalisation is produced in local places, and what I'm trying to argue for is a geography of the understanding of that. And London is one of the key places in which globalisation is produced. That means that we in London can't say, 'We must defend our local place against global outside forces' (and that is said a lot. It's said in the London Plan on numerous occasions). We also have to take responsibility for the production of the globalisation that we're now fighting on the streets. So there's a way in which we have to think about the local production of the global as well as the global production of the local. It's what, more generally, I call a politics of place beyond place. When we're thinking about our places, we shouldn't just be defensive about them; we should not just think about what's going on within them. We should try and plot what the impacts of those places are around the rest of the planet and in some senses try and take some kind of political responsibility for that, both in street-level campaigning and through local councils and such.

RK   Can you say a little bit more in terms of politics? When we talked about politics from six o'clock till midnight, there was a real sense of ineffectuality and powerlessness. Do you see a way in which people like us could be effective in resisting some of these things at this moment, against the seemingly overwhelming, seemingly satanic, seemingly unstoppable?

DM   I was part of the GLC of the 1980s, and I think that moment was really crucial. At that moment it wasn't inevitable, it somehow wasn't already pre-given, that Neo-liberal globalisation and finance would come to dominate. We lost that moment in all kinds of ways, not only through the GLC being abolished, but across a whole set of social struggles; we lost that moment. Neo-liberal dogma, and this new, vastly wealthy elite that you yourself, both of you, write about, came to dominate the social scene. What that meant was that London pursued a particular path. It also meant, I think, the victory of a part of London over the rest of the country, which is another issue. So now twenty, thirty years later, we have another Greater London group, this time an Assembly, with much reduced powers. Because, of course, Labour was as much opposed to the GLC as the Tories ever were – they saw it as far too radical. But this time, as well as having reduced powers, it's in a situation where Neo-liberalism is well established and it's very much harder to buck the trend. If you look at all the plans and the documents that are being produced, they all basically accept that. The London Plan says London has reinvented itself. Those are the terms that are used in the documents and the way in which it has reinvented itself is as this global financial capital and the Plan says 'Go ahead with it'.

Yet I think there are things we can do. The situation is glum, no doubt. The last interviewee said things were fine; I definitely do not think that. I feel incredibly depressed at times. But I do think there are things that can be done. We can question the dominance of finance. Even calling London a 'global city' in that way is to prioritise, in our imagination of the place, just that bit of it that's finance – it is quite a lot of it, but it isn't all of it. There are a hell of a lot of other things that go on in London that are also part of this place, so it's a kind of substitution of the part for the whole, a synecdoche. The rest of us are made invisible by that designation of London as a financial city above everything else. So we can challenge that. We can get debates around our dependence upon immigration in the difficult way I spoke of before onto the streets as live debates. We can plot and map. There's an arts group, Platform, that's done a lot of work just plotting the role of London and London-based institutions in what happened in the Niger Delta over the years through Ken Saro-Wiwa's execution and the current politics of oil. There's a lovely map at the end of their book *The Next Gulf* [2005] called 'the Niger Delta in London'. It shows a host of institutions, here in London, that are linked to what's happening in the Niger Delta now. In other words, the things that are part of our daily infrastructure, part of our daily lives, absolutely essential to the city in which we live, and yet producing such havoc and chaos in other parts of the world. So I think at all kinds of levels there are campaigns that can be waged and debates that can be provoked, yes. You can't afford, basically, to be so despondent that you don't do anything.

HUO   It's what we can actually do that I wanted to ask you about. I was wondering if you had any dreams for London or any projects in terms of the future of London?

DM   I don't think I'm that megalomaniac. I'm much more street-level in my thinking. Actually, that's not entirely true because I try and engage in debate at – I still accidentally continue to call it the GLC; that's a Freudian slip – at the GLA level. I do think we should have arguments about the London Plan, criticisms of the London Plan that are not only about its likely effects within the city, but which also think about the effects of London in the country as a whole and on the planet as a whole. So I do believe we need to engage at that level, and I don't think it's a battle that's impossible to win and get some changes.

RK   In this context, how do you see the Olympics? As the death-knell or potential new direction or bifurcation?

DM   I wasn't in favour of the Olympic bid, no – in part because the Olympics has become such a marketing vehicle for a small number of major corporations. And it's a way of engineering the body into something you almost don't want it to be; people are so hyped up into being top athletes. So the question is, is that the only way we can regenerate the Lea Valley and the East End? No, of course it's not. There are other ways of doing it that are much more bottom-up, that are much more street level, that are much more community-based. And that was what I think in the 1980s, not just in London but in lots of cities – the old Municipal Left, as we used to call it – that's what we were trying to do. When the social democratic consensus broke down in this country between the 1960s, 1970s, 1980s, there were different ways out of it. There was Thatcherism and Neo-liberalism on the Far Right and there was a breakout of the Left. Some of the municipal socialism of that period was trying to think about what that might be. The Labour Party, of course, was terrified by any idea like that and found itself in this vacuum called the Third Way, refused to stand up for the Left alternative, and Thatcherism won out. And here we are. That's how I'd see that trajectory. So yes, times are tough!

HUO   Preparing the Marathon, one of the first meetings was with Eric Hobsbawm and he said that in order to resist amnesia we should stage a protest against forgetting. We've followed his advice and asked all the speakers if there are toolboxes from the past that they think, in terms of their own field, are particularly relevant. You, as a professor of geography, venture into all kinds of other fields. Many artists such as Olafur Eliasson are inspired by your books and I was wondering what your inspirations were. Who are your heroes?

DM   Yes, I heard you ask earlier about heroes and I thought, 'My God!' because I don't have heroes. There are other lives that I find fascinating, like Tina Modotti, a photographer, who mixed art, politics, a weird life of continual commitment and travelling everywhere and died in a taxi on the way home from a party at a rather early age. As lives go, that seemed to me to be pretty impressive. She was in Spain for the Civil War, she was in Mexico for the Revolution and so forth. But I don't have heroes. I think Eric's right about forgetting and I think there are projects to make us forget. There have been an awful lot of attempts to make us forget even the 1960s and then again the GLC of the 1980s. The ways in which these get referenced in hegemonic discourses is through dismissal, as jokey; people are dismissive about them.

RK   They're regarded as absurd.

DM   Absolutely. It's a deliberate strategy of erasure from our memory of some of those times when we did have hope, when there were ideas – little ones, not great big ones, not utopian strategies – but things happening. We mustn't let them do that; we mustn't let them wipe those from our memories. Or maybe it's not so much wiping out memories, as reworking the past in such a way that it can no longer inspire. More on the side of my work as a geographer, which you mentioned, I think we underestimate the challenge of space itself, of spatiality itself. There's a lot of understanding of the challenge of time as the dimension of change, as the dimension in which we will all die and all that kind of stuff, and one of my long, long struggles has been to reawaken and to put on the agenda the challenge of space. If time is the dimension of change, then space is the dimension of multiplicity. It's the dimension in which more than one thing can exist at once. In fact, if that wasn't true, there wouldn't even be space. So it's space, in a sense, that's the necessary dimension for the social; space is the dimension in which we encounter the other.

If we fully recognise space then we have to respect the other in the sense of acknowledging their co-eval existence. Jacques Derrida associated space with the attitude of respect, that full recognition of the absolute co-existence now, at this same moment, of others. We adopt strategies all the time to evade that. When we think about globalisation, we talk about 'developed countries' and 'developing countries', but that's like saying that those other countries aren't different from us now, they're just behind us in some singular historical queue. So Nicaragua or Mozambique or somewhere, they're behind, they're developing, they'll one day be just like us, and that's to deny their actually existing difference. It's to say that there's only one way of developing, and it's also, of course, absolutely to occlude our own involvement in their lack of economic development. And that to me isn't taking space seriously; it's turning space into time, turning the contemporaneous differentiation of space into one singular historical queue. And that's just one little example of the ways in which, I think, through our implicit political imaginations, we evade the challenge of space.

RK   Is the space you're talking about the same space that architects work in?
DM   *[Laughs]* I've wondered about that for donkey's years because I've worked with architects a lot.

RK   Or can it be?
DM   Can it be related? I think it can be related. What I'm on about is space as a dimension in the same way as time is a dimension, so in the end it's probably more abstract. I'm not thinking about spaces in quite the same way as you may be as architects. However, one aspect of space as a dimension that I would want to stress is that it's always in the process of production. Quite often we think of time as like all process, change, becoming, and space is seen as just a dead flat, already finished cut through time, a slice through time. I want to emphasise the fact that space is not a surface; it's actually a cut through millions of stories. In that book (*For Space*), I call it 'a simultaneity of stories so far'. It is the fact that right now in Lebanon it's just after midday, and right now something is happening in Lebanon that we'll hear on the news tonight; right now in the Antarctic it's dark and there's this frozen stillness of midwinter; right now in Latin America it's still midnight or just after. It's that feeling of the multiplicity of space, a multiplicity of ongoing sto-

ries, that I want to get hold of. If we think of space like that, then the way it relates to architectural practice is, I think, in terms of space as the intersection of stories, as socially produced, as always moving. One of the essential contradictions then within architecture is that, in a sense, you're enclosing it, pinning it down, carving off bits of it, and that's just a tension, but it's related to the space I'm talking about.

HUO   Many thanks Doreen Massey.
DM   Thank you very much.

Applause, end of interview

Hans Ulrich Obrist   It's a great pleasure to introduce our next speaker, Mary Midgley. Welcome.

Preparing this conversation, we spoke the day before yesterday and you mentioned that the city doesn't play an essential role in your books. But we found something I thought would be very interesting to talk about, which is the idea that cities consume a big percentage of the energy of the universe, I think more than eighty per cent, and so it's easy to conclude that cities are also some form of parasite. I was wondering, in relation to your whole idea of the earth as a self-organisation and Gaia, how you would think about the city as a parasite.

Mary Midgley   Yes, I'm afraid now you've raised this question I shall have to say a lot of rather depressing things. Of course, I love many cities and I know splendid things have gone on in them, but ever since they've been around they've eaten up the territory surrounding them, haven't they? It's striking how people find a city like Angkor Wat, a great ruin, abandoned in the forest, and they say, 'Oh dear! How can anybody have abandoned so vast and splendid a city?'. It turns out that such cities eat up all the territory around them; they use up all the crops and they use up all the wood until in the end they lapse. I suppose in a way one might say this isn't tragic, it's just part of life. Everything is impermanent, as the Buddhists rightly point out. It's not only Angkor Wat, of course; all over the Middle East the ruins of cities have been found, which have apparently eaten up their surroundings in the same sort of way. If some sort of brake could be put on the growth of cities, I suppose something could be done about it. Of course, over the centuries a lot of cities have gone on at a reasonable size and a reasonable pace and haven't done this. Athens is still there, though the Athenians are doing their best to get rid of it in the same sort of way. But now that the extent to which we can eat up is so greatly enlarged that we can eat up the resources from the whole earth and not just around us, it's rather hard to see how unfortunate Gaia, who is a big, hospitable hostess and has done her best over many centuries for the animals that produce this kind of effect, can continue this service. That's my first thought, and I'm sorry, as I say, if it's not a very jolly one.

HUO   I'd be very interested to hear more about this notion of self-organisation and cities from you. It's something we've addressed in numerous previous conversations, but I think your approach is very different; it comes down to self-organisation. I was wondering if there's a link to someone like Lynn Margulis in science, who also talks a lot about Gaia and self-organisation in relation to the city.

MM   Well, yes, I'm always fascinated by our continuity with the whole of the rest of the biosphere and this is a very interesting case of it, because right from the beginning of life a whole lot of self-organisation has had to go on, hasn't it? People who study the origins of life are now pointing out that what looked like very modest molecules managed to organise themselves successively into more and more complex shapes until 'bing', one day, it's alive. It's not a sudden frontier. And then they get more and more complex and one day, 'bing', it's conscious. But I'm not sure that one's so sudden, either. We don't know whether insects are conscious. To my mind consciousness is just a more extreme form of life, so to speak. Life is highly organised activity and as it gets more and more organised it kind of reflects on itself. I don't feel that something quite separate came in when consciousness did, although that used to be the official view. Then when you get your people they organise themselves and 'bing', one day it's a city. Again it's a continuous process, isn't it, and a very fascinating one. Being gloomy at the start about the future of cities, I don't want to underestimate the splendours that those cities have shown over many centuries. It has to be like an organism, doesn't it? And at first it is quite like an organism in that all the parts have to agree more or less, but of course, even by the time of ancient Athens, that was becoming less true; it's a democracy but not for the women and not for the slaves. The consent of all is being asked in a rather special kind of way. The larger it gets, the harder it is for this story about self-organisation to be true, isn't it? Is London organising itself? Well, it is, in a sort of a way; that is, all of the people in it have some sort of indirect role, but it's very hard to make it really work. The cities that we admire most today, I guess, are those of which that's most true; that is, where all the members, all the parts, are most able to take part and where decisions aren't taken regardless of everybody else. This is, again, my first thought about cities and self-organisation. Does that make sense?

HUO   Yes, absolutely. Thank you very much. I'm also curious to hear you speak more about London, because you told me that you'd lived in London about fifty years ago. How do you see the changes in London?

MM   It's still the same London, but like all cities now, the traffic's bloody awful. I can't modify my views about this; I just hate it. I live in Newcastle, which is also an ancient city and is also pretty good except there's too much traffic. I don't know if there's any way of, as it were, training oneself to rejoice in this and seeing it as one more splendid communal activity, but that doesn't come very naturally to me. Apart from that, the only time I really lived in London was early in the Second World War when I was a civil servant. I was living in Kingston, but I was working in London, so I came up to London every day, and often spent my lunch hours looking at the city churches, of which I'm particularly fond, and thinking, 'I hope we can keep that one, but at any rate I've seen St Lawrence, Jewry, now, if it does happen to go'. The thing that bothers me now is that you can hardly find those churches if you haven't got a map. Before, it was all towers: they stuck up as they always had done. You could see this was a city to which the churches were fairly important. Now it's the banks; no mistake, it's a city where the banks are the most important thing. But, of course, that's how life is. Things have to change and I don't get too cross about it.

I wish to put up a psalm of joy about the London parks. This one's lovely and the other day my sons and I were sitting in Green Park in the evening and it's absolutely gorgeous. What we owe to those Victorian people who fought for those parks can't be exaggerated, I think. A city without parks is dreadful. I was in São Paulo once. I don't know if anyone else here has had that appalling experience. São Paulo, though it's very old, has been built absolutely continuously house next to house. Someone I knew had a house in São Paulo that did have a garden and everybody was saying to them, 'When are you going to build on that plot?'. We have in London a city that's not like that. It seems to me an endless cause for delight.

Rem Koolhaas   You've already spoken about churches and I've been trying without success to get our previous guests to say something about religion. You seem to be the first person that we might even hope to elicit a comment from on religion.

MM   *[Laughs]* What angle would you like? I suppose there are two angles that I could say something about. I could say something about Gaia and religion. What I'm actually working on at the moment is trying to understand the theory of intelligent design. That's made me aware, as I wasn't before, of how much the American attitude to religion is influential in politics at present. That may be rather a political topic – would you like…?

RK   Please, go ahead.

MM   You like that one?
        [Laughter]

RK   Yes.

MM   *[Laughs]* Where will I start?

RK   I like your phrasing: that you're 'trying to understand the theory of intelligent design'. I think we all are.

MM   I knew that this was being put forward as a sort of compromise between the Creationist view that the whole of the Bible is literally true and some kind of modern science, and I knew that the modern scientists say, 'Sorry, chum, it hasn't worked'. And I found that still to be true the more I investigated. But the interesting thing is why it's being attempted. I didn't realise how far the American public is, and has always been, deeply dedicated to that Biblical story, particularly to the literal interpretation of Genesis and also to the Book of Revelation, which is much worse because it's prophecy. The Book of Revelation says there'll be a thousand years when Christ will rule and that will be the end of everything. It seems that a great mass of the American people have a view of this, which is really not common over here, which is that Christ will only rule after the end of the world, as it were. There will come a terrific catastrophe, an Armageddon, and a lot of war and only after that can Christ come and rule. The only thing to do before that is to see to one's own salvation. An enormous number of Protestant sects that emigrated to America because they weren't welcome in Europe or were thrown out and so forth, had these extreme Protestant views: that the Bible is terribly important and what the Bible said was that there would be this frightful Armageddon and so forth, so anyone who dedicates themselves to trying to improve things is wasting their time. The idea that by improving things you could bring about this wonderful thousand years is held to be heathen and pagan and very unsatisfactory. All you can do is wait and the notion of the rapture, which has come up quite lately, that you will be rapt up in heaven if you're saved, really is pretty influential.

I'm sorry, I'm going to sound a bit alarmist about this, but I'm feeling a bit alarmed. A lot of Americans, of course, don't believe a word of this any more than most of us do, but they do tend to be on the East Coast, in the North or in the large cities. They tend to be intellectuals and are deeply suspected by the millennialist people. The figure that's sticking in my mind, and I'll stop after that, is that when asked what sort of science should be taught in schools, forty-five per cent will say direct Creationism, forty per cent will say intelligent design and you can teach both – you can teach ordinary evolution and intelligent design. Twelve per cent only will say that ordinary evolution of the kind that every paid-up scientist believes in should be taught. This is a gap and it's a political and moral gap much more than an intellectual gap, I think. It's a gap between the tribes that people seem to belong to. So I'm not sure if I'm talking about religion, really, when I talk about this, because I think it's a strange form of religion. I certainly want to say that Christianity as such doesn't call for this at all. My father was a parson who had no question about evolution, thought it was perfectly alright and always had. In fact in 1980 when the State of Arkansas passed a law saying that evolution should not be taught in schools, those prosecuting the State of Arkansas were the American Civil Liberties Union and twelve theological bodies; only one scientific body bothered. There's an awful difficulty, I think, with people talking to each other and understanding what the other is doing, because it's this great tribal divide. I think it's very bad now that people like Richard Dawkins are identifying Darwinism with atheism.

HUO   That's exactly what I wanted to ask you, because you've taken very combative positions against a reductivist scientific paradigm and also against a kind of mechanistic view of the genome, a very opposed position to Richard Dawkins.

MM   I'm often in trouble for having been a bit sharp with him, but he's been sharp with other people, so I don't feel too bad about that. I think it's like this: that he's done a monumental and very good job of showing the continuity of humans with the rest of creation: that the same sort of natural selection and other processes that have made us have made all the other creatures and we're really part of that continuum. This is terribly important to me; I think very highly of it and I think he's done that very well and got it through to many people. He's got a view about genetics that's, in the view of many geneticists, a bit one-sided and extreme: namely, that it's genes that the selection is among and not groups or individuals, but that doesn't matter so much. What really bothers me is the rhetoric, the language of selfishness and investment, because people pick that up inevitably in its ordinary, every-day meaning. He says it's only a metaphor, but metaphors are terribly important, especially the dominant, noisy metaphors that you put on your book covers. The idea that the genes are selfish is not, in fact, compatible with individuals being selfish. The idea is that your genes will make you unselfish if that will cause you to have more children and therefore to become a prevalent trend in evolution. In principle, it shouldn't mean that at all but people do take it that way. As the age was in any case greatly prejudiced in favour of selfishness, you know it's a highly individualistic sort of age; this wasn't something that needed saying. People do identify evolution itself with selfishness, with the survival of the fittest in the sense that everybody's out for their own ends and nobody ever bothers about anybody else. He has himself often used the word in that sense. And it's not only him, of course, it's socio-biologists generally, but I got very excited when that book *The Selfish Gene* came out and I wrote an article about it – I've not done it again – a very cross article that was by no means fair to Dawkins. But I do think individualism is a terrible danger to us because, although we've had excellent things out of it since the Enlightenment, lots of individual freedom and regard for each person on their own, if you carry that too far you lose the whole communal sense, the social glue that binds us, the sense of the importance of the whole, and I'm sure that we've fallen too far that way.

HUO   Following up on the question about religion, it would be really interesting to hear if you think Gaia is a religion.

MM   Well, it isn't a religion in the sense of being a sect with temples and priests and Ten Commandments; it's not meant to be like that at all. The word 'Gaia' is used to mean the Earth considered as a self-maintaining whole, a continuous being of which we're all part. When James

Lovelock invented that idea, he found people didn't understand it very well. He complained of this to his friend William Golding, the novelist, and I think he said, 'I want a four-letter word'. William Golding said, 'Why don't you call it Gaia, which is the ancient Greek goddess of the Earth?' But there never has been any suggestion of putting up temples. It's just that I think the idea of the Earth as our parent got through to people imaginatively and they then were able to pick this up. There are all sorts of difficulties, but I think, you see, that when the Greeks regarded the Earth as the mother of gods and men, they were taking an attitude to it that was a very proper attitude, though we wouldn't express it like that today. It's a matter of awe, gratitude, reverence, for something much greater than us, of which we're part, and you see it really does correct the sort of idea that's been around since the seventeenth century: that matter is inert stuff, just billiard balls, little blocks that bang off each other, and we bring in the spirit, which causes all the movement. That contemptuous, really, attitude to the rest of nature is what we've been brought up with, though we haven't noticed it as much as we should have done, and I think that the imagery of Gaia is good in so far as it corrects that. It really isn't a matter of setting up a sect.

HUO   Speaking with Charles Jencks, who knows your work very well, and reading your book *Beast and Man* [1978], we wondered if you think that there's a human nature.

MM   Oh, absolutely, yes! I've spent an awful lot of ink and time saying so. The idea that there's no such thing as human nature was part of a grotesque exaggeration that the Behaviourists made: that everything was due to society. Well where does society come from? Social conditioning. There's got to be somebody doing it. We're an animal like other animals with a marked emotional constitution. On top of that, of course, we do have a lot of culture; we do have much more complex and interesting ways of guiding and shifting and shaping this in the course of our lives than most animals do, and that, of course, is terribly important. But that isn't the side that's been exaggerated. Marx similarly said there wasn't any such thing as human nature, meaning that it's economics that does it all. Similarly, what's economics? The behaviour of men in markets. People are there behind all that. I've made a lot of effort in *Beast and Man* and everywhere else to make people feel alright with the idea of human nature, to say that it's not an oppressive kind of idea. Freedom is quite compatible with our having a natural constitution; indeed, if we didn't have any natural constitution we presumably wouldn't have the motives to cause us to want to be free. To get rid of that conflict has been, I think, my main writing interest.

HUO Many, many thanks Mary Midgley.
MM   Thank you.

Applause, end of interview

Rem Koolhaas I'd like to welcome now a combination that we've generated, who may be surprised to be paired, but who've generously consented to it. Mark Cousins, who's working at the Architectural Association and is responsible for its intellectual content, and Patrick Keiller, who's a film- and television-maker.

Can I start with you, Mark, just because I know you the best and there's a particular aspect of your recent interest that I find really important. You're giving a course on 'the ugly', and you're identifying the ugly as a category that's not necessarily the opposite of beauty, or not even dependent on beauty. I think that if you listen with a kind of metaphysical anxiety to the twenty-four hours, there's a very noticeable absence of weight, a preference for pleasantness and beauty and collectively, perhaps, a denial of the ugly. Can you describe the ugly or give us an impression of what its virtues are or what it has to offer us at this point?

Mark Cousins Well, if I can just try very briefly to summarise it, I've long held the position that within aesthetic discourse it's quite wrong to oppose beauty and ugliness, but if you think about it that's precisely what happens throughout the history of philosophy. If one goes back to any kind of antiquity or to Christian philosophy, then essentially you have this trinity of positive concepts: truth, beauty and good. In a sense they also define their opposites: error, the ugly and the evil. It's still, of course, the case that many writers tend to be sentimentally wafted away by this trinity of the good, the beautiful and the true, which is ludicrously anachronistic within modernity in the first place, but my point here would be that it defines the ugly as the negative of beauty. So you don't have to know anything about the ugly, as it were; it's already defined for you – you just strike out the plus and put in the minus. So if in antiquity beauty was defined initially as a totality, then ugliness will have its first draft as being fragments. It's not only that. It means that under that whole metaphysical dispensation the negatives are all themselves tied together, so that what is ugly is also erroneous and is also wicked. If we ask under what conditions might we treat very ugly people cruelly it's precisely that dispensation.

I define, then, the ugly as independent of the question of the beautiful. I define it as something that is there but is experienced as if it should not; or the special case of something that's not there that is thought should be. The point of that definition and the investigation that surrounds it, that hangs from it, I find quite a useful way of looking at a lot of phenomena. Let me give you one example. In the novel of Gaston Leroux, *The Phantom of the Opera*, the girls of the *corp de ballet* describe having seen the ghost of Room 54 and they say, describing the kind of skeletal frame of the ghost, that the ghost seems to have no eyes. Then the scene-shifter, who has seen the ghost, says, 'And he has no nose and that no nose is a hideous thing to look at'. That itself is an important observation because it enters us into the whole observation of negative or invisible objects as part of our investigation. It's not that I think this should simply be inverted and we should call the ugly the beautiful; on the contrary. It's rather that the ugly is something there to be tolerated; that's to say, it poses a threat to us. That which is there and is thought shouldn't be, or that which is not there and we experience as should be, poses us with a difficulty, but it's a difficulty which is worth, indeed is vital, for all of us to surmount and survive within, shall we say, the experience of the city. It doesn't have to mean that every proposal for the city is a kind of ceaseless beautification and jollification, but also an elaboration of the value of the experience that can come about by being threatened, unnerved, presented with some kind of obstacle to surmount. Ultimately, my account of what it is that's being surmounted doesn't really matter; it's actually a way of coming to terms with one's own finitude. We can use the city as a way of coming to terms with that finitude, with that mortality, in a creative rather than depressed way by actually surviving those negative elements of the city that don't belong simply to beautification and jollification.

RK Do you think Neo-liberalism and the market are compatible with ugliness or do you think that they drive the horror of ugliness?

MC I think they're unintentionally capable of ugliness; that's to say, when they try to do something beautiful, from my point of view it usually has the inadvertent quality of being ugly. I think it's a problem in architecture schools that terms like 'regeneration' or 'improvement' still have a somewhat unthought naïve quality of beautification, even though architects are quick to say, 'I don't mean that in an aesthetic sense'.

What possible sense could you mean in it? I think it would be quite difficult in schools of architecture to say, 'I present this as a project that presents people with the inevitable difficulties of overcoming their experience of it'.

RK	Is the ugly in your definition fundamentally different from the abject in Bataille?
MC	It's not derived from that, but it's somewhat consistent with it, or somewhat consistent with the abject in Kristeva. In all these writers, you can find an exploration, an attempt to deal with negativity – not, on the one hand, in a dialectical way, in a Hegelian way, where it's subsumed into something kind of good, nor on the other hand, in a simply negative way – but actually seeing it as a permanent condition that in being tolerated finds its kind of virtue. I think one of the problems is that we don't really have a language for urban experience save that of improvement. It would seem quite capricious, quite perverse, almost anti-social, to propose something negative in the city as having a value.
RK	Is London a good case-study for ugliness, and does it continue to be, or is it losing that capacity?
MC	I'm a user of the city and I'm not an authority on the city. I think the ratio's changed very much in thirty years. I think there have been perfectly reasonable improvements, but there's still a great space for a sort of anonymous negativity. When, as it were, we face a situation where the whole built environment becomes one managed plot, then that becomes a very important kind of issue: what is to be left alone? Where is the non-improved to be?
Hans Ulrich Obrist	We were talking about memory and I've always been fascinated that your medium is more the lecture, or more the speech, than the book. There seems to be a form of resistance against the idea of a book, so could you tell us about this?
RK	Is this intentional?
MC	[Laughs] Yes, well. Oh dear. [Laughs] I'm tempted to say that's a secret, but I'll try to share it. Maybe I could start by saying something about memory, actually, because listening to Doreen and hearing her quote Eric Hobsbawm, while I'm sure all that stuff is kind of true, I'd slightly like to bend the stick back the other way and say that in some sense I think

we ought occasionally to cultivate our capacity to forget. As Nietzsche pointed out in his text on the abuse of history, a culture that becomes merely saturated with historical memory is one that loses any kind of cultural indiscretion, any capacity to actually intervene in a new and brave way, that in a sense the example of the past becomes itself a kind of inhibition. Nor do I think one's political capacity to engage and identify with injustice and to act against it is necessarily improved by memory. Obviously many of these things have got condensed in a dramatic fashion around issues of Holocaust memorials, but when Holocaust memorials proliferate so much… I can't remember what town, it is in Germany, has in its baroque square a little black box by Sol LeWitt that's a Holocaust memorial – but nobody can remember what the little black box is supposed to be reminding you of. Secondly, the Holocaust memorial in Germany is undoubtedly a way of allowing the German middle classes to continue in their dreadful identification with their own collective guilt, a form of guilt for which I for one would have no time at all. So I think one has to be aware of the dangers of memory.

Passing to the question of publication, there is far too much publication and although I shall have to join it at some point, every morning I postpone that day.

[Laughter]

HUO   It's actually nice to hear that sort of comment after listening to Eleanor Bron about the publication that she edited of Cedric Price's work where the books were dispersed and it was more about the list and not the books as an object.

We have many questions for Patrick Keiller and then perhaps at the end we could bring the two conversations together. Your work has often been associated with resistance and also anger in relation to urban conditions. Could you talk a little bit about that?

Patrick Keiller   It's very kind of you to say that, Hans Ulrich, but it's not really my anger it's the anger of a fictional character, you have to understand. Do you really think it's anger? I find that difficult. What I try to do in the work that you are referring to, which is, I think, these two films which are now quite old, it should be said, is not so much get angry but I have set out an exposition of the way things were. The first of the films, which is called *London*, which was photographed in 1992 and released in 1994 was based, I think, on a critique of London which was probably formed in the 1980s and to some extent the 1970s and was answered almost as soon as the film was complete, actually. Almost humorously, as soon as the print was in the cinema a kind of complaint about public space was dealt with very swiftly by the market and all sorts of things arrived from Seattle and everybody's been happy ever since. Now the other one, *Robinson in Space*, was a little bit more of a journey of discovery and was an attempt to answer various questions about the UK's material economy, specifically the imagined plight of its manufacturing industry, in that the UK was, by the mid-1990s, seen as an economy in which production was not really an issue any more and had vanished to far-flung parts of the globe. I wondered how this was sustainable economically because all through the 1980s we had been faced with visible industrial decay. You only had to look out of a railway train window to see derelict factories. The whole of Birmingham was laid waste and then gradually supermarkets appeared where some of the factories had been. I had the idea that the whole landscape had turned into one of a consumer economy and that production was something that happened elsewhere, and I wondered how it was possible for people to go on eating when they had nothing to export. But in fact this proved to be an illusion and the UK was an extremely successful manufacturing economy; it was just that its exports were things that didn't employ very many people to make. This for me was a kind of revelation, so it wasn't so much anger, it was a question of understanding and the revelation, such as it was, was that we were not living through a period of industrial decline or economic decline, we were living through a period of extraordinary economic success. *Robinson in Space* was photographed in 1995 and it was released in 1997. 1997 was the last year, and also the first year for many years, when the UK had an export surplus, a very small export surplus it must be said, but it did have an export surplus in 1997 and it had been tending towards that for several years. So there was this whole stereotype of an economy that doesn't produce any manufactured goods and is reliant on financial services. Going back to what Doreen was talking about, we were fed this line that the City was somehow important for the UK's economy. The City exports virtually nothing. We could manage quite easily without it and still have half the south of England driving around in imported cars, as so many people do. So it wasn't so much about getting angry as an attempt to reveal the condition of the UK's material economy.

I should say, also, that I thought that this situation would last, that the form of globalisation which we encountered in 1995 was kind of a future, it was a modernity, and one of the reasons for making the film was to try and portray a modernity after a period of restructuring that looked as if it would be durable to some extent. But this proved, of course, to be an illusion and 1995 was a *moment*, if you will forgive me, in a much more elaborate historical process, as I think probably became clear fairly soon afterwards, certainly by the millennium. It was clear that this idea of a consumerist future, which you might not like but it kind of works, soon stopped working. *[Laughs]* And now we have this other thing which I must confess that I am at something of a loss to figure out, except that it seems that what we used to think of as globalisation was in fact something else and it was to do with the United States and to some extent still is, except that everybody seems to think that's not going to last either. So watch this space!

If I make another film, which I rather hope to do, I think the things that exercise me are, on the one hand, the revival of what we experience here as Gordon Brown's interest in Britishness, which seems to me entirely misguided and completely hopeless and in fact totally at odds with anything one might even consider to be Britishness, because the whole point of Britishness, if there is any point to it, is that you don't have one. The other thing is the implications of the increased demand for and possible peak in production of oil, which seems to me might continue to affect these questions of production. I should explain why I keep banging on about production. It's not just because I was a little boy in the 1950s and had a Meccano set, although that could have something to do with it, it's to do with the idea that the quality of life in some respects depends on the ability to produce artefacts, or to have some involvement at least in the production of artefacts other than just purchasing them. That's probably a rather old-fashioned and naïve belief but I think that's why I continually return to this question of production. It has to do, obviously, with the built environment. One of the reasons that new houses in this country are so despicable is that we are, by and large, an economy that declines to produce its own artefacts so when we have to, which is what we have to do with houses, we are not very good at it.

Sorry, that was a very long answer.

RK At the end of the biography we received, which is probably a rehash of many CVs, there is an indication that you are now working on a study of the former Victoria Terminus in Mumbai and that you are also working on an installation *Londres, Bombay: Villes du Futur*.

PK   Yes. *[Laughs]* These are the same thing.

RK   A preoccupation with Bombay/Mumbai.

PK   This was a commission, Rem. Somebody rang me up from Lille last autumn and asked me to propose a video installation for an exhibition which was already called *Londres, Bombay: Villes du Futur?* The question mark is important. I said, 'Why do you think London and Bombay are the cities of the future?' I still haven't had a good answer, I have to say, so I made up my own answer, which is something to do with the submarine telegraph and Neo-liberalism and all these kinds of things that we talked about and then thought: 'What on earth can you possibly do?' At about the same time I read the novel *Austerlitz* and also I read an essay by Roger Luckhurst which is called 'The Contemporary London Gothic and the Limits of the "Spectral Turn"', so I came rather belatedly to this idea of Contemporary Gothic. I'd always been interested in urban Gothic of the nineteenth century, the 1890s of Dracula and so forth, which cropped up in the films. And there's this interesting game one can play which is to spot the similarities between the two *fins de siècle*, the fear of terrorism and so forth. Knowing very little about Bombay/Mumbai, I could think of no better idea than to attempt to rebuild its railway station in Lille as a 30-screen video installation, which I am currently doing.

HUO   Maybe to conclude, a question to both of you. I was wondering if you had any dreams for London or projects for London which have not yet been realised.

PK   After you. I've got one!

MC   Well I think I have to, in a sense, refuse the question because I think one can dream of spaces but I'm not sure exactly that you can dream of places, or rather if you dream of places they are always a substitute for somewhere else. That is to say, the dream of a place very rarely turns out in any sense to be about the place itself, so I think the real question here is substitution. Dreaming of places is really a wish to connect them to a series of substitutions, which is kind of valuable in itself. I think that stands very much against another tradition of looking at the idea of place, which is that it has its own essential integrity and that's been influential in a certain, to my mind, conservative architectural kind of thought and urbanist thought and really can't be abandoned too soon because I think we are extraordinarily disabled if we think that place is given under some kind of essential Aristotelian notions of *topos*. Actually the cosmos is considerably more open than that.

PK   I think we need – I don't know if it's a dream – a proper metropolitan government and a lot of public sector housing. I don't know whether we are going to get it but it seems to me pretty obvious that it would be a very good thing to have both these.

HUO   Many thanks Mark Cousins and Patrick Keiller.

Applause, end of interview

Rem Koolhaas

Our next guest, and the last guest in this block, is Jonathan Glancey, currently the architecture critic of *The Guardian* and, before that, the architecture critic of *The Independent*.

I have read your book *London: Bread and Circuses* [2003] and I was really astonished how frank, honest, direct and occasionally brutal it was. If I compare it to your architecture reviews I notice a huge gap – I don't know whether it's sincerity or freedom – in terms of articulating a genuinely critical point of view. Can you talk about that?

Jonathan Glancey

Sure. That's a very interesting notion. The media is not free; it never has been, even newspapers that set themselves up, like *The Independent* in 1986, to be just that – independent – or *The Guardian*, which is owned by a charitable trust rather than a commercial monster like Rupert Murdoch. These newspapers are theoretically free to publish whatever they like, to discuss things in any way they like, but actually there's a kind of passive force at work which I've been hyper-aware of for a number of years now that tries to bring arguments down – especially in cultural coverage – to a safe, comfortable level of gentle, easy 'massage'.

If you're working as a journalist, or as a critic, and you go to section editors of newspapers, they don't really want you to let rip with ideas unless your given job at that particular moment is to be the columnist who is sanctioned to let rip. Then you would be labelled, or 'branded', as the paper's 'controversial' critic. If you want to be a critic with a spectrum of moods and you want to discuss something complex like architecture and planning, you will actually be told in a very gentle way – it's very strange – not to be too tough. In fact, the way this is done is not by saying you can't write about certain things, but by saying you should only be writing about certain things. In other words, architecture at the moment, as the media sees it, is largely about nice, shiny, glamorous buildings. Most of them, these days, are called 'iconic'. Rem designs some himself, and the more exciting the buildings are, the more excited commissioning editors are.

Equally, if they don't have big 'iconic' buildings to publish, then they want lovely, shiny houses, the sorts of houses you've all built yourselves or converted, the lovely, gorgeous flat you somehow 'found' in a skip and converted and made very charming; that's what the media wants. In other words, a happy, shiny, passive world with a bit of maverick design by Zaha Hadid, Daniel Libeskind, Rem Koolhaas and so on. To be truly free to write what you really want to, you have to write books. You write the book and then you can get a feature article published on the back of the book. It's a very, very strange publishing system, and it's consistent throughout the mass media.

Hans Ulrich Obrist   We've asked many of the speakers about a theory of London and the idea of London being too complex to have a theory. Your book *Bread and Circuses* is almost manifesto about London now. I was wondering if you could try to tell us, starting from *Bread and Circuses*, but bringing it right into the present, how you see this city now.

JG   When a city gets to a certain size, and I think ancient Rome was the first city to get to this size – over a million people – it develops a certain characteristic, which is a desire to do more and more things. So the bigger a city, the more activity it has. Exponentially. A city like London with eight million people today has a tremendous number of activities, including such things as a twenty-four hour 'talkathon' here at the Serpentine. Extraordinary events like this happen when a city gets so big. People in big cities want to do more and more and more. And, as these cities get wealthier, people want to be constantly excited. Roman emperors and the Roman patrician class understood early on that there's a danger of people getting bored and when they get too bored they start kicking balls around the street and then kicking heads around the street. Prosperity doesn't necessarily lead to peace.

London itself, when it became a very exciting and prosperous city in the eighteenth century, was one of the most violent places in the Western world; its riots were famous, its mob was famous. At times it was actually a very vicious place indeed. The response, on the one hand, from the authorities was to be vicious back, and there were more ways of getting yourself executed in London in the mid-eighteenth century than there were in many European cities; tiny crimes could lead to a public execution. The public executions themselves were, of course, great entertainments; they excited the crowd, they were a way of releasing violence. That was later replaced by Association Football and other events and today by, of course, Culture. Culture has grown and grown and grown to become a great mass entertainment, whether television or public events or museums or art galleries, or coming up now, the Olympics. To run a city today, to stop people from being bored, you must keep them entertained to stop them becoming violent. If you look at what's happened in London over the past twenty years it's fascinating. There are virtually no political demonstrations. Very occasionally – there was one about the Iraq War. The events that do happen tend to be small. People aren't out there saying, 'We want to change the world' or simply, 'We protest'. They can all be bought off. Sunday shopping. How wonderful; what a great thing! Surfing the Internet, wonderful! Downloading your i-Pod, going to the Tate Modern, going to a 'talkathon', whatever it is, just keep the people amused. Shopping malls: keep building them bigger and bigger and shinier and shinier, and people will act out a passive, easy life. I think that's what has happened to London. It's exciting in some ways, because pretty much everyone has access to all these new technologies and goods, but it's a deeply passive existence with none of that thrilling, raw energy it once had.

HUO   One of the topics you've addressed particularly strongly is the problematic notion of regeneration.

JG   Regeneration is a word used by politicians and quangos.

HUO   Exactly. I thought it would be interesting to talk about this because I think it is something you are working on right now.

JG   Very much. Let's take the example in London of how to excite people, of how to make them feel there's something happening in the future. The two big projects in London for architecture planning and culture and political excitement are the 2012 Olympics and the Thames Gateway. They are both wrapped around this idea of regeneration. Traditionally, of course, this was a spiritual notion, to regenerate yourself in soul and your spirit. Today it means something quite different: it's a word used by these endlessly growing quangos and other official bodies. Just while I'm talking I can imagine a new quango being formed there, and another one there with twenty-five people and, probably many more, being given new jobs talking about 'regeneration', 'accessibility', 'twenty-four hour lifestyles', yakkey-yakkety-yak… and these organizations and the jargon they use will continue to grow.

The 2012 Olympics and Thames Gateway are extraordinarily cynical ways of trying to keep Londoners entertained. They are cynical partly because they are property development wrapped up in smart-sounding words; it's a way of making London a deeply passive, property development-led, business-led city, which of course it always has been. But the new notion of regeneration is not real; it's not about making the city a better place, it's about making more opportunities for business, for property development and for keeping people rooted in their passive, Sunday-shopping way of life.

RK   Are we victims?

JG   Yes.

RK   Are you a victim?

JG   Sure. I'm a Londoner, so of course I am. Londoners in history, though, do tend to fight back every so often.

RK   I would like to compare your presentation to Doreen Massey's. Did you hear that a little earlier? She is sitting over there.

Doreen Massey   Hi!

JG   Hello!

RK   Do you know her?

JG   No.

RK   She is a professor of geography, and presented a critique of London which is on the one hand more precise and, let's say, less apocalyptic, and on the other hand more political. How do you think your rhetoric helps us?

JG   You need to be political.

RK   Or, what do you want to achieve with your rhetoric? Because, on the one hand you have told us you cannot say what you want to say in the paper, but you say it here in a very eloquent way and in a way which is almost contradictory to your seeming powerless in the media.

JG   Interesting. I'm with you, Rem. There's no question that there are a lot of delightful new buildings or developments to show people in the media and to say 'these are good things'. When one actually likes them and thinks they're a good thing, one can write about them in a gently positive way. There's no problem with that. Balancing this with the big political picture, the problem is there's not enough of that kind of positive development, planning and architecture. We're talking about a very political subject – architecture, planning – it's hugely political, and we can't get away from this. The danger is the media tries to de-politicise these subjects by making them the stuff of fluffy 'Culture' and smart entertainment.

RK	Are you re-politicising it?
JG	Yes.
RK	With this book.
JG	Sure. I'm following up with another book that will look at the whole notion of regeneration. There are several ways of looking at this, looking at the language it's presented in, its rhetoric, and then looking at the way a lot of the hot air used to talk about it is a smokescreen to look after property development. If you look at what's happening out in the Thames Gateway area, it's extraordinary. I don't know how many of you have been to any of these conferences about regeneration. They are wonderful to go to; you will be absolutely bored stiff after the second hour, but it's very entertaining to listen to the language used and to watch the people who are regenerating your cities for you.
RK	Introduced by John Prescott.
JG	Well John Prescott's involvement is a joke. Meanwhile, on the subject of quangos and regeneration bodies, there are many people whose job in life is to be a professional quango-person, and they're trying to create worlds where they can tick boxes and nurture neat developments they can say are 'happy', 'twenty-four-hour', 'accessible', 'cappuccino culture', lah-de-dah, when, in fact, they're just building a kind of purgatory.
RK	Did you choose your title yourself?
JG	Yes.
RK	We have been confronted with a number of people who have been forced to change their titles. *London: Bread and Circuses*; is that metaphor not a little bit on the neat side?
JG	It's very much on the neat side, but there was a point. It was towards the late eighteenth century, and into the nineteenth century, where many people living in London, and certainly running London, started to be aware, as Britain developed its empire, of this notion that London was the new Rome. At its height, Rome was a city that was both planned and chaotic, and London is both planned and chaotic. They had some of the same problems, too. I couldn't help feeling that the way, today, of trying to keep everybody living this happy, shiny, calm, consumerist way of life is, in a certain way, very similar to the way the Romans organised a bread and circuses way of life to keep people amused, and passive, with shopping, hand-outs and sport.

HUO   We are trying to make a list of toolboxes from previous generations at the end of the Marathon; so I was wondering, if you look at the urban condition of London now, what models you think could be interesting to mention.

JG   London's a funny city. It's a mercantile city, of course, rapaciously mercantile. It's a city based, from Queen Elizabeth I, on piracy, on big business, cutting a swaggering swathe through the world of commerce, of ships going out – ships that later formed the Royal Navy – raiding other ships, sinking the Spaniards, and bringing the gold home. This piratical rapaciousness has been London's great strength, financially. At the moment it's going through a phase where this is the predominant force working in the city; a ruthless commercialness. There are moments where it tries to be morally good, but these are few and far between. My favourite moment is almost totally incomprehensible to anyone who doesn't know how the city was more than fifty years ago. It was that wonderful moment where you had public authorities, public bodies, a public realm that was growing and run by very decent people who really believed you could do something with this city, and its great wealth, to improve its public life. They were, of course, the London County Council, which ran from 1889 and became the Greater London Council, and was destroyed by Mrs Thatcher, and the London Passenger Transport Board formed in 1933. I bang on about this in *Bread and Circuses*. Can you imagine that London Transport was one of the greatest civilising agents in Western Europe for a period of about twenty years? Almost impossible to imagine the notion that you all. Here was a moment when you had public bodies, people working in a public realm, who genuinely believed in it. Those people have been cleared out, very successfully, today and we are back in our rapacious, piratical world.

RK   We had a conversation with the new manager of public transport.

JG   Tim O'Toole.

RK   Your description is identical, and he definitely wants a return of that moment.

JG   Well, he would. You've seen how piratical our public services are today. Just look at that poor man, Tim O'Toole, trying to run the London Underground today, or Peter Hendy, the Commissioner for Transport in London. They're not allowed to do what they want to run the thing as well as they want to. Their maintenance contracts have been sold off to cowboy businesses to make someone a fast buck, to top up pension funds and so they can play golf and retire to smart villas abroad. It's utterly, utterly cynical, but our public services are run this way now, and this breaking-up of the public realm by is something that creates deep cynicism, and anger, amongst many of us. Certainly some have watched the New Labour movement in power at Westminster suffering very badly in the last few years as it's plunged into this world of ultra-capitalism, that's not, in the end, what any of us truly want.

HUO   Thank you very much, Jonathan Glancey.
JG   Thank you very much.

Applause, end of interview

Gustav Metzger
Isaac Julien
Gautam Malkani
Richard Hamilton
Peter Cook
Chantal Mouffe

Hans Ulrich Obrist	It's a great pleasure to introduce our next guest. Welcome Gustav Metzger. *[Applause]* Gustav Metzger is the only guest of our Marathon who has actually been here since the very first moment.
Rem Koolhaas	That's why they are applauding…
HUO	One of the first times we met was in Café Cosmo, when you told me about your very long relation to London, about your arrival as a refugee in the 1930s and about your studies with David Bomberg. I think it would be very interesting if you could tell us a little bit about your beginnings in London.
Gustav Metzger	Well, my first contact with London was in a bus coming from the coast, where five hundred refugee children, including my elder brother, Max Mendel, and myself were travelling from the Hook of Holland to Harwich. After a few weeks on the coast we were transported into London and my first image of London is thousands of lights as we passed through the traffic, looking back onto this array of traffic lights, which of course I had never seen before, coming from a relatively small town, Nuremberg, in Germany. The next strong memory was every Sunday we refugee children were transported to the grandest cinema in London at the time, the Gaumont State, Kilburn, where we were given the best balcony seating for nothing, as a gift. So these are the first memories. Some months after the end of the war we both came back to London and started our studies, which went on for seven or eight years. I don't think there is time to tell you more.
HUO	It would be good to hear more about David Bomberg because we have heard a lot about…
RK	… schools.
HUO	Yes, and we've heard about memory and transmission.
GM	Again, let me start with a first impression. We had problems finding enough life classes to complete our studies so in the end we had, my brother and I, attended four different classes, including one in Hammersmith, and we were told to go to the Borough Polytechnic as one other school; the problem was heating the life classes at that time of

scarcity. I remember walking into the life room and there was a small man who looked very unprepossessing and that was David Bomberg, but within a few weeks one realised this was not an ordinary person. He was charismatic, he had enormous experience, and he was, I think, a great artist. He did his utmost to teach everyone, literally everyone in that thirty, forty-strong class, whatever was possible. For years beyond 1945 I would attend his classes. At the end he had evening classes only, from 1950–53; I lived outside London much of the time and at night would travel in just for the two hours' study with him. So I can't be more positive on Bomberg; whatever I said, it wouldn't reach the level of significance he had for me and for so many others.

RK   If I may skip a number of phases, I understand you were a kind of member of Fluxus. Were you officially a member of Fluxus, or unofficially?

GM   Actually that is a bit of a misunderstanding. The essential facts are that Daniel Spoerri and Robert Filliou agreed to organise an exhibition in London and this took place at Gallery One in October 1962. In that exhibition there were Ben Vautier, Arthur Köpcke and Robin Page. In the end there were four or five people who would be going into Fluxus, which barely existed at that point, certainly not in England. So, since I took part in the exhibition indirectly and definitely took part in an evening at the ICA, where we were joined by Dick Higgins and his wife, Alison Knowles, who were absolutely Fluxus at that time, it is said that this evening was the first Fluxus event in England and I think that's a reasonable thing to say. But beyond that, I never had any direct contact either with Fluxus or with the participants in that event.

HUO   What is interesting is that you wrote your own manifestos and that is something we have discussed a lot in previous interviews. We are living now in a time where there are less manifestos. You told me previously you have been influenced by Wyndham Lewis. I was wondering if you could tell us a little bit about your manifestos and to which extent they were related to an earlier twentieth-century notion of manifesto, such as those of Wyndham Lewis, or to which extent there was a difference.

GM   Well, both. The answer is the case as you put it, inevitably. I eagerly sought out any avant-garde movement going and studied it as a very young student, and it must have influenced my later development when it came to the point of me writing manifestos.

HUO   What was the first manifesto you wrote?

GM   That was the autumn of 1959, 'Auto-destructive Art'.

HUO   One of the things this Marathon tries to cope with is the impossibility of a portrait of London and yet we have had a lot of different points of view over the last seventeen hours. We were wondering how you see London now and what your perspective on the city is, and how it changed in six decades.

GM   It changed enormously. Once I walked late at night from one of these big squares near Victoria all the way to Brick Lane near where I lived, and it was just like walking in a village. This was in early 1946, in winter. Just the moonlight. I don't remember seeing a car. Today we have the night buses – let me put it like that. This is the contrast. That's my early experience of London, which was very beautiful. Even the bombsites had a certain beauty. My brother and I worked at the John Cass Institute in Aldgate on a bombsite, carving bombsite stones. This was 1946 and for a couple of years we carved on that bombsite.

RK   You have attended this event, where there has been an enormous amount of representation from the art world. Can you comment on your closeness or distance from the artists you have heard? I try to imagine how somebody like you, who organised an art strike, would look at the current generation of artists. I would like to know your feeling of closeness or distance and simply your comment.

GM   That's difficult. There is now so much going on in this country, not only in London. All over the country artistic activity is expanding enormously – manifestations, performances, exhibitions, in places that spring up every few weeks... To judge that is actually impossible for anybody, certainly for me. But a few general points. I do believe there is quite much weakness. When I go round some of the art school diploma exhibitions I see a lot of weakness and playfulness which do not in the least correspond to the reality of life, either in this country or worldwide. And that is worrying, extremely worrying. The tendency to be light about the world and cynical, ironical, is just not adequate to the challenge we are faced with. That is one point, certainly of criticism, I would make about quite a lot of art, not just among the art students but more generally speaking in the exhibitions of younger people.

HUO   Another interesting point is your unique positioning in relation to the art world. You have actually had an amazing influence on young artists over generations. However, you have always placed yourself in a unique position and often been resistant towards the art world. Your position is very independent, not related to the art market, proclaiming at one moment an art strike and also occasionally disappearing from the art world.

GM   Yes. I think it's necessary to bring in the experiences I had before becoming an artist, and that was an intense involvement with revolutionary politics: left wing, socialist, communist ideas and ideals. This took place between the ages of sixteen and eighteen. When I then came out of the idea of becoming a political animal I chose to be an artist but I maintained my interest in politics, in revolutionary politics. I still maintain that interest and it influences me constantly, this early excitement and attachment. So that is the basis of the continuing criticism I have of art and of society. If I could, perhaps, bring in some points that you might not ask me about.

HUO   Absolutely. That is a very good idea.

GM   I have just made a couple of notes. We are in the middle of a number of paradigm shifts concerned with consciousness and the difficulty of going beyond where we are now in understanding our present situation. There is an enormous gap between generations, one with exponential aspects. By the way, all that I am talking about is what I read in the media; I am not a very clever man, I am responding to and quoting what I read in the media. Let us spend a few minutes on the significance of having the elder people who are not in touch with the actual experience; they cannot even get the experience. The gap is exponential, in that every day the young, and the very young, are moving into and the parents and grandparents are not moving; so there is this exponential gap now. This is very important and relates to the earlier point, that is, the way we (in the broad sense) look at reality is so limited compared to the reality as it has actually taken place, compared to the speed of the changes that are potential, that are happening. Our ways of understanding are simply too slow and too limited. This is one of my great interests and I think that is something that society, especially those elements of society who desire a change in quality and significance, need to constantly discuss, proceed to understand and communicate.

The other point I would make is that it is absolutely essential that people act. We have endless talks – I mean, I am not criticising what is happening here, I think it is right that this has happened. But there is endless talk among people in the media: 'What shall we do?' It's a waste of time. I am proposing an action within the art world, which is to introduce a world campaign on the slogan, 'Reduce art flights'. I believe a good point to start would be the upcoming Frieze Art Fair. What I am saying is, we as a kind of community can't just talk about the problems but we have the opportunity, and I believe the absolute necessity, to act on what we know. We can't go to Beirut and put ourselves physically between the combatants. But we can go to Frieze Art Fair and the Miami Art Fair, and wherever these art fairs are, which all depend on art flights, and say, 'We want you to, not to stop (you can't stop it) but to reduce, just bring it down'. That is a campaign I hope to go on to and I hope it will meet with some kind of response in worldwide art systems.

HUO   It's very interesting because it's the third campaign we've had in this Marathon. It started out with Eric Hobsbawm, who said we should have a campaign against forgetting; we then had Gilbert & George who proclaimed a campaign against the rucksack. And now we have the campaign to reduce the number of art flights. In relation to Eric Hobsbawm, whom I know you appreciate very much, I wanted you to comment on his suggestion that we should have a campaign against forgetting.

GM   I'm increasingly concerned with these issues and my last works were in that field. The room at Cubitt Gallery was stating we must remember the ten thousand and more Jewish, particularly Jewish, intellectuals and artists who were forced to flee and who were destroyed [*Eichmann and the Angel*, 2005]. And the second work, *In Memoriam*, made for Basel Kunsthalle early this year, was all about recording the memory of millions of Jews destroyed. So this is one direct line I have been working on as an artist in the last year or two and I intend to continue in that direction.

HUO   Many, many thanks, Gustav Metzger.

Applause, end of interview

Rem Koolhaas	Our next guest is Isaac Julien. I want to discuss with you, or verify whether it is true, that at some point you could be described as a documentary filmmaker and that now you don't strictly work in that domain any more and you are working in art. This is something that Hans Ulrich suggested to me, so I don't take any responsibility for the theory.
Isaac Julien	*[Laughs]*
RK	You can deny or contradict it if you want, but is there something to it that you went from one ambition to another one?
IJ	I'm thinking about moving images that were in an area of indexicality where, in a sense, all filming is documentary or documenting an event of some kind or other. Obviously I think about moving images in terms of genres but essentially in these genres you have the documentary mode, which is a very important mode. I was quite interested in that as a mode of expression because it was at the pinnacle of trying to relate something about the world which didn't have that much to do with art. It was about lives and about political questions or issues and in this sense it was a catalyst for trying to propagate or create a position. I think in an earlier stage of my career I wanted to really project what I saw, as certain voices which were not part of the main bastion of different institutions. So in a way the documentary mode is still a mode I'm committed to. I'm now making a documentary, actually, on Derek Jarman, which I hope to complete next year. So in this sense there's still a certain commitment to that, and even if I think about some of my latest work like *Fantôme Afrique*, there is a clear documentary element which I think is very important, as opposed to something that looks artistic. But of course I always think that the different ways of describing these genres are really inadequate for communicating what it is one is interested in doing. Invariably that is always the thing that is more important than just the form.
RK	We have promised each other that we will look beyond those genres and we will also make an effort to look at the different economies of the art world and how these economies enable work to be produced. Would you say that those genres have different economies and that, for instance

a documentary has, presumably, somebody who commissions it and that some other genres are more free and therefore operating in a different economic sphere?

IJ Well, yes. I think in an ideal world, absolutely. I'd agree with that but I think what we've come across in this moment especially is one space where we were actually able to make certain works, which was in broadcasting. This whole area of, if you like, reality television, as a way of thinking about a documentary mode, is something which has completely exacerbated what could be a creative artistic autonomy in terms of making work. So though I think questions of economy are centrally important to the ways in which we might want to think about work or value work or making work, we also have to think about the ways in which, even in these various scenarios, the question of autonomy is one that has become really very important. That brings us back to a position where one might find oneself between, say, film or working in one area, into a sort of art area where there is a different value put on that notion. It seems to me that this has been one of the main difficulties, but of course economies of scale are really important and one of the things that are really refreshing about working in different contexts is when you don't have that economic argument. That's one of the horrible things about the film industry, you know, that it's economics which is absolutely at the vanguard of trying to express this artistic medium and in a sense has, in this country at least, become very problematic and very narrow in the ways in which one might think about certain possibilities. I know you had Ken Loach speaking as part of this Marathon and I think he is one of the single authors, film directors, who have been very committed to making a certain political cinema, but not one that has been greatly supported within his own locale.

Hans Ulrich Obrist One question related to that is about format and the freedom of all kinds of possible formats the art world offers for moving image which the world of cinema doesn't, where there is just one given format in terms of time. In the 1990s it seemed as if video would become the new golden frame, it was just a projector on the wall, but in the last five to ten years through protagonists like you and a few other artists, there has been an amazing variety of different temporalities and also of display features. I want to ask you to talk about this.

IJ   I think really the question revolves around the notion of time. The question of time has been fundamental to moving images in contemporary practice. One of the main attributes, we could say, is that perhaps the orthodoxy which has developed is something that one could ascribe to the ways in which certain critics have posed the question around the very problematic nature of video projection and the idea of the scale. We are familiar with the various critiques but I think one of the exciting things in relation to what I see is the way in which one has been able to tie certain political interventions and to suture that with a form that could try to make various interventions in thinking about politics and the world and generally try to shift a certain empathy. In a way, the Documenta 11 project was part of that aspect, trying to shift that away from a completely market-driven focus in terms of the ways in which one thought generally about contemporary art and hence the complaints about taking too much time to look at the various moving image forms, etc. I think we have this development of a certain orthodoxy on the one hand and at the same time this particular moment where one can, perhaps, utilise that for different political ends.

HUO   One of the recurrent issues of this Marathon is an idea of a partial mapping of London through a polyphony of participants. I was wondering what kind of role London plays for you in terms of your work. Earlier, Ken Loach talked about the professional difficulties London presents in relation to his films. I was wondering if you could talk about your relation to London and how it maybe changed in time, and if you feel London is changing.

IJ   I think undoubtedly London is changing. In terms of the social fabric London is incredibly eclectic and cosmopolitan. One of the things around London for me, however, was during the mid-1990s: I literally wanted to escape London. I was born here and I began to detest London in relation to the previous government that we had, and obviously when I was teaching in America at New York University, at Harvard University, there was a certain celebration, as it were, a mood of optimism with New Labour. I felt very sceptical about that particular moment but returned to London and indeed London, I think, had a certain sort of energy. I would say that perhaps now things have shifted somewhat and that shift has been about the ways in which there is a certain corporate, global development, and of course part of that is precisely in the announcement of bigger museums and that sort of general celebratory tone of what is to be bought in 2012 and that general impetus mixed with general apathy and general silencing around dissidence. There's a certain numbing effect about that. I think one of the things one thinks about is whether this idea of dissidence is something one can find in an art world context or whether that is seen as something which is desirable. I think there is that ambivalence at this particular moment in this city.

RK   Do any of you know when the term 'art world' was first used and by whom? Is it ten years old or twenty?

IJ   I think it had something to do with aeroplanes.

RK   So Gustav Metzger's idea of reducing art flights makes sense…

IJ   I think the idea of speed is significant or the idea of what has become a world which is certainly fairly solipsistic, certainly quite narcissistic, certainly very self-interested, and particularly interested in, as it were, trying to be at the forefront of making certain cultural arguments which are connected to economic arguments but not necessarily interested in developmental ideas or other social questions. Of course that's very complex because I deplore the whole New Labour rhetoric of the way in which art should somehow help police crime, that somehow art can solve these sorts of problems; but nonetheless it seems to me there is a certain synonymous aspect with the way the art world thinks of itself and, if you like, this separation around certain conversations that can be carried on and certain conversations which may seem undesirable. I think that leads itself to certain works and certain ideas. Of course you don't want one to be the mere illustration of the other, but I think this tension is the thing which is quite useful and that's something that is not pushed in a particular way.

HUO   That leads to the next question about the impact of globalisation on the art world, something we are going to discuss in the next Marathon as one of the key topics. Obviously the next Marathon will have a very different format; it has to be a reinvention. Writing about creolisation, but also globalisation, Édouard Glissant talks about the idea of *mondialité*, which would be a globalisation which enhances difference. I wondered what your take would be on that. Yes, his idea of *mondialité* as opposed to homogenizing globalisation. I was wondering if Glissant is important for you.

IJ Glissant has obviously been centrally important for having a very nuanced way of thinking about globalisation, and he is very interested in islands. I remember being at a debate with him in Germany recently where he said that islands could never be the centre of globalisation forces and somebody said, 'England's an island and that's at the centre of a certain globalisation force'. His answer to that was, 'England's not really an island'. I thought that was really quite interesting in terms of the way he was thinking about south and north, and thinking about the question of power. Certainly one of the main aspects around the notion of creolisation has been the ways in which one can think about movement and certain subjects and languages, the way that can come together in thinking about the ways we might face the contemporary or the present. That's something I have been working through in various works; *True North*, *Fantôme Afrique*, and *Fantôme Créole* are works which try to develop that notion as a certain aesthetic, political difference.

RK How important is teaching to you?

IJ Teaching is incredibly important. I'm usually not asked to teach in Britain, I have taught in various universities in the States and I have recently been asked to teach in Germany. For me teaching is really important because of the ways students force you to re-think your position. I remember in 2002 making my piece for Documenta 11, *Paradise Omeros*, working in the meanwhile on the documentary about our cinema project and also doing *Baltimore* all in one year, and also teaching at Harvard in both the Spring and Fall terms. That was exhausting but also exhilarating and in a way my work became very interpolated by that experience. I think you've had a similar experience as well; it's something which has been centrally important in your early work. I think that kind of relationship is really important for continuing, for linking, this inter-generational aspect which was spoken about earlier and I think is part of that dialogue.

RK And what are the tools? I think tools are the best gift you can transmit to a student. What do you think are currently the most important tools in the art world?

IJ I think it's really the notion of criticality and where you can try to embed that certain way of looking and thinking about how something is made. I think one of the things I'm always struck by in this situation is really the ways in which you have people who may not have economic advantages but have amazingly brilliant ideas and the ways those can resonate. It's really about how you can secure that relationship rather than this exposure that one gets in an art context, where perhaps those things won't be valued, or dissipate or disappear. I believe it's trying to keep that notion of criticality alive and to promote that, to encourage that.

HUO The question about the tools of today leads us to the question of tools from the past. One of the things we have established over the last eighteen hours from participants is a list of tools and toolboxes from the past which are still of use now. Are there examples you could give from your own practice of artists from the past or institutions or schools?

IJ Interesting question. For me one of the most important persons who has been at the forefront and who has used his own life as a tool is Stuart Hall. I think he has been at the forefront of trying to both position a paradigm shift in the Humanities and at the same time he has been at the forefront of being incredibly generous with his time in terms of trying to campaign for the new building that David Adjaye is going to be designing for Iniva and Autograph. I think the way that someone like Stuart uses his mind and his body, someone who actually has dialysis three times a week and literally at the same time has this incredible mind. For me his writings and his example in terms of his general generosity and humbleness are very inspiring.

HUO Many, many thanks Isaac Julien.

Applause, end of interview

Hans Ulrich Obrist

It's a great pleasure to introduce our next speaker, Gautam Malkani. Welcome.

Gautam Malkani

Thank you.

HUO

Gautam has also been advising us for the Marathon on all kinds of other disciplines such as economics and media. You have been working for the *Financial Times* and at the same time writing a novel. I was wondering if you could tell us about these two practices and how it came about that you wrote this first book.

GM

Well, I think the hardest thing when it came to doing both the day job at the *Financial Times* and then writing this novel was switching between the different languages because the language I use for the *Financial Times* is pretty straightforward but the language in the book is a mixture of Hip-Hop slang and Punjabi slang and American slang. So it was very difficult to write for the *Financial Times* during the day and then come home in the evening and completely switch. But at the same time, being at the *Financial Times* was quite helpful because, as you said, I was covering the media industry and one of the things I tried to do with the novel was to show the extent to which the characters in the book – the guys in the London rude-boy scene that I was writing about – construct their identity using the media. Instead of your usual three-dimensional characters I wanted to have two-dimensional characters whose personalities were projected onto them by the media, Bollywood, Hollywood, MTV, advertising for designer fashion brands, that kind of thing. That's how the two related.

HUO

You told us in a previous conversation that the title came before the book. It would be interesting to hear how *Londonstani* as a title was a generator of your novel.

GM

The research behind the novel goes back many years because it started off as an undergraduate dissertation. During the research, I heard a couple of kids refer to themselves as Londonstanis and that kind of struck me because it wasn't a very widespread term like rude-boy or Desi or other self-referential terms that kids had. What struck me about it was that it was such a celebratory term. These guys were proud to be British, they were proud to be Asian and they were proud to be Londoners; so the word stuck in my mind and I decided that whether I wrote the book up as fiction or non-fiction I would call it *Londonstani*. Of course, after the bombings of July last year, the word Londonstani, or rather the word Londonistan and variations of that, took on more negative connotations but I was still keen to use it. When I first heard the word it was a positive term, it said something positive about London's multiculturalism. So I was very stubborn about sticking with it and not letting it be hijacked by any anti-multiculturalism agenda.

HUO   Who were the authors who inspired you when you wrote the novel?

GM   I was trying to write something that would get people reading who would not normally read, so I was thinking about writers that I read when I was growing up who pulled me away from my Nintendo. S. E. Hinton, who wrote *Rumble Fish* and *The Outsiders*, was really important in that respect. I think that was probably the main influence. There was another writer in America called Junot Díaz, who wrote a collection of short stories called *Drown*. What was great about that book and the reason it was so inspiring was the way it examined race and identity and all those big issues but in a really subtle way. It wasn't so 'in your face'. I guess I get influenced by everyone I read, but I'm a big fan of the American writers Bret Easton Ellis and Chuck Palahniuk, so they were important as well.

Rem Koolhaas   You write for the *Financial Times* and you have written a novel, and those are at least two different worlds or two different genres, but they both have economic aspects. According to rumour you have been very successful as a novelist in terms of the economy of your first book.

GM   *[Laughs]* That's been exaggerated, but yes.

RK   Can you talk about that? We are really trying to see how money and how the potential connection to the market are affecting a number of domains, including writing, art, etc.

GM   You are referring to the money that I got for the manuscript – is that right?

RK   Well, I'm not asking you to explain anything. Let's say that your expertise in one world helped you in the other world.

GM OK. Sorry. I'm misunderstanding the question. In the book, I did look at the role of money – the role of hyper-materialism in today's Urban and Hip-Hop youth culture and how that relates to the wider economy. We've had youth sub-cultures before but this seems to me the first one that, rather than being a counter-culture that sets itself up in opposition to global capitalism and corporate life, instead actually promotes it, accentuates it and glorifies it. So I was keen to explore the implications of this in the book. This is a sub-culture that worships affluence, that's becoming mainstream culture; if you look at record sales, Urban music now outsells rock. So I think it's important and what I look at in the book, through some of the characters, is the implications for general assumptions about economic life. As I said, youth cultures are traditionally associated with ripped jeans but now suddenly it's *designer* ripped jeans. This struck me as something that had been overlooked. In the book the characters call it 'bling-bling economics' – this idea that we don't have a good handle on measuring inflation in a world where worshipping affluence is not just a niche thing, it's becoming mainstream for a lot of kids coming up through schools nowadays. And it's not just an ethnic thing – we've got the 'chav' phenomenon in Britain. So that's where my fascination with economics at the *Financial Times* is used in the book.

HUO Speaking some months ago in a fax interview with J. G. Ballard, I asked him about the future of the city. He talked a lot about surveillance (something we've also explored here through Tim Newburn) and he talked about London becoming a kind of Orwellian nightmare disguised as a public service. Ballard also talked about forms of early twenty-first century cities (something Scott Lash also hinted at) such as unrestricted urban sprawl, a decentred metropolis, transient airport culture, gated communities and absence of traditional civic pride. I was wondering how you would see the future of the city of London. Would you be more optimistic?

GM Insofar as I have been researching and writing about an anti-assimilation ethic – or an anti-integration ethic – one of the forms that it takes is that a lot of young people don't subscribe to public services, for example they don't want to take public transport. Again it's part of this bling-bling economics thing. This worship of affluence means kids want their own cars and access to exclusive clubs rather than shared civic spaces – including of course school. I feel this is quite a depressing thing. The more people I interviewed, the more worried I got about it because obviously cities don't work without infrastructures and infrastructures don't work without some sort of subscription to them. One of the other symbols for this anti-assimilation ethic in the book is the way the parents of these guys avoid taxes. The whole idea of tax avoidance ties in with the idea of the civic system being seen as an enemy that people don't subscribe to. In the book I focus on that as a British–Asian, Desi, rude-boy phenomenon but I'm not sure that it's restricted to race.

On a more optimistic front – and this *is* about race, because it was what I was researching and thinking about – what I think has been good about London is that London has always been a hotbed of youth sub-cultures. From Punk, Goths, it's been a great place for sub-cultures to thrive, and what I think we've seen amongst British–Asian kids is that anti-assimilation, very assertive ethnic identity that I try and capture in the book, eventually morphs into a sub-cultural identity, and that's very much…

RK   … in a British tradition.

GM   It's a British sub-culture, absolutely, yes. That's the thing about it. By retreating and volunteering for segregation, my community ended up developing a sub-culture that fused aggressive Gangster Rap and Bangra music with other less aggressive styles. Basically you ended up with this Desi-beat sub-culture, and that's the channel through which the kids in the book re-integrate with mainstream society and then develop a kind of affiliation with mainstream society because the sub-cultural identity, as you said, is as British as it is Asian. When I was doing the interviews for the book I was struck by the extent to which the guys were so proud of the way their Desi subculture had been appropriated by the British mainstream media, by the BBC. The BBC has really embraced this kind of sub-culture. So that's the optimistic and pessimistic way of looking at it.

HUO   What role did the interviews play when you wrote the book?

GM   As I said, the book started off as an undergraduate dissertation. The problem with the undergraduate dissertation was it had to be only 20,000 words and I got so much into it (in fact it was probably the only decent thing I did at university) that I over-researched it. So I left university with all these tapes of interviews that I'd done not just with guys, but

British–Asian girls as well, about this scene, about this identity. I had so many cassettes that when it came to writing it up as a novel it was a great resource to have. I had the issues, I had the anecdotes and I also had the language to really immerse myself in. Whilst at university, when I did the research I was feeling a bit stupid for having over-researched the thing and done a ridiculous number of interviews, many more interviews than I needed to have done – although I don't know if it's as many as you guys are doing over the Marathon! When it came to trying to capture this thing in a novel I was so grateful that I had all those cassettes.

HUO   Many, many thanks, Gautam Malkani.

Applause, end of interview

Hans Ulrich Obrist   It's a great pleasure to welcome Richard Hamilton. As this interview Marathon is the London Marathon and we are somehow trying to map different aspects of the city, I wanted to start with some questions about London. I wanted to know why you actually left London in the 1970s and if London is still a source of inspiration for you now.

Richard Hamilton   I've been asked the question before. Some months after the move I met Bill Turnbull at an opening and he said, 'What's this I hear about you leaving London. You are supposed to be a devotee of the city, a sort of prophet of urbanisation, and now you've gone rural'. He saw it as a betrayal. I had to find an explanation then, so I'm ready for your question now. *[Laughs]*. The reason was that I felt there wasn't really much difference in being an hour to the West of London and being in Highgate. It took me an hour to get to the centre of London when I lived in Highgate and, if I choose my time, it takes me an hour to get into town now that I am near the M40 between London and Oxford. I can get to Heathrow in half an hour, half the time it takes by car from London. The main reason for leaving was that I needed more space. I had been living in the same place for twenty-five years and when it became obvious that it would be good to have a bigger studio I began a long search. Every time I found something that seemed to make sense, like Romney's beautiful studio in Hampstead (where Lord Nelson liked to get together with Lady Hamilton) things got difficult. That was a bit ambitious I admit, but it became available so I thought it would be worth a try. Finally I was told by my accountant to 'Forget it! You could live in the Isle of Man, that would be a tax advantage, or you could live in Jersey, but don't even think about Hampstead'. Neither the Isle of Man, nor Jersey appealed to me very much, so I decided to stick around and look further afield. In my research I realized that an hour is just the right distance to be from the centre of London. I had friends who had done the same thing. Marcel Duchamp's wife, Teeny, moved to a beautiful village near Fontainebleau, an hour south of Paris; that was perfect. Jasper Johns was living an hour north of New York at Stony Point. IBM's Eastern headquarters was about an hour upstate of New York. A sleek black building viewed through the trees from an Expressway.

HUO   That is a very interesting new statistic for our lists.

RH   *[Laughs]* To my surprise I found that there were unexpected advantages. I was able to buy a derelict building described in the auction particulars as an 'eighteenth-century farmhouse awaiting the restoration of which it is conspicuously deserving'. It went with eighteen acres of land and outbuildings that I have spent thirty years converting to exactly what I need for working purposes: it's a pretty good location. The remarkable thing is that some facilities are more widely available, in High Wycombe or Reading or even Marlow. A week or two ago I accompanied my wife Rita, whom I love, to get her neon problem resolved. Neon is not a medium favoured by artists these days so she had to search around on the Internet and found a place in Bray, which is about fifteen minutes drive from home. We discovered a very good craftsman working alone in a shed in his garden. If I want computer parts I can get them more easily on the Internet than in Reading or London. I needed a sound proof cabinet for an Apple network server and a raid, a big storage device with lots of hard discs, recently. We sourced only two manufacturers on the net. One was in the US and their only competitor was a small company in Marlow making a similar product. Now that the Internet exists there is not much difference in the availability of services anywhere and I don't miss the social and cultural life. It's easy to get into London when I want to: which is not that often.

HUO   Do you feel that London has changed its identity to a more global city? Do you feel that there is a strong change?

RH   It has become less pleasant than it was. *[Laughs]* If that means more global, I must say yes.

HUO   We have had a lot of discussions here about art and architecture, actually mostly about dialogues, about collaboration. We are also interested in the conflict that might exist, maybe collision. I remember a couple of years ago that you were very, very upset about certain aspects of the Venturi building in London. I thought it might be interesting to talk about this.

RH   I wasn't upset by the Venturi building. I rather admire it in a way. But some very perverse effects emerge in that building. It's an interesting question for me. You know, I went to the States in the 1970s and found myself sitting next to somebody before dinner at Yale, it was a very academic kind of evening, and this person said, 'How does it feel to be one of the fathers of postmodernism?'. I didn't know what postmodernism was. I felt a bit stupid to be a father of something I'd never heard of – like a donor to a sperm bank being confronted by a dysfunctional offspring on his doorstep, I went into denial. Postmodernism? I was blamed for it and I didn't even know what it was. It's not like 'Cubism' or 'Futurism', you know what they stand for, but 'postmodernism' is a bit like saying post-contemporary, it's a conflict of terms. It took me ages to work out what it meant. I have architect friends and I am interested in what they do, I am also fascinated by industrial design. I wanted to find out why the work of a designer like Dieter Rams should have the ability to move me. Why were his creations more interesting than a hamburger? All these things were going round in my mind. What is Pop Art? Did Pop Art have to be about vulgar things exclusively, or could something more high-style be thought of as Pop? It became a problem for me in the sense that on the one hand I was sometimes painting figurative subjects and at other times trying to do something that I thought of as a product. These products could be very close to being artworks. Even a table I made for myself raised interesting questions: 'I have devoted to this object the kind of technical skills and mental effort that I would give to a painting, so is it a work of art? How do these things relate?' I think I am talking too much! *[Laughs]*

HUO   No, it's great.

Rem Koolhaas   The first time I knew about you and saw your work was in connection with the Smithsons and it was particularly one collage with a bodybuilder that established your connection to architecture: *Just what is it that makes today's homes so different, so appealing?*. To what extent were you an ally and to what extent did you have a collective aim with them?

RH   We had rather opposed aims. When I look back at the 1956 exhibition and think of the so-called Fun House I did with John Voelcker and John McHale and compare it with the contribution of the Smithsons, Eduardo Paolozzi and Nigel Henderson, I ask myself, 'Why did they do something so archaic?' Their idea was, 'We will make a fence around our space to mark out our territory, and we will put a shed inside the fenced area'. It was a simplistic philosophical statement about architecture: they defined a space and put a shed in it: an expression of the Smithsons' naked light bulb doctrine. The shed was inhabited by Nigel Henderson's wonderful photo-collage symbolizing man and Eduardo filled the garden with pseudo-fossils. It was an elegant solution. But I still think, 'What is the point? How far back do you have to go to be modern?' I was not at the meeting when the decision was made to call the show *This is Tomorrow*. If I had been there I might have argued against it but I was commuting to Newcastle and didn't attend all the meetings that were held. When I came back from Newcastle one weekend and heard that the exhibition was to be called *This is Tomorrow* I thought, 'How can we do anything about tomorrow? Shouldn't we at least find out what is going on today?'. My whole concern was the present, yet some of the so-called groups were doing things that were rather passé to my way of thinking – a belated version of Constructivism or a distinctly Modernist programme. They hadn't caught up with today, so why should we claim to be representing tomorrow?

RK   I probably recognise this absurdity of architecture that is always claiming, excluding, defining and therefore closing. Do you think that is inevitable, or not necessarily?

RH   I don't think it is inevitable because I have always been interested in something more inclusive than architecture – the area of art that I have chosen, that is to say painting. My interests lie in a pretty wide range of objects, not so much objects as subjects. In fact my concern has been to look at subject matter and find the right pictorial solutions for that subject. I began to feel that what was needed was a kind of aesthetic general theory of relativity. Looking for a theory that tied everything together. That sounds a little pretentious.

HUO   You have talked about the present and I wanted to ask you about the future. We exchanged e-mails about that earlier. Could you talk a little bit about the future?

RH   At the age of eighty-four there is hardly any point in talking about the future. *[Laughs]* My future is somewhat limited. My friends are dying like flies around me, Marcel Broodthaers, Dieter Roth, John Latham, just to name a few. I feel somewhat alone. When I began to assemble the group of paintings that I hope to bring to completion I was amused to think of them as 'the late paintings'. They are in some ways absurd, rétro rather than late. I have become interested in the idea of beauty. The creatures I am painting, I call them angels, are inspired by Fra Angelico. They are pictures of stripped-off young women. Angels are famously unsexed but my angels are women because I am more interested in painting girls than in painting young men. I also know that Fra Angelico wouldn't have dreamt of painting a naked woman. My compositions are contrived from the outcome of sessions with a camera and they are completely self-indulgent. I find that I get so much pleasure from working in my studio these days. I am past any thought of sex, my subjects are purposefully chaste and beautiful – not at all erotic. It is, in some ways, an eccentric group of paintings, but when friends come to my studio, they manage to express some interest in what is going on. *[Laughs]*

RK   Thank you very much.

HUO   Can I have one more question? I thought it was very beautiful that you mentioned John Latham and when we spoke with Eric Hobsbawm preparing for this interview Marathon he said we should not forget about memory; he wants to protest against forgetting. I would be very, very happy if you could tell us a little bit about John Latham. I remember that there was a time when many people could not cope with the complexity of John Latham's work, but John Latham told me that you are one of the very few people, if not the only person, in the world who understands him. So I think it would be wonderful to hear a little bit about John.

RH   I knew John for fifty years and was always excited by what he did. I remember going to a basement in Better Books on Charing Cross Road. It must have been the late 1950s or early 1960s. John had made a machine that tore up paper; newspapers, magazines, pages from books, anything printed, and spewed it all over the room with great force. That was an extraordinary event experienced by twenty or thirty people. Everything he has ever done has a buzz about it. But his work is demanding, because the ideas he is trying to come to grips with are abstruse. I received many wonderful documents over the years, they just appeared in the post like memos from outer space. Then there was a fantastic Arts Council exhibition at the Hayward Gallery that he designed an exquisitely printed catalogue for: it was a brochure that looked exactly like a large company's Annual Report. There were many columns of figures but the figures were all zeros. The only piece of print I know that can compare with it is a great publication by Marcel Broodthaers.

Marcel made a replica of the Mallarmé poem *Un coup de dés* but instead of printing the lines of poetry he put black lines of precisely the same length as the lines of the poem: it was as though it had been censored. What we see is only the beauty of the positioning of lines on the page. John's piece somehow measures up to that in my mind. John often asked me to attend meetings where his ideas were discussed, they were amazing occasions but I couldn't figure out what the hell he was talking about and it didn't appear as if anybody else could. Hansjörg Mayer, the publisher, was asked by John to do a book. Much as he liked John and admired his work, he refused. He explained to me, 'Everybody has so much trouble with John, it's just not worth getting involved in that kind of difficulty'. I said, 'Hansjörg, you should persevere because John is worth the aggravation; he will do something wonderful, I know it'. So the project was begun and it took a lot of effort. The result is a masterpiece called *Report of a Surveyor*. Of course it didn't end there. John complained to me that nobody had reviewed it. He asked if I would do a review to which I replied, 'I don't write reviews of books if I can help it'. He insisted, saying that *The Observer* was waiting for a review and would surely print it. I thought hard for a couple of weeks and got one paragraph written. Then he telephoned to ask how far I had got. I said, 'I've done a paragraph'. He was desperate to see it so I sent him the paragraph. It took eight more months to complete a few pages with John calling me regularly and all I could do was give him another sentence or two. It puzzled me that he didn't discuss anything I wrote; he didn't help me. There was just one worrying moment when he expressed the opinion that I was being flippant about his use of the word God. My text was never printed as a book review but it was published later in the catalogue for an exhibition at the Lisson Gallery [in 1987] and I was pleased and proud to learn that John liked it. The task of writing had forced me to think intensely about his work and his mind. Deciphering John was a labour of love, and it was immensely rewarding.

HUO   Many, many thanks for the interview.

Applause, end of interview

Rem Koolhaas   Our next guest is Peter Cook, one of the members of Archigram and in the last decades also a builder of his own architectures. Peter, you have been incredibly adamant about building. With the Kunsthaus in Graz you have realised a very noticeable and unique building. Can you say what kind of satisfaction it has given you?

Peter Cook   I think it gives you information, speaking as somebody I see listed as a writer and teacher and all these other things and sort of pontificator and somebody who likes drawing – I'm not a good drawer but I like drawing – and I like making things. Simply at the level of research, simply at the level of information, simply at the level of finding out, there are certain things that don't happen until you actually see the stuff. We are sitting inside a piece of stuff. We see the diagram, we see the image in every evening newspaper, we know some of the conversation, but then I find myself sitting in here looking at the wallpaper above me, I look at the joint, I look at the way one's head comes under the door or not. The funny thing that you get from built stuff is actually more to do with the presence of the object. It is very strange that you can draw and draw and draw and you can have excruciating conversations with your colleagues about a three and half degree shift or picking up the size of the cathedral on the hill, or carrying out some sort of philosophical statement, and then you go inside the space and you say, 'Oh! It's a bit lighter than we thought or a bit narrower than we thought and that radiator or beam…'. If I can take one of your buildings, which is a favourite of mine, the Kunsthalle in Rotterdam, one is fascinated as an architect by the degree to which you can see through your feet or the way that you deal with the triangulated corner. The diagram sure as hell, we can discuss it in books. The funniest thing that ever happened to me was staying near Helsinki in some university apartment looking out of the window in the morning and thinking, 'I know that thing. I know that thing'. I couldn't place it until I went inside it and realised I'd used the plan of it in a book. But the plan of it in the book and the thing itself were, in a sense, different and that's something which you don't get until you start building. You can make models, you can have all these wonderful computer projections that have a reflection of a reflection of a reflection and marvellous geometrical things going on, but the stuff, the presence of the object is rather like meeting somebody in the flesh. It's extraordinary, isn't it, with all the devices that we have, that people like ourselves are expected to show up on platform? I'm not quite sure why. Do they want to see the wart on your nose or whether you go to the loo in the middle or something? It's to do with some extra sensory thing. We can only digitalise, we can only hypothesise to a degree, I think.

RK   Are you building buildings now, and how many are you building?

PC   Yes. I'm building one building at the moment and hopefully a second one.

RK   Can you tell us something about it?

PC   I'm building social housing, as a matter of fact. It's going to be blue. It's going to be blue building number three. Of course social housing has a lot of strictures upon it, particularly if you're building in Spain, where they seem to be stiffer, strangely enough, in a sense more secretly traditional than in Germany or Japan or the UK. It's quite curious. You might be building there as well; everybody else seems to be on this Vallecas site. You go there and it's flat; it's about two square miles of nothing and it's dusty. They drive you there and say, 'This is your site'. Of course, what one didn't realise is that, though I would not think of myself particularly as a contextualist, one grows up with all those useful props. Graz in a way was easy because there were so many funny things hugging it and one knew the town and one knew some of the idiosyncrasies of the town, but there was plenty to get off on and you can be more radical in a way if you know from which you jump. But you go to a flat site with nothing there and they can't even tell you who is going to be across the street because they keep changing who is going to be across the street. A *tabula rasa* is the worst possible thing. So what you do is take something out of your back pocket; you take a previous scheme which wasn't built but did in fact invent a series of urban contexts. I think one returns to something that my own teachers (who were Richard's contemporaries, in fact his friends) would do, and possibly my generation did, which was that every building which you proposed – and if you were lucky every one you did – was a prototype of a piece of the city. If you take the Smithsons' Economist Building [1964], it was in fact a piece of their Hauptstadt, Berlin competition entry [1957]; they just happened to build that bit. And in a sense that's what I've done in Vallecas. I've said, 'Right. This is a prototype of what would be a larger statement about cities', and in fact we have been leaning over backwards to incorporate into it ramshackle kiosks, the idea of lifting the building above the ground, ten floors of building, and then you have the ground running through (which is not exactly the Corbusian model) because then you encourage a lot of flotsam and jetsam to come inside it. You then say the top, which is a bit Corbusier, is a piece of free, open space that can be usable and controlled in a way, so you want people to kick balls around and jump up and down on rubber floors and stuff. So one has this sandwich, this sort of hamburger where the car parking and the building are the bread, so to speak, and then the filling is the ground, which is all this rubbish coming in, and the top is the topping. The only trouble is they then ask you to design the crack. They say, 'Would you design the kiosks and stuff as well?' Which is not quite the point. So seven years of expensive architectural education, you try and pretend that they didn't exist because for good or bad you do grow up with all sorts of overtones of taste or anti-taste or whatever it is.

RK   Talking about expensive architectural education, although I never was your student you were very influential in the school where I was a student and I heard you many times. I am wondering in retrospect whether the persona that you then represented, which was somebody almost aggressively provincial, not particularly interested in taste and advocating virtues of some kind of English, misunderstood compromised fudge, whether you were deliberately using that persona as an incentive for us to react to.

PC   It's so long ago! I think one was consciously using it and one was consciously enjoying it. I was just reflecting this morning, because I thought you might ask questions about cities, to make a comment that though I've still lived in London longer than anywhere else by times two, I still am psychologically provincial in that I hate not looking out on a tree when I wake up in the morning. I once, for about five months, lived somewhere in the centre of London which didn't have a view of a tree and I hated it. So I carry my provinciality with me but you put it then in special boxes because the last twenty or more years of my life I have spent a lot of time in non-English cities, in other cities; I am married to a foreigner, and so on. In fact in my address book I have far more people who are not English, and certainly not English provincials, or pretending not to be. I still have a fear of provinciality. One of the things that make me scream (but I am also attracted by it) is when I visit a number of cities I know well with people I know well, usually cities of about – I don't mean LA, New York, Tokyo or Berlin – a million, give or take; they are fascinating. They just have enough things going so you can probably eat well, listen to intelligent people, etc. but there is still an element of provinciality. If you go to two bars you have 'met everybody': kind of provinciality. It reminds me of Leicester or Bournemouth or Norwich on a wet Thursday. I still suddenly, in my worst moments, think, 'That's what provinciality is about: that you cannot choose to hide but you cannot find anywhere that's open and you're forced to talk to people who you don't really have very much in common with. But some people say that's very good for you.

In a way, there's also another provinciality which I think we carry with us, and a lot of famous architects carry with them, interestingly, but several people you and I know very well still have very few friends even though they get on a plane and land in the next city. They carry the gossip from city A to city B but with that same small group of friends; they are concerned about what is happening to them. And then suddenly a new name is mentioned and they say, 'Who is that?'. Whereas everybody in that city would know who that was. So there are layers of provinciality which – I am saying it's more of a usable concept and is a protection, sometimes. I'm not sure that total globalisation is always useful.

Hans Ulrich Obrist How do you see the future of the city now? Somehow you have always been a relentless optimist. In all our conversations in the past and in all the texts and interviews that concern you there is a relentless optimism about the future of the city.

PC I think the trick is to find somewhere, something you can be optimistic about. We all have friends, particularly in places like Austria, who immediately see the gloom factor in any conversation. It enjoys me to irritate such people by being optimistic! Seriously, I think Richard said something quite interesting about living in Buckinghamshire or whatever. He was born in London, I remember this, I was not and therefore once after twenty years or whatever one got to London one said, 'I'm not the fuck going to leave. That's it.' But I think he made a very interesting point, which was that many of the aspects of the organism of the city, the urban aspect of the city – he can find neon lights in the nearest small town, he can probably get, if he's into French cheeses or a certain kind of literature, whatever it might be – that's probably available, though Buckinghamshire isn't the top of Scotland. There is also this extraordinary thing that so many people, just as they pay a lot of money to go to a health club, will spend two and a half hours in a car twice at the weekend in order to get to somewhere where, when they get there, they are so exhausted they are sitting there watching the same television but maybe there's a view of the sea or of a windmill or something. I'm very cynical about all these things because I think they are interesting constructs. Ideally the organism of about a one-million-size city has many advantages over the organism of an eight- to twenty-million city, but it has the down side that I talked about earlier. I think this is a problem for architects because we still, all of us, use physicality. Like I just said about Vallecas, there is nothing to see so you have to invent something, but we are reluctant to do that invention unless absolutely forced to. We would rather say, 'Because there is an urban grid or because there is a certain number of people or because there is a certain buzz, therefore, therefore, therefore…'.

RK Hans has been asking every single participant a question about memory. The incentive was Hobsbawm asking us to launch a campaign against forgetting. Mark Cousins has also been talking about memory and actually mentioned the virtues of forgetting.

HUO And the danger of memory.

RK You were part of one of the most famous avant-garde architectural groups when you were very young. To what extent did you have to forget that and to what extent do you have to remember it to create your own freedom?

PC I think there is a short answer and a long answer. The short answer is that I get very irritated by my contemporaries who can only talk about whatever they perceived to be their finest moment, just as the generation in front of me remembered the war. Bugger the war! I don't want to hear about it. There is also the thing, as a sort of academic professional, which is you get asked about Archigram and then you find some art historian sitting in the background who thinks that they know about it better than you. In fact you tell them what really to your own memory mattered and they don't want to hear that because it's not particularly about politics, it's not particularly about art movements, it's not even necessarily about provincialism. It might actually be about technics; it might be about things that you did with stuff. You watch them glaze over because that they don't want to hear.

The other thing is, I think, whilst one has senior moments from time to time and just can't remember somebody's name, there is selective memory. I think you can play selective memory and decide that day, 'I am not going to talk about the 1950s because I am perversely not remembering it'. The next day talking to somebody else you'll say, 'Ah! But what you don't realise is that blah blah blah was happening'. I think Richard, for example, was wonderful because he was absolutely in control of his memory. I hope fifteen years hence I will also be as much in control. I think you can play it, just like you can play the business of being an urbane person, being an academic. What has always amused me is things like when for tax purposes or for somebody's CV they say, 'What are you?'. As it says here, academic, lecturer, builder, and what amuses you is to be not the thing that they wanted you to be. They've got you in there as a commentator, and I suspect that you being somebody who is intrigued by the perverse in your own way can understand this, that there's nothing more irritating than being pigeon-holed because then you are like a trapped pigeon and I think Archigram was always about – if one remembers that – always about breaking out of the trap, architecture being trapped into a certain sort of precision.

RK   Yes. Has the situation for you become more complicated or less complicated now that your past is not only a burden or responsibility of memory but also represents a considerable financial quantity?

PC   *[Laughs]* I'm not sure about that! Nobody's signed the cheque.

RK   There has been a lot of news about the archive of Archigram.

PC   I haven't actually given – not being the innocent – I haven't particularly given that thought. I think I am more relaxed about all of that.

RK   Who owns the archives of Archigram?

PC   It's held mostly by the individuals, so it's a series of pieces of archive. And museums own a lot of it. A lot of it sits in museums where you have to pay money or plead to have a look at your own drawings. But in sense I think I am more relaxed about that. There was the inevitab.

thing of being totally out of fashion. The worst period, I suppose, was the late 1970s, early 1980s, and one has a biased view of that, which was that from where I was sitting it was also the dullest period of the English scene, and then in the 1990s it started cheering up again. Or was that simply because people started being nice about what one had done? But that's also a trap because it's too easy to say that you simply want that to happen. My criticism of my own early drawings is that they were too consistent. The idea was about inconsistency but the mannerism was consistent. One doesn't want to do stuff that is as consistent as that.

HUO   This idea of resisting being pinned down to just being an architect and to have a more expanded notion of different identities also becomes clear on the Bartlett website. It says, 'Peter Cook is an architect, he is an educator, he is a writer and commentator, he is a rainmaker and he is an evangelist for the forward development of cities'. I was curious about the rainmaker notion.

RK   And then the evangelist.

PC   I was rather flattered – I didn't write that – *[Laughs]* I was rather flattered because the person who both Rem and I remember well was Alvin Boyarsky, who was always being referred to as a rainmaker and I think he was already dead by the time that was written. So I felt rather honoured that somebody thought I was a rainmaker. I think I know what it's sort of getting at, which is that you take a creative interest not only in stuff and things and your own opinion but also in the creativity of others, and that's not an entirely self-sacrificing position, if you think it through. At first it sounds terribly nice – he cares more for his students and his fellow teachers than himself. Actually, no, because without them you ossify. I've always enjoyed the fact that there's been somebody smarter, a better drawer, a better designer possibly, than me down the corridor. It gets you going. In a sense it's selfish in a roundabout way. You need the rain in order to breathe, that being the point.

RK   What has been for me perhaps the most impressive thing about Archigram, and it is really something that in the current representation of Archigram is never very visible, is that you were not really an architectural movement but you were a magazine, weren't you?

PC   Yes.

RK   And you were a medium rather than architecture.

PC   Well, you know, we didn't call ourselves Archigram until so many people started calling us it. We sat down one morning and said we thought we'd better register the name because everyone calls us this. It was sort of reluctant and in a way it was a kind of coalition. A lot of people had been intrigued by the fact that, if I take a particular example, David Greene and I have very different views. He tends to be very English and gloomy in a creative way and I tend to be very – I don't know what – not gloomy! We did a thing about half a year ago at the Royal College of Art and what emerged at the end of the evening was we were still an alliance but an alliance of two slightly different approaches. I think that was the virtue, the fact that we were ten years apart if you took the age range, no two people had gone to the same college, no two people had the same taste in music, the politics were broadly middle Left, but we were very different people. Some went to football, some couldn't stand football, some were listening to Sibelius, some were listening to Miles Davis, some were listening to God knows what. And I think that is a strength; so many groups come out of a rather consistent corner of a year at college, or whatever it may be. They must bore each other.

HUO   That leads to Metabolism in an interesting way. Rem and I visited the Metabolists in Japan and that was also more a coalition than a movement. If they did manifestos they did them as a parody or in an ironic way. How do you situate the manifestos of Archigram? Was there a notion of parody there?

PC   No. There was a wonderful phrase – this has been quoted many times – it was a phrase that we would use from time to time apropos a project or apropos something somebody might write or show, which is, 'This will upset them'. We never said who the 'them' were but we knew they were the great unwashed, the Philistine, but we never said they are this, this and this. We knew who the 'them' were and said, 'This will upset them'. I was listening to an earlier conversation when you asked is it necessary in architecture to have a hate figure, is it necessary to be hitting. I can remember as a student reading a lot about the English movements in the nineteenth century, where the Romanticists and the Classicists clearly hated each other and perhaps this is a politically incorrect thing to say, but a certain amount of hate sometimes gets you going, actually says, 'Right! This is what we're not doing.' Until you find that there is an architectural position that turns on itself, rather like Herzog & de Meuron now. What has fascinated me in the last eight years is all the straight up and down acolytes who treated them as heroes, and you would know the reasons which I don't but I'm fascinated. Did they just get bored? I think that highly intelligent people often just get bored. And then all the followers are left with their trousers down, which is wonderful if you're sitting observing it. Sorry, I digress! *[Laughs]*

RK   Can you confirm Archigram was a magazine?

PC   We became a magazine.

RK   I think the deeply attractive thing as a student was that you could own you. Whatever you thought of you as a movement, whatever you thought of you as human beings, the fact that you could lay your hands on a publication of Archigram, that there was this thing called Archigram that was distributed through the mail, was an unbelievably strong aspect of the attraction.

PC   That's a funny one. I don't quite know what to say to that. I think it became a magazine; at that point maybe it was the moment to stop it. On the other hand, subsequent generations became much cleverer at leaving their mark. I think most of the people sitting in this room, whoever they are, would be much better at knowing how to market, whether you leave a visiting card, whether you leave a beer mat, whether you make a piece of smoke, whether you whisper in somebody's ear or whether you just happen to be in the right bar at the right time or with the right person on your arm. I think they've become infinitely more sophisticated than we were about signalling and controlled signalling. I think that's something which civilization has acquired for good or ill. Probably there's a slight sadness that then, of course, the means were a secondary consideration. You can't print anything crappily any more, not that one necessarily wants to but it would be nice to be able to, offices have to have a smart front, everybody has to have a certain means of communication, and often a lot of creative energy goes into that but the actual ideas are rather boring. So I suppose in an old-style Puritan way I would say the idea is much more important than if you communicate it well. That's great, but sooner or later if there's no idea there…

HUO   I was wondering now that you actually build architecture, is there an unrealised project you would like to see realised?

PC   Yes. I would like to do a building in which there was a progression from solidity through to total transparency without the tyranny of the window. I've always wanted to do such a building. It sounds a very narrow objective in a sense; it's an architectural idea. But I'm fascinated by the tyranny of certain aspects of architecture, that we still have to make things with sticks, we talk about fluid structures but in the end you still have to have bits of stick. There's still a square sitting over our head with a dangle on it. That sort of thing interests me. So I suppose one's aim is still a very tectonic aim. I think architecture is still extremely narrow in its vocabulary, actually, despite all the waves.

HUO   Thanks, Peter Cook. Thank you so much.

Applause, end of interview

Hans Ulrich Obrist   It's a great pleasure to introduce our next speaker, Chantal Mouffe, whom we have already quoted many times in this Marathon. Welcome.

Rem Koolhaas   Chantal, we need your help at this point. We are deeply exhausted and we are actually a little bit scared because I know how fiercely intelligent, eloquent and impressive you are, and at this moment we cannot hope to be your equal. We surrender happily to our inferiority. At this point can I ask you about the two books here that are published with an interval of…

Chantal Mouffe   … ten years, or more. *On the Political* was published in 2005. *The Return of the Political* of course, is a new edition of a book that was published – I can't remember when it was published – ten years ago, certainly.

RK   There is a quote I would like to read because it is an idea that hasn't been mentioned yet and I believe it's a very important concept. 'I think there is no way to avoid such a situation and we have to face its implications. A project of radical and plural democracy has to come to terms with the dimension of conflict and antagonism within the political and has to accept the consequences of the irreducible plurality of values. This must be the starting point of our attempt to radicalise the liberal democratic regime and to extend the democratic revolution to an increasing number of social relations. And then, instead of shying away from the component of violence and hostility inherent in social relations, the task is to think how to create the conditions under which those aggressive forces can be diffused and averted and a pluralist democratic order made possible.' I think also in the newer book you insisted on conflict and a way of dealing with conflict; incorporating conflict remains critical to your thinking. Can you elaborate on that? I should also say that we have heard a number of eulogies on London, on the incredible ability of London to absorb minorities, the incredible ability of London for many different cultures to co-exist, and the idea of conflict has been studiously avoided and been an absent factor.

CM   Yes, well if there is one thing that is common to all my work from the beginning till this book it is precisely that idea that what I propose to call 'the political' has to do with the dimension of conflict, antagonism, hostility, which I take as ineradicable in human societies. My critique of current political theories is that they are not dealing with that dimension. I consider that if we want to really understand what the task of democracy is, we need to realise that democracy is not a set of institutions whose aim is to establish consensus, because consensus in politics is not possible. The task of democracy, and this is central to what I call the agonistic model, is to establish a set of institutions which will, so to speak, tame the dimension of antagonism and permit a co-existence between different views so that people are not going to treat each other as enemies but as what I call 'adversaries'. Antagonism is a dimension that is always potentially present; it can always erupt into societies. That is the point of my reference to the work of Carl Schmitt, which sometimes is taken as very provocative. But I think that Schmitt really understood something fundamental about politics when he said that politics has to do with the friend/enemy distinction.

My problem with Schmitt is that he dismissed the possibility of a pluralist democracy and my whole project is to show that pluralism is in fact possible, even if we accept that the dimension of antagonism is ineradicable. My aim is to envisage under which conditions a democratic co-existence among a plurality of views is possible. My central argument is that the dimension of antagonism can be played in two different ways. One is antagonism, strictly speaking, a relation of friend/enemy; the other is what I call 'agonism', in which we are not dealing with enemies but with adversaries. The main difference between an enemy and an adversary is that adversaries acknowledge the legitimacy of their opponents. They do not believe, however, that it's possible to arrive at a rational consensus and this is why the dimension of antagonism is still there. But adversaries accept that the others have the right to have different points of view and to fight for them. This means that there exists among adversaries a common symbolic space. What I refer to as a conflictual consensus, a consensus which must leave space for dissensus, for conflictual interpretations of the shared ethical and political principles which inform the democratic political association.

HUO　It's very interesting because it leads us to discussions we've had about London and the city in the early twenty-first century, where there is the question of a permanent state of exception. I wanted to ask you a little more about Carl Schmitt. You write in *The Return of the Political* that the reason for engaging with the work of Carl Schmitt is that revealing the deficiencies of liberalism can help us to identify the issues that need to be addressed and thereby to gain a better understanding of the nature of modern democracy. You say, 'My objective is to think with Schmitt against Schmitt'. Can you explain a little bit more about this idea of thinking with Schmitt against Schmitt and maybe link that, if possible, to the permanent state of exception.

CM　I did say already a little bit about that in my answer to Rem. I distinguish what I call 'the political' from politics. 'The political' is this dimension of antagonism. By politics I understand the manifold of institutional practices whose aim is to establish a specific form of human co-existence. To use an Heideggerian terminology, we could say that 'the political' belongs to the ontological level, while politics belongs to the ontic one. I agree with Schmitt that 'the political' has to do with the dimension of conflict, the friend and enemy discrimination. But of course, as I said previously, as a consequence Schmitt believed that we cannot imagine a society that allows pluralism to exist in its midst. This is because he only can imagine antagonism on the mode of a friend and enemy relation. To allow pluralism in a society would therefore necessarily lead to civil war and to the destruction of the political association. But my point is that Schmitt does not realise that there is another way in which antagonism can manifest itself, in the form of agonism. The task for a pluralist democracy is to establish institutions allowing for conflict to take the form of agonism. Where such institutions are available, when conflict happens it is less likely to emerge in an antagonistic form.

Schmitt is nevertheless right in his critique of the liberal tradition for not acknowledging the ineradicability of antagonism. There are two reasons for such an avoidance. The first one is that liberalism is dominated by a rationalist approach which asserts that it is possible to find a rational solution to political problems. Liberalism, when it envisages pluralism, envisages it as a multiplicity of points of view in a society that, when put together, constitute an harmonious whole. In my view however, and here I clearly locate myself on the side of Weber or

Nietzsche, pluralism necessarily implies conflict. For instance, Weber speaks of the *polytheism* of values and Nietzsche of the war of gods. If you accept pluralism, you need to accept that there will be conflict. Pluralism cannot be conceived in a harmonious way as liberals would like us to believe.

The other problem with liberalism is its individualism. This is a serious shortcoming because politics always has to do with collective identities. In the field of politics we act always as part of a group. Of course it is the individual who acts, but as part of a wider community. And this means that if you deal only with atomistic individuals, you are not able to understand the formation of collective identities, and one of the fundamental dimensions of politics will necessarily escape you. It is therefore no surprise that the nature of nationalism or of mass movement is something that has never been properly understood by liberal discourse.

Where I disagree with Schmitt is that I do not want to completely reject liberalism understood as the recognition of pluralism and individual liberty. This is something which is central for me and that I want to defend. In my view, modern democracy, pluralist democracy, must acknowledge the importance of the liberal tradition, but of course we must also acknowledge its limitations and I think Schmitt is important here because he helps us to understand what those limitations are and how to remedy them. Instead of rejecting the liberal tradition like Schmitt, what I want is to contribute to the elaboration of a liberalism that will be really political. This is why I have always said that I'm thinking 'with Schmitt against Schmitt': because I want to derive exactly the opposite conclusion from the same starting point.

HUO   In relation to this idea of the antagonistic political position you evoke, how can art, architecture or literature actually contribute in the shaping of a more mature antagonistic political position in your opinion?

CM   That's a question that is not easy to answer in general, but I have noticed that several architects have been getting interested in my work. I spoke at Bartlett College with a group of architects not long ago and I was pleased to realise that they found my idea of agonism very inspiring. I have also been involved at one point in a project with Teresa Hoskyns, an architect who has been trying to imagine what an agonistic space would be. We were planning to design such a space for the

Making Things Public exhibition organized by Bruno Latour and Peter Weibel at the ZKM; but finally our project was too expensive and it could not be realized because their budget was drastically reduced. The idea was to construct two spaces, an Habermasian space and an agonistic one. For the Habermasian space we were thinking to ask people entering the room to cover themselves with a white dress to dissimulate their identity. Indeed this is an approach that requires that we leave aside all our particularities in order to coincide with our rational self. So the idea was to keep the space completely minimalist, all white and to stage it like a tribunal. The agonistic space was going to be completely different, with lots of colour and a bit chaotic, with a multiplicity of conflicting voices. Unfortunately we were not able to do it.

HUO   That's an unrealised project.

CM   It's an unrealised project. *[Laughs]*

RK   I have a question and it is maybe an unspeakable vulgarity but almost every word you say has a resonance with the most compelling and urgent, seemingly immediate issues that we are facing today – and those are obviously politics, in their most crude manner. Nevertheless many of us are extremely interested in having a blueprint or a map or a guide to intervene or to act or even interpret the current moment. How can your story help us?

CM   Unfortunately, I can't give recipes. It's not simply that I can't; I don't think there are recipes. I must say that I am very concerned with the state of our societies today because we are living in what I call a 'post-political' time; what I mean by that is not that politics has disappeared but that we have become unable to think politically. In *On the Political* I've got a chapter in which I criticise the Third Way, particularly theorists like Anthony Giddens and Ulrich Beck who declare that the adversarial model of politics has become obsolete. According to them, this model might have been relevant for the last century but we are now, they say, in a different type of society that they call 'reflexive modernity' or 'second modernity', in which old antagonisms do not exist any more. So a consensus at the centre is now possible.

It is in the context of this post-political Zeitgeist that I have been trying to understand the reasons for the rise and success of right-wing populist movements in Europe recently. My thesis is that this is a consequence of the consensus at the centre that exists nowadays. Socialist parties today define themselves as 'centre left', and there is no fundamental difference between the politics advocated by centre left and centre right parties. A consequence of this lack of alternative is that people do not vote; they are not interested in politics, why should they be? There is no possibility for them to have a real choice. This has created a favourable terrain for right-wing demagogues who pretend that there is an alternative and that they are going to give back to the people the possibility to decide. We touch here on another important aspect of my reflection which concerns the role of passions in politics. By passions I do not mean individual passions but all the affects that are at work in collective forms of identification and in the creation of collective identities. The problem today is not that people have become so individualistic and that they are not interested any more in collective action, but that they do not have the possibility to identify with a variety of political projects within the democratic spectrum. This explains why they can be attracted by the rhetoric of right-wing populists who are trying to mobilize passions in an anti-establishment direction.

If you are asking me what I would suggest, I think it's very important for the left to abandon this idea that the adversarial model has been overcome and to realise that in the field of politics we are always dealing with conflicts and passionate attachments. A left project must mobilise passions, it must give to people the possibility of identifying with an alternative. The idea that, because of globalisation, there is no alternative to the present order, is fatal for democracy.

RK   Is this true for democracies only or does it also apply to China, to Russia, to the Arab world?

CM   My work so far has been mainly concerned with developing this agonistic model in domestic politics but I have become more and more convinced that this agonistic model is also relevant for the way we should envisage Europe and also in the field of international relations. At the end of *On the Political*, when I am criticising the cosmopolitan model, I have begun o suggest what could be called an agonistic approach to international relations. In my view this would require the creation of a multi-polar world in which regional blocks like Europe, Latin America, China, India and others would establish among themselves an agonistic relation. This means accepting that there is not a single model that should be implemented worldwide but a variety of legitimate ones. A multi-polar order would aim at a form of co-existence that is enriching for all the poles.

With respect to Europe, I have been thinking of what an agonistic Europe will look like. In fact, the creation of the European Community is a very good example of what I call a transformation of antagonism into agonism, which I take to be the aim of democracy. Indeed if we think of Jean Monnet and Robert Schuman who were at the origin of the project of European unification after the Second World War, it is clear that their aim was to create the institutional conditions that would impede that a conflict between Germany and France could take place again. Their idea – and I think it was a brilliant idea –was to establish institutions to link these countries through common economic and defence projects, so that they would not be enemies any more but adversaries. So far this project has really worked, even if of course we should never take for granted that it cannot collapse.

The question today is what does an agonistic approach tell us for the kind of institutions that are more suitable for the development of the European community. In my view it tells us that we should not think of the EU as some kind of super-state, on the mode of a post-national entity composed of individuals who have left aside their national allegiance to become citizens of an homogeneous European demos. Much of the current opposition to the EU comes from resistances to such a conception.

An agonistic Europe will respect the diversity of the different European nations and try to find a way to create forms of commonality within this heterogeneity. We find some interesting ideas at that respect in the work of Kalypso Nicolaidis, a political theorist who has proposed to envisage the EU in terms of a 'demoicracy'. Obviously in order to have democracy you need a demos, but this demos does not need to be one single, homogeneous demos: it can be composed of a multiplicity of demoi. This is what a 'demoicracy' would mean. I really like this idea. Another interesting idea has been put forward by Massimo Cacciari the Mayor of Venice who advocates a 'federalism from below' instead of having it imposed from the top. Cacciari also argues that an European federalism from below should not be envisaged as composed only of nations-states, but that cities and regions could have a place in it. Moreover, he indicates that those regions could be drawn across nations, for instance across Italy and France, France and Spain, or Austria and Italy. In this case we would have a 'demoicracy' that would not be composed only of nation states. It would be really a very heterogeneous form of 'demoicracy'. I think that's definitely a type of reflection that is very promising for thinking of the future of the European union.

HUO   Many, many thanks, Chantal Mouffe.

Applause, end of interview

Eyal Weizman
Hussein Chalayan
Tariq Ali
Marina Warner
Milan Rai
Doris Lessing

Rem Koolhaas   You have been preoccupied, to use a polite word, with studying the ways in which architects and planners have been complicit in devising military strategies in the whole settlement programme in Israel and you have been making a very interesting connection between architecture and crime in that context. Therefore it is inevitable to ask you what you think of the current events (the Lebanon war has just broken out), that if anything seem to be an escalation of the already radical suffering that you have documented.

Eyal Weizman   Yes. I could try to answer this question but not as an architect because, besides the enormous destruction of neighbourhoods, I don't immediately see the 'architectural' dimension of the conflict that is happening within Lebanon and Gaza right now. But it seems to me as well to be a product of a set of ideas and conceptions that have entered the Israeli military and the Israeli government recently. I think that current military thinking seeks to mobilize the West's sensitivity to the humanitarian situation. It thus creates a 'humanitarian situation' that will force an intervention in Lebanese politics and the politics of the region. There seems to be a calculated move here by which the seven hundred thousand Lebanese refugees are made to flee, so that their suffering is mediatized in a way that would appeal to a Western intervention. In effect there is a very cynical game which is being played out on the backs of civilians.

RK   You mentioned the complicity of architects and planners in that whole process has now shifted to some extent and that there is a specific interest in urban theory on part of the military.

EW   Yes.

RK   I think that is a very important shift.

EW   Yes. I believe that the military, and not only the Israeli one, but different militaries around the world, have gradually got to the understanding that most conflict, most war, is actually an urban war, primarily taking place within Third World cities. And they realise that they must understand the city in order to govern it.

RK   Is, or will be, urban?

EW   It already is; since the early 1990s most conflict actually takes place in cities. However, both military doctrine and equipment is not geared to deal with that situation, therefore in an almost panic reaction militaries around the world have started to set up a network of think tanks and institutions that are geared to study and teach urbanism and to understand the way in which cities have developed and are still developing, mutating, the way in which they are growing and the way in which they reflect high degrees of contradictions and complexity within them. This will allow the soldiers to operate within the urban environment. I think to a large extent, most urban research that is taking place right now is not in universities but in the military. There is almost a shadow world to the one that we know, to the network of elite or other architectural institutions, which are relating to each other, which are sharing knowledge. There is a shadow world of military research institutes that are operating pretty much with a similar system of conferences, publications, guest lecturers, etc. where a lot of urban theory…

RK   … do you know which theory?

EW   A lot of the urban theory that has become instrumental to militaries is actually what we used to think were subversive theories conceived around 1968 and thereafter. I know here it has been discussed quite a lot: Situationist theory. The work of Deleuze and Guattari, other so-called radical left theories, that used to understand the city as the site of capitalist spectacle and repression, and this called for transgressive actions by these thinkers and practitioners. It is paradoxical that it is these very transgressive theories that have now completely been abused and actually re-articulated by military thinkers as modes of attack on the enemy city. So that if a lot of the Situationist project was trying to undo the order of the urban syntax, to see gaps and subvert bits of the urban environment, that is exactly the kind of toolbox that is being thought of and used by soldiers as they are moving through the city.

RK   So, is *Dérive* a military manoeuvre?

EW   In a kind of roundabout way, yes. Initially one has to differentiate between the field of knowledge which is now assembled and discussed within militaries, which includes those readings I mentioned, as well as other examples of architectural theory. I was very surprised to hear a soldier/architecture theorist I interviewed talking with much passion about Bernard Tschumi's *Manhattan Transcripts*. I have actually had one Israeli Brigadier General who has translated that book into Hebrew and claimed that the system of notation – and the thinking that Tschumi developed around the notion of the 'event' – is more adequate to plan attack on an urban environment than any other traditional tools (like maps) that the military has. I know it sounds really bizarre to the degree of being hysterical, but there is that particular military institute that is using this and other post-Structuralist theories in order to conceive of methods to 'transgress', so to speak, the enemy city. Their problem is that they cannot come now overtly – all guns blazing – in the same way in which urban warfare was conducted fifty years ago. They have to start manipulating different elements that already exist within the city, different conflicts that a city actually fosters – every city is a field of conflict between the different groups that inhabit it, the presence of media, the presence of NGOs of humanitarians. It becomes an incredibly complicated field and somehow the military have realised that the toolbox they had before is completely inadequate in order to operate within the environment now.

Hans Ulrich Obrist
I was curious to know more about the mapping, because we have spoken a lot about mapping during the last twenty hours. You have actually written before about the geometry of the Occupation and that can only be perceived or understood in a three-dimensional understanding. I wondered if you could explain how this conflict can actually be mapped three-dimensionally.

EW
Initially that project was conceived as a human rights project that I undertook with an organisation called B'Tselem, where the aim was to implicate the work of architects and planners in the mechanism of occupation. The question was whether we could actually relate the very architectural methods and tools that they were using: the way they have been drawing maps or plans and the way in which a road is made to curve, the way a settlement is made to bend and in a sense cut and bisect great wedges through the environment. That led to a long process of collection of architectural plans that took more than a year, where we were basically jumping from one settlement to another and assembling the plans in order to, again, relate the very architectural methods with an intention, a negative intention, to dominate the area. So here there was a clear implication of the very methodologies of architecture. Another part of the way that I work is that I tend to see architectural

341

research not as something that produces a kind of toolbox – look at something, make it a concept, the concept turns into a tool, the tool is going to be applied in a building somewhere else – but as a form of witnessing. I think when you are dealing with a situation that is horrific to such a degree, instead of architecture being an interventionist praxis, it becomes a form of producing professional testimony. In that respect we were starting to look at situations that were not directly architectural but perhaps geopolitical and look at them through an architectural framework. And therefore the three-dimensional, or 'the politics of verticality', is an understanding of the conflict that has emerged where it seems that both people who were working for the occupation and people who were trying to offer solutions for it, started to imagine Jerusalem in particular and the West Bank in general, not as a flat surface on which things are placed but as a three-dimensional reality. The sub-terrain, anything that is under the surface, is seen as a different constituency than the surface of the terrain and, again, the air space over it is seen differently. You can see that now in the evacuation of Gaza, where effectively Israel has evacuated the surface of the terrain. Everything over it, the air space, is still Israel's sovereign territory. The aquifers under it are still to a certain degree, through a very complex bureaucratic process, controlled by Israel. So that in effect you start to imagine a territory in borders not only as lines on maps but as things which enclose volumes. And borders become vertical.

HUO   I would like to know more about how this three-dimensional reading of these maps gets translated, because you have organised exhibitions. How does that translate into exhibitions?

EW   The moment the project took another life, was – and I think somehow it must have coincided with – a developing of aesthetic sensibilities in the art world towards documentary forms and political issues. After the banning of my original exhibition in 2002, I got a number of invitations and somewhat some means to undertake research. Somehow, our relationship with the art world initially was quite utilitarian, in the sense that all of a sudden there were these institutional bodies that were willing to finance research that could not have been otherwise conceived. To develop new forms of knowledge in relation to the conflict that would have no place in either human rights organisations or universities. As such, the art world was a great platform. But somehow through the process of spatialising the exhibition, of putting it in space, working with curators and people who have different aesthetic sensibility to the visual and a different way of seeing, interpreting and analysing images as sites of knowledge, I am happy to say that a lot of these have become extremely productive, also in the politics of this work. They were folded into the project itself. So what initially started as a quite pragmatic project ended up as a very unique collaboration in which we can say that, in a way, we learnt to see anew.

RK   There was a moment where it seemed possible to use the moment of transition and withdrawal from Gaza as the occasion of an intervention there.

EW   Yes.

RK   And you could say an appropriation of a settlement for a Palestinian institution.

EW   Yes.

RK   What has happened to that effort?

EW   The entire complexity of that project has been flattened into the rubble of the settlements destruction now. Throughout this conflict there were still moments of optimism where the mode of our work shifted from a witnessing, from a professional testimony, to a mode of intervention. There was an opening in 2005, a few months leading to the August 2005 evacuation in Gaza, where the biggest geopolitical players seemed to have been interested in architecture. You had The World Bank, the IMF, the Americans even put in, discussing what to do with the buildings – mainly single-family house and garden – that will be left in a settlement. Somehow those silly-looking suburbias have become part of a geopolitical game. At that moment, together with my colleagues from the Palestinian Ministry of Planning with which I had been working already since 1995, we received a commission to think about a form of inhabiting this evacuated colonial architecture in a way that would not reproduce exactly the same kind of hierarchies in space.

The problem is that when colonial architecture is evacuated, many times it has been used by the newly-formed national regime in a very similar way to the way it was used by the colonialists. So the villas remain villas, the prisons stay as prisons, military camps are military camps. Here there was an attempt to liberate those suburbs and use the militarised geography that networked them. There was a very massive set of highways that created a kind of network of suburbs through Gaza, and our attempt was to convert them into a matrix of public institutions. We were looking for potential to spatialise in evacuated suburbias things like a university, a medical centre, an agricultural training centre and a cultural centre: each one a different suburb, each being one of those new programmes, and the question was how such a programme could spatialise itself into that very familiar, somehow mundane, suburban form. Imagine an entire suburban geography taking another meaning and use. In fact the plans reflected on the possible transformation of those institutions themselves. The fantasy was that if the settlements are nothing but an exaggeration of very known banal, mundane typologies that are being put in that extreme situation, is it not somehow a way to speculate about the future of suburbia at large? So there was this wild speculation at the time and I was happy that we could discuss that at that moment.

RK You are now here in London. What are you doing at Goldsmiths? What is the intention of your programme?

EW There is a new programme that we've set up. As a matter of fact we have just completed the first year of it. It's a PhD and MA in Research Architecture. Somehow that format has allowed us to think about the limitation of post-graduate architectural education, that seems locked in a very professional American way (either professional in terms of design or professional in terms of history and theory): the custodians of knowledge model, that is produced in the so-called elite schools in the States. Ours I hope is a more robust, action-based research. So in a sense it's a practice-driven theory course. It's action-based research in the sense that we understand that in order to force a system to reveal itself you have to interact with it to a certain degree, so it's very speculative and propositional as a form of research.

HUO Thank you so much. Many thanks.

Applause, end of interview

Hans Ulrich Obrist   We are very happy to welcome our next guest, Hussein Chalayan. I am curious about you and London and also about your being dislocated from Turkish North Cyprus. Could you tell us about this?

Hussein Chalayan   In terms of why?

HUO   Yes.

HC   I am actually the son of an immigrant; I am here because my father moved here in the 1960s. He became a restaurateur and my parents met in Cyprus, we came over when I was born. I then went back to Cyprus, came back again. I've been back and forth ever since. It's very loose, let's say, it hasn't been that stable. Now I'm thirty-five and I guess I will be mostly here but it really has to do with my father.

HUO   And what led to your decision to go to fashion school in London, rather than Paris or New York?

HC   I was already studying here so it felt like the natural thing to do. You have to remember if you have a family somewhere, you are in a place because of them and they support you. Also St Martins was the place where I wanted to be; I felt it was the best of any kind of college I could go to. I had done research on it so it really felt like the natural thing to do. In terms of afterwards, I guess what I do now has a lot more to do with other countries apart from London. I am based here but a lot of my relationships are outside London.

Rem Koolhaas   Can you elaborate?

HC   London doesn't really take, in my opinion, creative thinking and fashion that seriously. I feel that a lot of people can blossom here but really they can only sustain their livelihoods by creating connections with other European countries. For instance, if Italy didn't exist I couldn't really survive. I think that, of course, you can have a certain level of work you can do here but I don't feel within the kind of work that I'm doing I could have survived here had I not created these other connections. So I am only based here because I like the eclectic side of London and I can have friends from all different backgrounds. I think there is a certain level of liberalism that I enjoy.

RK   There was an earlier encounter with fashion in this Marathon and I was voicing my admiration for the efficiency of fashion. I think that many fashion designers produce three hundred prototypes a year and for each of them they maybe have an average of four tests, so a fashion designer has to decide about a thousand or fifteen hundred items. We have also been speaking to young artists who simply couldn't maintain the pace. I think that fashion is about the pace and therefore a very important prototype for all of us. Particularly in some of your work, most famously and perhaps in my eyes impressively, the demand at some point that each fashion item ends or begins as a piece of furniture, you seem to put yourself challenges that are highly unusual. Why do you resist efficiency? Or is it a form of resisting efficiency?

HC   I think there is a duality to what I do. I am definitely your classic fashion designer in one sense, where me and my team create a collection and we do fittings, etc. Then there's another side to what I do; sometimes I can incorporate them into my collections, which is like the pieces that you are talking about. Fashion is an industrial process, it's not really about art unless you are doing couture, it's about mass-producing and delivering on time and it's a seasonal project, you have to produce one after another. You constantly have to renew yourself; it's a very transient thing. Within that I try to, let's say, incorporate things that I feel are going to be more timeless for me and things that I feel I am going to enjoy doing. To be honest, enjoying is a really important thing; I think it shows through. If you have enjoyed something I think other people will enjoy it, too, somehow. I was doing one collection after another and I was feeling quite restricted and I felt I should really start to incorporate my other interests into what I was doing. I was kind of doing it in the early days and then I got caught up in this industrial thing that you're talking about which is very mechanical and exhausting and difficult. So I decided to incorporate other things into it and present them together and now I show my work in galleries and I also sell my clothes in fashion boutiques, so it's actually an interesting duality, at times hard because there are different concerns in each thing. But let's say the way I'm showing the work is different but the roots of ideas are very similar.

HUO   What is interesting is that we have had many speakers who talked about this boundarylessness of being in different activities or even different fields at the same time, yet there seems something very specific to your work that there is this moment of transformation where suddenly a skirt turns into a table, turns into something else. I was very curious to find out more about that.

HC Are you asking about boundaries in abstract things or boundaries?

HUO How this concretely works. It doesn't seem to be unusual now that there is a practice of design, at the same time a practice of fashion design, at the same time gallery exhibitions; these are parallel realities. But what is specific in your work is that the objects in themselves seem to be able to transform and suddenly a skirt becomes a design object.

HC I see. I am very interested in change, I am very interested in how something could evolve, how something could change form and change meaning as well. A lot of the clothes have a sense of life and I try to create a mini-narrative for each thing. So it's about how a garment might evolve or might have come from a story and it kind of marks that story and it's, in a way, a residue of that story. I guess that's the main thing I have. I like things to have a sense of life. I like to be able to look at something and understand maybe what it's been inspired by or where it's come from and maybe that moment is a segment of the life it's had. I guess this is my main interest and I'm excited by that.

RK I have a question and a confusion. You say you are exhibiting in boutiques and in galleries.

HC I am selling in boutiques, not exhibiting.

RK You mention the galleries and the art world as if it were a form of endorsement.

HC It's just different. I don't see it as endorsement; I see it as just a different platform because I think there's a big difference in people consuming what you do and them looking at it closely. I think what an art gallery does is give you the platform to look at something closely and when it's not a catwalk situation – our shows aren't really typical catwalks – but there, there is movement, it goes in five minutes. I think what a gallery environment does is help you look at something closely and I guess to enjoy it more or be able to analyse it more. I don't see it as an endorsement. I never said, 'Please show my work in galleries now'. It was something that evolved over the years. I have been given commissions and said, 'Why not? Let's do it'. One thing has led to another. I'm not one of those people who thinks fashion becomes more worthy or more important when it's in galleries.

HUO   I was curious about a utopian dimension of your work because in the video *Place to passage* one sees these futuristic capsules connecting Istanbul and London.

HC   That piece was again a commission and I felt at the time that it could combine a few of my interests together because I feel like a displaced person in a way, I'm always dreaming of either Istanbul or Cyprus and my family and what they are doing now and there has always been this curiosity as to the whereabouts of other people that I'm connected to or other places, and my existence here. So I think this project was about combining design and my thoughts. The capsule was something that started in London and travelled to Istanbul in this virtual environment; and the capsule was something that, in a way, represented a constant state of movement where the environment controlled also your activities or your being. Really it was also about going back into the womb because it gets filled up with water as it goes into the Bosphorus and it felt like this displacement to the extent where you go back into the womb. This was in my own abstract way, the initial idea, and I felt that I didn't need people to recognise this; it was just in some ways a banal journey, but these were my reasons for doing it. But again, processes are there for you to be inspired, you don't need to explain yourself each time. But this was my reason for doing it. Let's say it's a meditative film that starts from one place and goes to another and I guess Istanbul is a place where I spend a lot of time through my work and I have a fascination with it because I am a Turkish Cypriot. I speak Turkish but yet Istanbul is a place I am not a native person in. I am a voyeur but yet I can engage with it. So it was really, let's say, a meditative piece based on these ideas.

HUO   We haven't yet spoken about your link to architecture and there is very often an architectural dimension in your work. And yet you said in a recent interview, 'I can't say it's architectural but it relates to space, it creates an interplay between event and place. The clothes become a catalyst to create experiences at an event. I am questioning whether you have an event in a space that does turn it into a place'. You have actually opened your first Tokyo store and there you collaborated with an architecture group from London, Block Architecture.

HC   Yes.

HUO   I was wondering if you could tell us in more general terms about you relationship to architecture and then more specifically about this collaboration with Block.

HC   To be honest, I never thought I had this connection with the architectural world. People start reading into your work and your interest and they label you to create something to talk about, to be honest. I have got a general interest in space in relation to event and I am interested in form and structure. In this case with the shop in Tokyo what we wanted to do was to create this sense of being in one place and another at the same time, so I looked at my Cypriot background and basically I wanted to recreate that in this synthetic Japanese environment. This was what that project was about and it was also about the state of repose and the state of movement, so we had like a whole wing that cut through the building which was based on an aeroplane, so it suggested static movement. We had trees growing out of the floor and you sensed travel but it was static. I was interested in that contradiction as well. It was a really fruitful collaboration because it wasn't so clearly drawn by them and proposed to me and I would say yea or nay. It was really that we would exchange and go through ideas and it evolved. I guess because of my interests I couldn't have done it any other way.

RK   Right now there is a very large and important issue whether Turkey should be part of Europe.

HC   Surprise, surprise! This question was going to come up.

RK   Maybe it is more a European issue than a Turkish issue.

HC   Yes.

RK   In some ways Turkey seems to have already moved beyond and is forming other connections.

HC   Other connections with other parts of the world.

RK   Yes.

HC   Right.

RK   And doing it extremely well and energetically and intelligently.

HC   Yes.

RK   Somehow London is the part of the world where that issue and the whole issue of Europe is completely absent. Do you have an opinion of Turkey and Europe?

HC   My opinion about Turkey and the EU is much more on a cultural level. I think the more you isolate communities or countries, the worse things get. I think that an isolated Turkey – I don't know where it would go, to be honest. Just simply on that level, forgetting the rural Anatolia and how it needs to catch up with western Turkey, etc., just the idea of embracing is an important thing. I think for many Turkish people the way they feel isolated from the world is the biggest issue. They have always wanted, let's say, to become European – through Ottoman times, etc. Ottomans were a multi-ethnic empire and I think just on that level it's enough to try and include them if countries like Poland, and many years ago Spain, have been invited. I think it will take longer because it's a bigger country with a poor infrastructure in the East. I think it's a process. Looking at this climate right now in the world I think people are better off including Turkey, to be honest.

HUO   Eric Hobsbawm said when we prepared this Marathon that we should have a protest against forgetting. Is there any fashion designer out of the history of fashion design or designer or architect or any kind of other practitioner who for you is a toolbox for the present?

HC   There are various people but if I think about it, I haven't really looked at fashion as an inspiration. As I was growing up I always loved Hitchcock, always loved various other film directors like Krzysztof Kieslowski for example, who's a Polish director. I think that, to be honest, I haven't really had role models like that because I have such broad interests that I can't give you one person that's my star. I think film, because it's always about a narrative and I guess I'm like a story-teller myself. I guess that's the nearest thing I can relate to.

HUO   Do you write?

HC   I don't literally sit and write but of course I have a notebook and I make notes, but no, I don't. I can't say I write.

HUO   Is there an unrealised project of yours, a dream, something you always wanted to do, which you could tell us about?

HC   I would like to really belong to some kind of a group where things are constantly discussed, because I do actually feel quite isolated in London. I wish there was some kind of a body that I could belong to, in a way what you are doing now. I would like that to be part of real life because this is an event; it is not part of real life. I might know a few of the speakers today but actually everybody is in their own bubble. I think my biggest dream, and the most exciting thing, would be for me to belong to a group of people who are not so exclusive, who can invite other people constantly, where there can be things exchanged. Because, honestly, what you are doing today is really a synthetic event where people are brought together, but London is people living in little bubbles where there isn't much exchange going on, it's all very remote. This would be the most exciting thing for me.

HUO   Many, many thanks, Hussein Chalayan.

Applause, end of interview

Rem Koolhaas We will now talk to Tariq Ali. You need no introduction and I have said that of very few people. It is not a way of avoiding talking about your history but simply because it is an established fact. You have taken, with considerable courage and consistency, highly critical positions of the British Government and this civilization in general, and you have written a very angry book, *Rough Music*. Can you first talk about the title?

Tariq Ali When the bombings happened in London in July, like every other Londoner I was incredibly angry that they had happened, but I wanted to understand the causes of these bombings and at that time British culture, the dominant political culture, didn't want to listen. I tried to explain to them that even if you do not support the consequences you have to understand the causes, because unless you understand the causes these things will happen again. But they did not want to accept that the war in Iraq had anything to do with this and for two whole weeks the dominant culture of this country, the media, the BBC, was in total denial – 'It has nothing to do with Iraq'. And then gradually, as they began to conduct opinion polls, they found out that the views I expressed in the *Guardian* the following day – saying this is a big tragedy, it's unacceptable, the carnage we don't accept, but it has a reason, and the reason is this government's decision to go to war in Iraq and occupy another country – this was also, as it turned out, the view of sixty-six per cent of the British people. This came out two or three weeks later, but the fact that it was covered up made me angry and the fact that we then witnessed a public execution on the British Underground when a young Brazilian electrician was killed for no rhyme or reason angered me even more. I just felt that if this went on in this way the civil liberties of British citizens, not even people who are all that political like the Brazilian electrician, are under threat. So I sat down and wrote this book, *Rough Music* in a real rage and in anger. Thank God that Verso, this radical publishing house, exists and they published it. That's all, really. It was something that should have been said by the media, by lots of pundits, by television, saying, 'This is why it's happened and let's try and stop it happening again'. But because the political elite didn't want to accept that they were completely out of step with the country as a whole, as they are today when they go in and support what the Israelis and Americans green-lighted in Lebanon. They are completely out of touch. The bulk of the population of this country does not agree with it, and the political elite doesn't represent it.

[Applause]

RK You have written it in a rage, as you say yourself, but nevertheless I am very surprised by how moderate your recommendations are because it ends with five recommendations. The first one is to withdraw from Iraq and Afghanistan; the second one is to stop financing religious schools; the third is to undo the connection between England and Great Britain; the fourth is to defend civil liberties and the fifth one is a peasant revolt.

[Laughter]

You surely must mean that metaphorically but I was wondering whether this agenda doesn't deserve an update because the repertoire is familiar. Very few people disagree with it and I am wondering whether there is not currently exactly this discrepancy you describe, which is actually not about the government keeping anything secret but the government having a separate life from the population.

TA This is it, as you say. The five points that I make at the end of *Rough Music* are, relatively speaking, moderate, and for me very moderate indeed. But the fact that they still cannot be accepted by the political elite, either Labour or Conservative in this country, that's what's deeply shocking. What you increasingly see now is a real anger with this government in Britain; large numbers of people, even people who are not so political, absolutely loathe Tony Blair. And the response of the Labour Party to this is if you loathe Tony Blair we understand, we'll give you Gordon Brown. But we say that Gordon Brown has exactly the same politics as Tony Blair. It's not a personal thing against Blair; it's not the cut of his clothes or how he looks, it's what he does, so we don't want a politician who repeats what Blair does in a slightly different way. We want a different sort of politics and that's what these five points are there for. But the fact that the political elite cannot accept them indicates, if you like, the disjuncture between what people want and what the political elite can give. In Latin America this disjuncture has led to a whole rise of popular and populist movements challenging traditional politics and that's why I wrote that we need a peasants' revolt, that British citizens should see themselves like Latin American peasants in

Peru and Bolivia and learn from them, because they are in a way more advanced than you are.

Hans Ulrich Obrist How do you see the current moment in summer 2006?

TA The current moment I think is a big tragedy that we have, as Eyal Weizman was saying a few minutes ago, a country which can get away with murder. It can get away with destroying the social infrastructure of states, it can get away with reducing Gaza to the status of a large prison camp. It can do whatever it wants and no-one in the so-called international community is permitted to challenge it and if you challenge it you are attacked, saying, 'How dare you challenge it because of the crimes committed against the Jewish people in Europe during the Second World War?' Which were, if you like, the 'crimes' of European civilization. Why should the Palestinians or the Lebanese be the victims and be punished for those crimes? Europe cannot speak up any more; they go along with it. We have a situation where they say, 'Bomb for another two weeks and then we might have to stop you', and meanwhile the entire social infrastructure of Lebanon has been destroyed.

I would just like to say something else on this which affects architecture, it really does. When you have architects beginning to organise against this horrific wall which has been built and is being built in Palestine/Israel, people get very nervous: you can't object, you can't speak up against it. And I have to say that I was deeply shocked when an architect of the stature of Richard Rogers – let me give him his proper title, Sir Richard Rogers – or his firm, was attacked when he went to New York to build the Jacob Javits Centre and they said, 'We will not give you this contract because in your office a meeting took place of Palestinian/Israeli architects who are not in favour of the wall'. Instead of saying, 'I believe in the freedom of architects as any other citizen to think what they like', he completely capitulated, hired a public relations guy to describe in a statement a defence of that wall and saying that this wall is necessary to fight against terrorism. That is a level of intimidation which exists in this world today and the fact that people like him, who are extremely wealthy and don't need too much money, gave in to this I find deeply shocking.

RK I think we have so far avoided *ad hominem* discussions today and I think in this case it is better since he is not here to defend himself.

TA   Well, we should have a debate with him. I am in favour of a big public debate with him saying, 'Why did you do that?'. I like him. He is someone I know.

RK   But he is not here.

TA   We should say to him, 'Why did you do it?'.

RK   We invited him but he is not here.

TA   I am sorry.

[Laughter]

HUO   You brought up architecture, and I want to ask you the same question we asked Chantal Mouffe before, which is how you think that art, architecture and literature can contribute to the shaping of a more mature antagonistic political position. And also why, besides the type of book like *Rough Music* Rem mentioned, you write fiction as well.

TA   I started writing fiction in the early 1990s and the set of novels which are translated all over the world is known as the *Islam Quintet*. This is a set of novels I started writing after the First Gulf War when I heard a commentator on the BBC, who should have known better, saying that the Arabs were people without a culture. Just hearing that remark angered me so much that I wanted to reply to it and I felt one couldn't reply to it just like that; one had to think and reflect and research. So I went to Spain and Portugal and spent months there researching the medieval period when Jews, Muslims and Christians lived together and what happened and then seeing the architecture which remains of that period, especially in Spain, in Granada, in Cordoba. In Cordoba you have an amazing mosque, the Grand Mosque and in the heart of that mosque there is a church, as if the mosque has been raped by the church and the Spanish king who came to see the church said to the architects, 'You have destroyed something which is unique and inserted your mosque in'. But what he didn't understand was that if they hadn't put the mosque in the church, the mosque would have been destroyed. So that, seeing the architecture of medieval Spain and what had survived, I decided to write a novel about it to try and reconstruct that civilization and its last days and what happened to it.

    That's how I started writing fiction and then the late Edward Said, the dear friend who read it, said, 'You can't stop now. You have to tell the whole bloody story of the clashes between Islamic civilization and Western Christendom'. So the four novels have been done: the first is on

Spain; the second is on the Crusades, the fictional memoirs of Saladin; the third is the Ottoman Empire and its decline; and the fourth is the very little-known story of the Arab period in Sicily, *A Sultan in Palermo*, of how even after Arab civilization in Sicily was defeated, for a hundred and fifty years Arab culture remained. The Normans who took over spoke Arabic and educated their kids in Arabic because this was the language of learning. And this was my response to that ignorant commentator who said that Arabs are people without a political culture. So that's what caused me to write them. The fifth novel has to be set in the modern world, which is going to be a problem, because all civilizations are in a state of deep crisis, in my opinion, not just Islam but also Christianity and Judaism.

RK   I want to make one more effort. I think that all your opinions are probably shared by the vast majority in this room but to try to take the temperature in terms of willingness to undertake political action or a political imagination, there is perhaps not a despair but a real sense of inadequacy or powerlessness. There I still find your proposal that we become peasants, and particularly South American peasants, a little bit wanting.

TA   *[Laughs]* Obviously, I don't believe that the people of England, Wales and Scotland can actually revert to peasant status physically or sociologically, but I think they might actually benefit if they did revert to it in terms of rebellion. Some of the most amazing rebellions we've seen against this new liberal economic system: for instance, against water privatisation in Bolivia, against electricity privatisation in Cuzco, against landlords in Brazil, against slum dwellers in Venezuela, against the collapse of the whole system in Argentina. These are things which the British or European trade union movement could learn a great deal from but I think they are stuck, I think they cannot learn any more. A new generation has to arise which comes up with a different style and a different form of politics which says, 'Enough of you people, enough of the way in which you run the world and run this country and run Europe. We are going to try something else'. We can't will it into being in a voluntaristic fashion but it's something that has to come and that is why Latin America is what excites me.

RK   And do you see any signs here?

TA   I see very few signs here, actually. I think within the younger generation there is now a growing anger but if you look at the country where we've just had a change of government in Europe, Italy, the removal of Berlusconi and that whole thing has brought a new government into office that is doing very similar things. We have a situation where democracy itself has been hollowed out in the United States and in Europe and where the differences between centre left and centre right hardly exist any more. And the big tragedy for me is that all this is alienating whole generations from any political engagement. In the last two general elections in Britain, the majority of people between the ages of eighteen and twenty-six did not vote and they are the future of this country and the rest of the world. I am optimistic because I think if changes take place in one part of the world, slowly the news begins to seep through and spread, but what I do not believe is that religions or religious politics are the answer in any way. I think that's a disaster for whoever, whether it's Muslims, Jews, Christians. Going into politics exclusively through a religious prism doesn't take you anywhere. And that's why the situation in the Middle East is also quite depressing.

HUO   A very last question, which is whether you have any unrealised projects, dreams.

TA   My unrealised project is the overthrow of this system.
[Laughter. Applause]

HUO   Many thanks, Tariq Ali. Thank you very much.

Applause, end of interview

Hans Ulrich Obrist   It's a great pleasure to welcome Marina Warner, our next speaker. Marina also certainly does not need an introduction here. You have some visuals to show us to begin.

Marina Warner   I just thought that as you'd raised a pavilion in the park it seemed a way into the question of illusion, which I think lies so much behind the question of belief. I thought somehow your bubble, which floats and is a temporary structure and is gathering us together in a temporary space for a certain amount of fluid time, connected to one of the most remarkable mirages that occur in nature, which is Fata Morgana. So I just thought I'd show you one or two pictures of Fata Morgana and I think in some ways even your frieze inside, though I think it's leaves, has something to bear on it because it seems a refraction and a series of reflections, which is what Fata Morgana is. This, which you probably can't see on the plasma screens, is a very rare eighteenth-century print showing the effects in the Straits of Messina. You won't be able to see it so we'll go to the next one. What happens is that bands of different temperature air create mirrors in the sky and these reflect in the water and reflect on the clouds. This is an actual photograph of Fata Morgana occurring in the Arctic Circle; it's either very hot temperatures or very low temperatures that cause these mirrors in the air. In the next one you'll see a close-up. That's enormously high; that's towering into the sky as high as you can ever imagine as high. It's known to the Norsemen in myth as a *hillingar* and they thought they were castles raised by the gods.

The next one. This is the point I am making: those are just meteorological phenomena, they are natural wonders, but in the Christian tradition these wonders in the sky were interpreted as portents. You can see here the relationship between these bands of clouds stretching across and the phenomena of reflections. This is a very characteristic one of a battle occurring in the sky, lots of horsemen, lots of armies fighting and some images that are Christian have a Christ image at the top. If we have the next one, bloody heads in the cloud and a drawn sword, again a Fata Morgana mirage but particularly interpreted by a collective group – this is important at this point – by a crowd, seen as a sign from the heavens that something terrible is going to happen. Sometimes a victory is going to happen, too. Next one. There are heavenly ships, a very common one because actually that's a very common reflection that occurs: ships floating on the sea. Their image is reflected up on the clouds. The next one is a leap. This one is just a tiny stone, it's an agate, and it belonged to somebody (you were asking people who inspired them), it belonged to Roger Caillois, who is a writer I'm interested in. It's just a split through an agate but almost everyone in this room will see a face in that and also a particular kind of face, a kind of phantasmagoric face, some sort of cat-ghost type. The stone is known as – it's only about this size [large orange] – *petit fantôme*, little ghost. The point about that in terms of belief and illusion is that the brain finds it extremely hard to resist the illusion. It is very hard to see that as a stone unless you're told to. So in some ways I wanted to draw attention to that. We are much more drawn by the structures of our brain that make us perceive certain things and the wider circles around that are the ideologies and belief systems that shape our perceptions. I think that this kind of situation is one we very much live in today. That's it.

HUO   Many thanks. What you have just shown us leads directly to our first question because we were wondering about the relation between the city and phantoms or ghosts.

MW   *[Laughs]* Well, as you know, there has become a tremendously strong element in a lot of writing about London and I think it belongs to a new secular metaphysics of some of the people who were resisting religious metaphysics. It's also to do with trying to tell stories about the past that will, perhaps, awaken certain ghosts who might actually help. So two things are happening: one is that the kind of hauntings that people excavate – if you like, a writer like Sebald will do that, though he didn't specialise in cities; Iain Sinclair, who is somebody who might have been here…

HUO   … he was here at 6.00 am.

MW   Yes, absolutely. Iain Sinclair is the great master of the London walker, the *dériveur*, the person who goes drifting through the city and hears the voices of the past. There are two things that I am particularly interested in: one is that memory can be constructive; it can be constructive because it can be critical so that you don't actually just inherit your memories but you question them, you interrogate them, you uncover them. That's an obvious process of any writer. At the same time, this is in a sense a newer point, and that is that a lot of writers in all media, and a lot of artists, are also engaged in trying to tell a new story. So they are trying to take that story from the past and say, 'Is there anything we can do with this?'. It's not quite fairytale, though fairytale is something I am very interested in because it's wishful thinking, but this kind of wishful thinking and mythological perspective-construction of the past, people who are atavistic, people who want to go back to some Ur project, some Ur text, the fundamentalists, will always dislike the prospective imagination at work. They will dislike the idea that you can look at a given data and what you interpret from it will always be phantasmagoric to some extent because that is how our minds work. We work with images and we work with symbols; that's how we are. So I think a lot of interesting writers are trying to take that and to some extent mix in a new story. Some of the people I heard this afternoon were saying that; Hussein Chalayan was saying it about his approach as a dress designer, that's as a couturier. It spreads through different fields; I happen to know more about writing.

HUO   I want to ask you about another link to the city related to immigration. In your book *The Leto Bundle* you write about immigrants in the city and I was wondering what your opinion is on the government's legislation on immigration.

MW   Every week brings another deplorable step that this government takes. I don't want to go into the details of the immigration laws but it's also an unholy relationship with the media. We do really have a very problematic representation of immigration and refugees and asylum seekers in our mass media so there is some attempt to counteract that. In *The Leto Bundle* I wanted to show that exclusion is a dynamic of society at any time; the only grain of hope that you can take from that is that it operates along different lines at different times, so it is in metamorphosis itself. One of the racist bases of our present immigration policy is that it tends to define people in a certain way, according to racial and national boundaries, ethnic divisions and so forth. It is a temporal thing – it has happened in history at a certain time and it only started happening recently. We can reverse it. The larger problem is that exclusion is this human thing: the drawing of borders, of boundaries, the pure, the impure, the permitted ritual, the non-permitted ritual, what is forbidden, what is not forbidden. How we deal with that and where we draw these divisions: it's our responsibility to attempt to draw them in an inclusive fashion. That's such a banal thing to say because how do we start doing it? But some people are trying.

HUO   Can I ask you more about London? You have been connected to London for such a long time and I was wondering how London has changed and how you think it will change in the next decades.

MW   The main thing that I have experienced as a change is property. London has become too expensive for many of its people to live in. The mixed housing which was a characteristic of London since the war, in which streets were mixed up with all kinds of different types of accommodation and housing, that has all been changed – you know much more about it than I do, of course, being an architect – but basically this is happening and it is moving towards an American style, property-banded city and that is catastrophic for the social cohesion of our communities. We need to have it layered and banded and different people living side by side. How we resist the march of the property market in an era of free market forces is really very difficult.

Rem Koolhaas   Your presentation is very precise and also very urgent and it seems to have the urgency of somebody who is trying to avert a disaster. Which disaster are you trying to avert by insisting on this ghostly dimension? And what are we to gain by recognising it?

MW   In response to Hans Ulrich's question about how London has changed, one of the greatest changes is not a material one, but one that I had not expected: it was the change to religious belief. I wrote a book in the 1970s about the Virgin Mary which ends with a prophecy that no-one will believe in the Virgin Mary by the end of the millennium. Well, I could not have been more wrong! [Laughs] Far from belief declining it is actually gaining pace. This apocalyptic note that you have quite rightly identified is in some sense a kind of echo of an apocalyptic discourse which I have been feeling for quite a long time. We all feel it. It is present in our politics. But I think there has been a growth of collusion between entertainment and political discourse, not only in the direct representation of religious wars in films – and they are religious wars, even if they are fantasy wars they are religious wars – but also in the spread (and this is why to some extent I am very interested in your kind of work, and particularly your work with textures and so forth) of a disengagement with embodiment. So, some of the apocalyptic elements in my work are that I feel people are haunted themselves with increasing numbers of spectres. These can take the form of celebrities. We are the first generation who know what we looked like when we were children because we have seen so many photographs of ourselves; our children know what they looked like moving, which our generation doesn't know. They know themselves when they are moving, so they know themselves in these spectral forms – but they are disembodied. And of course we also know many, many famous people, many political figures, as spectres who haunt us. So I think this disengages us with the reality of bodies and one of the problems with the wars that are going on, with the invasion of Lebanon and on many other fronts is that people scream blue murder that people are being killed because they've forgotten that's what happens in a war and that's what happens to bodies in a war. They scream because they want it to be a movie, they want it to be spectral.

[Applause]

HUO   Many thanks Marina Warner.

Applause, end of interview

Hans Ulrich Obrist   Welcome Milan Rai. We have all been reading your book 7/7. *The London Bombings. Islam & the Iraq War.* My first question was if we can treat 7/7 as history already.

Milan Rai   Well, I think we are asked to learn from history, we have a duty to learn from what happened a year ago; in that sense what happened on 7 July is very much a present issue, and as we found out on 21 July, it was not by any means a one-off event. It is both now something that has happened in the past and it is something we need to learn from, and it's also a warning about the future, a warning that has been delivered by two of the bombers in their video statements. I think that, particularly right now, it's very important for us to attend to the likely causes of the attacks that took place because if we want to prevent them from happening again we have to understand why they happened, otherwise we are not going to take the correct actions.

Marina Warner was just making a reference to the war in Lebanon and the anger that there is over that outrage. I think I have a slightly different perspective on it: I see a lot of anger and outrage about what's going on there because it seems like an exercise of unrestrained brutality, disproportionate brutality, illegality. For us here in London right now the biggest threat to security is our Prime Minister's support for what Israel is doing in Lebanon, and that's really the heart of what I was trying to write about because immediately after the 7 July attacks we found out a few things pretty rapidly. One of them was in the opinion polls in the *Daily Mirror* and in the *Guardian*: we found out in the *Mirror* it was eighty-five per cent and in the *Guardian* sixty-four per cent of the people in Britain felt there was a causal connection between the war in Iraq and the bombings that took place in this city. Then there was a later poll for the GLA which found only eight per cent of people didn't think that there was a connection. So there was a very early consensus in the city about that and it was the investigation of that topic, which we found a lot of evidence about, that was one of the main reasons I wanted to write the book.

HUO   Can you tell us about your arrest outside Downing Street last year?

MR   Sure.

Rem Koolhaas	And a larger issue, the whole issue of civil disobedience, which is a term that we haven't heard this entire day.
MR	OK.
RK	And even the term 'activism'.
MR	Activism, civil disobedience and how I got arrested on 25 October 2005. Three-part question! I think when people use the word 'activism' what they mainly mean is trying to struggle against established power, people who are using grass-roots mobilization, people who are using face-to-face work in their communities, horizontal networks to try to counteract the power of the state, counteract the power of corporations when they are doing wrong things. Civil disobedience is one of the modes of doing that; it can also be used to strengthen the power of the state or strengthen the power of corporations for objectives that I would think are against human rights and so on.

So civil disobedience as such is just about taking forms of action and forms of protest, about the risk of being arrested, being prosecuted and being tried and punished by the criminal justice system, not necessarily illegal. So, for example, on 25 October last year, along with Maya Evans, I was reading out the names of people who had died in Iraq as a result of the invasion and occupation. Maya was the first person to be convicted of participating in an unlawful demonstration in the vicinity of Parliament under the new 'Serious Organised Crime and Police Act', and I became the first person to be convicted of organising an unauthorised demonstration in the vicinity of Parliament. I was convicted of organising the two-person demonstration of me and Maya. What we were doing was trying to hold a remembrance ceremony to mark the anniversary of the report in *The Lancet*, the medical journal, the estimate that one hundred thousand Iraqis had died. So I was reading the names of Iraqi civilians who had died, Maya was reading the names of British soldiers who had died in Iraq as a result of the invasion and occupation.

When we notified the police that we wanted to go outside Downing Street to read these names, because that seemed to us a very fitting place to do it, we were told that there were new regulations and that we would have to apply in writing for permission to do this. Initially I was really focused on doing this remembrance ceremony; it was really important to me. But the more I thought about it, I realised that 'I can't cooperate with this law. I can't believe that you have to ask the police to remember the dead. I can't believe that is something which is criminally wrong'. So in the end I was arrested, I was convicted and I was fined and now the bailiffs are after me for five hundred pounds' worth of goods to seize from my property and I'm not going to cooperate with them. So probably it will end up with me going to prison. But that whole process, in my view, does not involve me in any illegality because I believe that the law that was passed by Parliament is in contravention of the European Convention on Human Rights in relation to freedom of assembly and expression and so on. I believe the law is wrong and what I have done is not illegal, it's civil obedience, which has, unfortunately in this instance, ended up with prosecution and so on.

RK   Are you going to take this to the European Court?

MR   Well, in the first instance you appeal to a divisional court. Anyway, there is an appeal in train about that, yes.

HUO   I want to ask you the same question I asked Marina: how has London changed and how do you think it will change in the next decades?

MR   I heard a bit of her answer to that and I think London has changed in a lot of the ways that the world has changed. London is a globalised city; it is very much connected to what is happening in the world, so in a sense the evolution of London and its fate are very much tied up with what's going to happen with the whole world. In particular, as I was saying earlier, the basic question facing people who live and work in London or who come here for other reasons, is: are we going to be physically secure, are we going to be allowed to live in London? I think this is the root question. If we continue to have US and British policies abroad who go on brutalising people around the world, giving them no hope of redress, then I think we are going to have an increasingly dangerous time here in London. That worries me greatly. I would guess that there are some people in this room who are anti-war, who are against the invasion and occupation of Iraq and maybe there are some people who are for those things. Nonetheless, I do believe that an honest inquiry into what happened on 7 July, an honest inquiry into Al Qaeda and the Bin Laden phenomenon lead to the conclusion of Michael Scheuer, who used to run the Bin Laden unit for the CIA until 1996. He says they are not attacking us because of our values and our freedom, they are attacking us because of our policies, particularly in the Middle East. He is the CIA's Bin Laden expert and I think that we have to attend to that. This means that if we want to be safer we have to change those policies.

HUO   You wrote a book on Chomsky, called *Chomsky's Politics*, in 1995.

MR   It wasn't the most poetic title, but it was descriptive.

HUO   And you have also contributed to the *Cambridge Chomsky Companion*. So I was wondering if Noam Chomsky, as a public intellectual, is a kind of role model for you.

MR   Well, you know, Chomsky is a major figure in the history of ideas for his contributions in cognitive psychology and linguistics; and he also works harder than pretty much any other commentator on contemporary affairs. So anyone who treated Chomsky as a role model would be setting themselves up for very high hurdles. Some of the ways in which Chomsky is exemplary, I think, are that he does take very seriously what the available evidence is and he eschews rhetoric and sticks very much to trying to summarise the available best knowledge about situations. That leads to radical conclusions, it turns out. Another way in which he's exemplary is that I think he is very honest, particularly about his own shortcomings. Chomsky is a very good role model to take.

RK   I want to read you a quotation from your book. It contains a citation of David Miliband, an up-and-coming Labour intellectual, so I assume it is with a necessary irony that you quote him. 'At the 2005 Labour Party Conference Miliband said the Government needed to act to prevent voters turning to extremism. Pointing to recent BNP successes in council elections in Burnley, Lancashire he said, "It is when people feel powerless, when they feel the system doesn't work for them, they don't just get apathetic, they get angry. When they turn to anger they turn to extremism". Miliband declared that to stay in power we have to release power. We know that the new enemy is a sense of powerlessness. And then he added, "I think the sense of powerlessness is a very profound thing to us to come to terms with"' – and this is a pretty obvious point for a politician – '"Over the next ten years the issue of power is going to be the core of politics"'. What I think is untrue in this statement is that many people, and many of us, have perhaps turned into apathetic people but few of us have turned into angry people, or at least people who are able to find a way to articulate that anger that is productive.

Do you have an explanation for that?

MR You are absolutely right. I was thinking that maybe you guys think the twenty-four hours is working harder than Chomsky kind of thing! I don't know. You are absolutely right. In that quotation David Miliband, who, as you say, is an up-and-coming Labour intellectual, talks about the Labour Party, the Labour Government, releasing power, saying powerlessness is the enemy, when it was precisely this government that has increased the sense of powerlessness amongst people, most dramatically in relation to the war in Iraq, but in so many other ways – from local government all the way up to international affairs. This government has been driven by the desire to centralise power and to increase powerlessness; people react to that in different ways, and you are right about that. Some people react with anger, some people react with defeatism and some people react to that by committing themselves to non-violence and some people react to that by committing themselves to violent actions and revenge. I think the last part of your question is why is it some people choose productive uses for their anger?

RK Yes, but why so few of us? And particularly in those parts of the population whose anger might actually be read or registered.

MR I believe this issue of powerlessness is not just about government policy. In a way we live in a culture of powerlessness because in this culture the most valued things are to be famous, to be wealthy, to be powerful; these are the things which are valued. The message we get from every corner of the culture, really, is there are about a dozen people who count, like Bush, Blair, Bono; there's a handful of people who count. What they say counts and the rest of us are just insects who can watch and maybe we can vote for one or go and see another one in a film or buy a record; we can applaud but our role is just to spectate. That is the message we are being given all the time from every direction. All this stuff about how come all of our children are so unhappy, we have a multi-billion pound industry which is telling all of us, including targeted at children, that we are ugly, unattractive, we are not popular enough. We've got a multi-pound industry which is there to make us feel bad and to make us feel that we are powerless and that we have to go to someone else in order to plug into what makes us worthwhile and so on. So, it's not just about policy; it's all the way through. I think even in our forms of education and so on, there's a message, what's been called 'the tacit curriculum', which is you have to learn to shut up and listen to other people *[Looks around at audience. Laughter]* for a long time without saying anything, without being disruptive and so. You see, it's all through the culture. So it's not surprising that the end result of that is that we have internalised our own oppression there. There are lots of factors, but one of the main things is that the powers that be give a sense of invulnerability and immovability.

I'd just like to finish by saying one thing: one crucial event of my lifetime in this country was the miners' strike, which very much gave the signal. We only found out years later that in the closing months of the strike, when everyone had given up, the Thatcher government was on the brink of defeat, but we didn't know that. She looked like she was unassailable, but in fact they were crumbling and they were very nearly defeated; it could have turned out totally differently. But the end result of that strike, the projection that we were given, was that it was an enormous blow to the confidence of the people in the Trades Union movement, an enormous blow to people in all sorts of popular movements.

HUO It's almost a great final statement. However, I have a very last question. What is your unrealised project?

MR Unrealised?

HUO Yes.

MR My filing system!
[Laughter]

HUO Thanks so much Milan Rai.

Applause, end of interview

Hans Ulrich Obrist	It's a great pleasure to welcome Doris Lessing.
	[Applause]
Doris Lessing	Thank you.

HUO Thank you so much for joining us. This is the finale of this interview Marathon and we thought that it could be interesting to talk to you about the city in your work. I wanted to start with *London Observed* and ask you how London matters in your writing.

DL Well, I've lived here since I was thirty, you know. It's my hometown, so of course it matters to me immensely. When I arrived here I had no money and a small child and London was very tough in those days, not like now when it overflows with milk and honey. People of my age looking at what London's like now, we can't believe it, the sheer fullness of everything; everything is here. What I came into was a place that had nothing; there was war damage and everyone was poor. Of course, this is a long time we are talking about, so it would have to matter a lot to me.

HUO You wrote a marvellous short story called *Report on the Threatened City* and when I interviewed you some months ago you emphasised very much this kind of threat but at the same time you said that we are rather good at dealing with this threat, at dealing with calamities. I wanted to ask you to tell us a little bit about this report on the threatened city and the way to cope with threat.

DL Well, I've just been reading James Lovelock and his cheerful theories about Gaia, that is the Earth, who is now supposed to be getting her own back for the way we treat her. This, of course, is in a lot of what I write because I think we are dancing around the edge of a precipice saying, 'Look at me! Look at me! Aren't we clever?' In actual fact we are not clever at all. James Lovelock is postulating all kinds of horrors – flooding, ice ages, you name it, the Greenland Current, you can go on for hours. But we don't really need Gaia to do us in because look what we do to ourselves. This is something I can talk about because it's something on my mind a lot but I don't think it's the right time for it. What we do to ourselves: at this very moment today I'm reading

369

about the forests in Brazil which we are doing in. We have known about this thirty or forty years. Does it stop us? It does not. In the same paper yesterday there was something about how we destroy the ocean by our methods of fishing; we know we shouldn't do it but we do do it. And so this is the thing that strikes me. We are an almost calamitously stupid species. That is what we are and we don't take that into account with our planning or how we look at ourselves. We are always testing the boundaries of everything and hoping for the best. Well, we might not get the best!

Rem Koolhaas	I have a question about what is called visionary fiction or science fiction. Why does it have such an appeal for you?
DL	Science fiction is not a little shelf of books, it's an enormous collection of different kinds of books now. There are some books that could be called science fiction and they're not. What are you going to do about Rushdie? It certainly isn't realism, is it? Or lots of books, they are certainly not realistic. When you say, 'Do you like science fiction?' we are talking about a universe of different kinds of writing. I don't think it's easy to talk about that so simply.
RK	No, but why do you yourself write it with intervals of, sometimes, twenty years?
DL	Why do I like writing it? Because if you're going to write about some kind of perspective you can't start a book saying, 'Fred Bloggs sat in his kitchen drinking some Typhoo tea on the 1st March 1937'. You can't do that. You have to spread it about a bit. You can't write about millions of years in a simple way. I have written a lot of books that are not realistic but I started off with the Jocasta series simply because somebody said to me nobody ever reads the great sacred books of the East one after the other, like our Bible, the Jewish Bible, the New Testament, the Qur'an, one after the other. If you do that you will feel this is all the same story with the same characters, the same anecdotes. But nobody does that because as far as we are concerned these religions are all fenced off from each other. So I thought it would be nice to write – it turned out to be Jocasta – about all the ideas that are in all these sacred books. You can't begin a book like that, as I say, 'Joe Bloggs preferred toast to muffins', you can't do it like that. That is why it turned into this great blockbuster of a book.

HUO To continue with science fiction, in a recent conversation you quoted science fiction writer Arthur C. Clarke who talked about the way the lives of human beings will be changed in the next century. In relation to that you made some analogies to Guttenberg. I wanted to ask you to explain that.

DL What I was saying was that the invention of the computers and all these new things is having as much an effect on our brains as the print revolution had in the Middle Ages. We have no idea at all where it is all going to end. We do know that the children's brains are changed; the scientists now tell us that the children's brains are altered. We know that people can't keep very much in their minds for very long, we have a very short attention span, and people can't read long books. What has happened is something has gone wrong with their brains, hasn't it? Everybody else used to read long books without any difficulty, so what's happened? So this is what I meant, that we have a complete revolution in our minds and we're not really taking it into account at all, we are not looking at it clearly.

HUO Rem was just pointing out that you have a text. We wondered if it would be nice if you read it.

DL If you had asked me I would have brought one. This piece of paper is because I have a very bad memory and I have key words down so that moment when I can't remember something I can look, you see. That's all this is. If you had asked me I'd have written a speech for you.
[Laughter]

HUO You were suggesting, and I think it's a very good idea also in relation to this threat you mentioned, that we talk about your recent books, *Mara and Dann* and the sequel, *The Story of General Dann and Mara's Daughter, Griot and The Snow Dog*. Could you tell us a little bit about these two books?

DL I wanted to write an adventure story. There are rules for adventure stories. I started off with Mara and Dann. The basic rules are you have children who are badly treated, they are in prison, with a bad stepmother, something or other, and they have to get out of the situation by their own cunning, wits and courage and they do and they go on this long series of adventures with some people helping them and other people not helping them. You have to have a villain – I think I have a very good villain in *Mara and Dann* – and it has to end more or less happily, though I have to say the ending of *Mara and Dann* is a bit ambiguous. Then I wrote *General Dann* because I got intrigued by this young man, who you would say, perhaps too easily, that he was schizophrenic or something like that. Good and bad are very tightly wound together in Dann. But I postulate, you see, that the coming Ice Age has swallowed up all of Europe. I did not want to write an adventure story of the modern kind, like James Bond, which is all about cars and machinery and that kind of thing, that is an adventure story now. You cannot write about the modern world without writing like that and that bores me, so I thought, 'OK, we'll get rid of Europe and our civilization under the Ice Age'. So we're in the future and we're back with a kind of primitive savagery, which is much easier, believe me, than writing about cars and helicopters.

It occurred to me afterwards that nobody in either of these books is not a refugee. Everybody is on the run from somewhere: a civil war, a flood, a drought, you name it. Everybody is running but I didn't realise that when I was actually writing it. So all these people are infinitely damaged, surviving people. I am now talking about *General Dann*. The thing that links up with them is our friend James Lovelock and Gaia. He postulates that quite soon, in a thousand years, five hundred years, there will be only warlords left with a few breeding women, because after all you have to have breeding women if you want the human race to go on. A warlord thinks one day that all these myths about us, we are all legend, amazing people, and he was watching a bird fly and thinking, 'That lot back there, these clever people, they flew, they flew in machines. How did they do that?' How is he going to find out what we were like? Is there, under the flood or under the ice, a room, within it instructions of how to make our civilization, MIT or Cambridge, England or somewhere? No, there is no place because it is so dispersed and spread about and the knowledge of how to make it is in a lot of different minds, it isn't in just one, not even on a computer, which is so extremely unreliable. So this warlord, you see, what he would like is to have a place where all that dead civilization is, so I invented it in Athenta, where all our artefacts are, but not the knowledge of how to do them.

HUO   It's very, very interesting because it's the second time today we have talked about James Lovelock and Gaia. Mary Midgley was here earlier and also evoked this issue. One other recent book I want to ask you about is *The Grandmothers*, which is a very different story. It is a kind of a portrait of a very extended family. Could you tell us about *The Grandmothers?*

DL   There are four long stories. They are all true and I put them together because they are true. *The Grandmothers* is a story that was told to me. The basic story is that there were two women whose husbands went off. Anyway they were by themselves with two boys. They had love affairs across; one woman had an affair with her friend's son, etc. This went on for ten years and then the women ended it. The young man who told me about it, and this was really interesting, was a friend of the two boys and he was extremely angry with the women for ending it. He kept saying, 'That's what women are like. They don't care about our feelings, they are just practical and stupid.' This is what I was listening to. I was listening to this shocking story, which it is. He was angry because the women were callous and brutal and ended it and I kept saying to him, 'Look, knowing what life is like, you do know that in, let's say, ten years after the time you were watching this the women would be old and it would come to an end in any case. You do realise that?' He said, 'No. I don't want to think about that. I don't want to know about that. This is how women talk, you see, this is how you talk. This is why you are so cold and heartless.' I thought, 'This man is a bit drunk and sending himself up'. I had to write that story. I cannot think of any writer I have ever met who would not want to write that story, so I did.

The story about the love child is true and the story about the black girl who lost her daughter to the middle classes happened to be American but this was interesting: when I changed the story from New York to London it was no longer a story about race – it was about class. In England race was not the important thing in that story, it was the fact that this little girl was going to go up into the middle classes and become a middle class person. I think it would be different in America; I have never lived there, but so we think.

RK   It's unbelievably exciting to hear you carried away by your own stories and so much more inspiring than many of the political harangues we have heard this afternoon.

DL   *[Laughs]*

HUO Eric Hobsbawm gave us the advice to protest against forgetting in this Marathon and to think about memory. Could you tell us about the notion of memory in relation to the current moment?

DL I wrote in my two autobiographies a lot about memory. I spent a lot of time thinking about it. I see they've got this series running on memory. But so far they haven't said anything that I hadn't said in my autobiography a long time ago, so I am waiting for them to say something that I haven't thought of myself.

HUO Do you have any unrealised projects, an unwritten book?

DL You know I am getting too old to have many unwritten projects. I do have one or two and I keep thinking, 'Am I ever going to write that?' Yes I do, of course, because I don't have any problem about ideas; my problem is that I never have enough time for everything and even less now, as you can see. I can't now say, 'I am going to write this, I am going to write that', because I won't, you know. It brings you up a bit short, doesn't it?

HUO I have a very last question. I re-read some time ago the very nice small book Rainer Maria Rilke wrote, which is *Advice to a Young Poet* and I was wondering what your advice would be to a young writer in 2006.

DL To a writer or poet?

HUO Either.

DL They are different animals. *[Laughter]* Very different. Well, novelists are much more down to earth and solid and earth-based than poets and poets tend to be at their best, most of them, fairly young, whereas I think that we do better from middle age onwards. We are completely different. Do you remember this Russian chap – here I go, I cannot remember a damn thing – Mandelstam – he said when a poem was coming he seemed to hear a kind of a buzz. He would talk to his wife, Nadezhda, and say, 'I've got my buzz. I can hear it'. And then they would turn into words. I don't think novelists are like that. We get excited with people and ideas and all that has to get done. A poet is different. I've known quite a few poets; they are not as earth-based as we are.

HUO Many, many thanks, Doris Lessing.

DL Thank you.

Applause, end of interview

POSTFACE *

Ghostwriter   So, I think following the interview Marathon, Ryan Gander wanted to turn the tables, so to speak, on the inquisitors. Therefore, in many respects this is an interview about an interview. So can I start by asking something about the Marathon itself? Which of you came up with the idea for a series of consecutive interviews over a 24-hour period?

Hans Ulrich Obrist   It started, basically, about a year and a half ago when I was invited to do something on Stuttgart, and I was thinking, following reading a lot of Italo Calvino and reflecting on this impossibility of making a synthetic image of the city, that it could be really interesting, through conversations with many different protagonists of the city, to draw an incomplete portrait of it. So we started to interview artists, architects, designers, composers and all other sorts of practitioners that formed the cultural life of Stuttgart over the last few decades. The idea was that it was not only about the now, but it also, somehow, addressed memory and a protest against forgetting. The idea was basically by having practitioners who have forgotten previous generations of pioneers. After Stuttgart we started to discuss with Rem how we could continue our interview project because we both, independently of each other, had pursued interviews for a long time, Rem much longer than me. He already, in the 1960s, recorded his first interviews with Le Corbusier and Dalí. I started to interview in the early 1990s, when I begun to work as a curator. I interviewed Vito Acconci, Félix González-Torres, and these were the beginnings of the development of a project in the art world. And at a certain moment, I teamed up with Rem and we started to do interviews together. So that's the sort of prehistory. Therefore our joint interview project started by us kind of visiting architects mainly, at the beginning, who had been important.

Ghostwriter   Well that's interesting. What were your selection criteria in choosing the people you were going to interview?

Rem Koolhaas   In London?

Ghostwriter   Yes, for this interview Marathon.

RK   It was a kind of randomness. I mean, basically, whoever was available from as many different areas as we could think of.

Ghostwriter	What were the areas you were looking at, specifically?
RK	We were looking at art, obviously, and architecture, basically our own territories, but we were particularly interested in going beyond them. So, politics, money, sociology, anthropology, writing and history in the end. And science became the important other category.
Ghostwriter	What were the precise objectives of the interview Marathon?
RK	I think what was important is that Hans Ulrich was new to London and, in a way, the project was based on the curiosity of somebody who is confronting a situation for the first time and trying to understand how many facets there were and what the facets meant. So it is also a discovery for Hans of London.
HUO	The first thing that Rem said is that architecture without content is a meaningless shape. The idea was to develop a content machine, so that the Pavilion would become a content machine for the whole summer. That was the driving idea Rem suggested for the Pavilion. From the very beginning we thought that it could be important that we devise a programme together. And so, for the first time, these interviews that we had been doing very occasionally before, in a more systematic and longer way…
RK	*[Off camera]* … and public way.
HUO	Yeah, and public way. And that happened throughout this summer.
RK	So the thing is designed to actually be the kind of ideal environment for an interview.
Ghostwriter	Now, Rem, when you conceived the Pavilion (I just want to clarify this), did you already have this Interview Marathon in mind?
RK	Yes.
Ghostwriter	It wasn't the other way around?
RK	No, not at all.
Ghostwriter	It's a common observation about this structure that it's reminiscent of a hot-air balloon.
RK	Actually, I don't like that association and you can see that in the balloon there's a number of structures and they aim to deform the balloon and make it less regular. If we had more time, it would have been more deformed and flatter and wider. But anyway, it was a shape that we wanted to redesign and we succeeded only imperfectly. But if you look care-

fully, you see it's asymmetrical, or a little bit warped, not exactly a balloon.

Ghostwriter Was it always meant as a forum for conversation?

RK Yeah, that was the intention.

Ghostwriter I'm intrigued by the absence of any form of separation between the people talking and the people who might be listening. What was your thinking behind that?

RK I think that we were trying to create the kind of situation where it would not be spectators and actors in a very emphatic way. And it is true that, by designing non-furniture, which is used by all of us, and by a circular arrangement, there is a sense of participation without necessarily talking. But you feel, if we are here in the centre, there is a lot of energy, and you get a very precise sense of how the audience reacts. And that's really the point of the whole set up, I think.

* Hans Ulrich Obrist and Rem Koolhaas, interviewed by a Ghostwriter.
An abridged transcription from "Ghostwriter Subtext" by Ryan Gander, 2006